DOJO

Magic and Exorcism in Modern Japan

STANFORD UNIVERSITY PRESS

STANFORD, CALIFORNIA

1980

DOJO

Magic and Exorcism in Modern Japan

WINSTON DAVIS

OVERLEAF
Okada Kōtama,
founder of Sūkyō Mahikari

Stanford University Press
Stanford, California

© *1980 by the Board of Trustees of the*
Leland Stanford Junior University

Printed in the United States of America
ISBN 0-8047-1053-8
LC 79-64219

For LINDA *and* COLIN
  who shared the adventure
  and
for MONICA
  who will share others

Preface

In March 1976 I went to Japan with my family to study Shinto festival organizations. While there, I accidentally came upon an exorcistic group called the True-Light Supra-Religious Organization. Known as Sūkyō Mahikari in Japanese, this sect turned out to be the most primitive religious community I had ever encountered in Japan. Although primitive may be too strong a word to use, it does express my immediate reaction to the group, its ideas and practices. The only thing that had prepared me for this experience was some work I had done on African magic and witchcraft as a graduate student at the University of Chicago.

I found little in Mahikari that I could empathize with personally. Its belief in spirit possession, its idea that "medicine is poison," its latent ethnocentrism and manifest occultism, taxed patience and scholarly objectivity alike. I must therefore admit that this book has grown out of a prolonged reflection on my own culture shock. Although professionally trained in the history of religions, I found myself asking again the simplest and most fundamental questions about religious experience. How is religion *possible*? What are the motivations, needs, satisfactions, meanings, and mechanisms that have enabled religions like Mahikari to come into existence and even thrive? How do such groups put together and sustain worldviews that, in so many respects, run against the grain of contemporary Japanese culture?

Madame de Staël's "*tout comprendre c'est tout pardonner*" is too demanding a rule to impose on realistic students of religion and society. More appropriate is the advice of Charles Dickens' Mr. Sleary: "I conthider that I lay down the philothophy of the thubject when I thay to you, Thquire, make the betht of uth: not the wurtht!" Although I could not always appreciate the ideas and practices of the religion, I have tried to keep Mr. Sleary's words in mind. Since some readers will find my presentation of Mahikari odd, a bit droll, or perhaps even repugnant, I must insist that I have at least tried to "make the betht" of the followers of the religion. When compelled to present material that is at odds with Western sensibilities, I have sought to do so charitably, or at least *sans commentaire*. In my concluding chapter I suggest that more important than the good and bad of the religion itself is the question of the rationality of the society that gave it birth.

Today, a liberal suspension of disbelief is becoming de rigueur in religious studies. But this approach, and the "I'm OK; you're OK" attitude it seems to entail, may not be the most authentic or productive way to understand a foreign religion. It is my opinion that one can understand a religion without believing in it, practicing it, or even "appreciating" it. In fact, I would go so far as to say that belief, practice, and appreciation have nothing whatsoever to do with understanding a religion. Some of the conclusions I have reached in this book would have been impossible, or at least unlikely, were it not for the luxurious distance that disbelief alone could afford. Because Mahikari does not use the word believer, I could legitimately call myself a member (*kamikumite*) without committing myself to anything in particular. I was perfectly open with members about my motives for joining the church. Most members, in turn, seemed quite satisfied that I had joined for no better reason than to do research. The leaders of the local church graciously enabled me to participate in the life of the group without making any profession of faith. Since Mahikari's founder had vented his wrath on philosophers but not on sociologists, my role in the church was relatively secure.

Unlike some accounts of popular Japanese religion, this book is not based on the "philosophical" account that leaders of the New Religions are wont to give to foreign visitors. Rather, it presents the Mahikari gospel as it is preached, believed, and practiced in a provincial congregation of unpretentious "common people." "Nakayama City" may not have been the best place to study Mahikari.* In Tokyo there is a much richer oral tradition about the deeds and sayings of the founder, Okada Kōtama. Because the headquarters of the church were still in the capital at the time I was doing my research, I would probably have been able to say much more about the national organization had I done my work there. On the other hand, working in a relatively remote place like Nakayama had its own rewards. Because Nakayama is still relatively provincial, many members of the local church are deeply rooted in the folk tradition from which the gospel arose. Being this close to the grass roots turned out to add not just local color, but real depth to my study.

Understanding a foreign culture presupposes both empathy and genuine distance. Simply putting that culture into the categories of one's own civilization inevitably causes distortion and misunderstanding. On the other hand, all goodwill and objectivity notwithstanding, it is also impossible to understand a foreign culture simply by introducing it into our thought world on its own terms. Introjection is not the same as interpretation. Understanding an alien culture or religion always involves an untidy compromise between three very different "languages." First, there is the language spoken by one's informants, sometimes called emic discourse by anthropologists. Then there is the language of scholarship, or the etic categories and distinctions that we superimpose upon what the "natives" say. And finally, there is the language of the researcher himself, in my case English. Because the values and religious traditions of a society always have repercussions in language, the idiosyncrasies of one's mother tongue are of crucial importance when trying to interpret another culture.

In this book the problem of the three languages becomes crucial at several points. For example, what Mahikari members call miracles is called magic by anthropologists and historians of religion. Many

---

* In order to protect the privacy of the members I interviewed, I have changed all names except those of the Savior and the two individuals who, as rivals, now claim the title of Spiritual Leader of the church. For the same reason, place names except for Osaka and Tokyo are fictitious. Japanese names, even when fictitious, are written in the Japanese order, i.e. family name first. Macrons will be used only when a term first appears in the text or when considerations of intelligibility dictate greater flexibility. They will also be used in the Japanese words that appear in the Index.

speakers of the English language, however, untutored in the sophistry of religion and anthropology, would call the same phenomenon base superstition. Because we are therefore compelled to compromise in our choice of words, the understanding of religions not our own must always be provisional. Under these circumstances, the only rule of thumb is to use words and concepts that distort the least and illuminate the most. Although this advice is as robust as any platitude, the result of our hermeneutical compromise may still be a bit messy. It may even ruffle a few feathers. Thus, if I call magic what Mahikari members call miracles, I can only excuse myself by saying that I have had to do my work in a complex hermeneutical triangle, each angle of which seemed to exert an almost magnetic attraction. For this reason, I beg members of the church to continue to show the same indulgence and forbearance to my choice of words in this book that they have already demonstrated in the face of my endless questions.

After I was initiated and had received my amulet, I was empowered, like all other members of Mahikari, to perform the same miracles once wrought by Jesus Christ and the Lord Buddha. Or so I was told. I must confess, however, that I was less than zealous in my own performance of miracles. Although I performed and received many "exorcisms" myself, I much preferred to sit quietly in the empty room beneath the church, interviewing members and recording their miracles and encounters with the spirit world one by one. This book is based on six months of observation and participation of this sort. I have made use of about forty formal (taped) interviews and field notes from many more informal ones. (Throughout the book, material cited from interviews and official church lectures is generally presented in condensed form.) I also distributed a questionnaire to four congregations in the Osaka area that was designed to survey members' spirit possession experiences, performance of miracles, church involvement, political and social attitudes, and such variables as age, sex, marital status, and income. From this survey, 688 usable replies were received and analyzed.

Many individuals helped make this study possible. First, I must thank the many members of the Nakayama dojo for their unfailing cooperation and, above all, "Yoshida Sensei"* and his wife and children for their friendship and generosity to me and my family during our stay in Nakayama City. The present Spiritual Leader of the church, Okada Keiju, and other staff members of the national headquarters provided valuable assistance in many ways. Regrettably, I can repay my debt of gratitude to these good people only by expressing my personal respect and affection for them as friends. In matters of faith and philosophy we go our separate ways. I would also like to express my gratitude to Professor and Mrs. Andō Seiichi and Mr. and Mrs. Ōta Seizō for their help in so many ways, large and small. Several people served as research assistants, performing a variety of invaluable services: Fujita Mariko, Kasahara Masao, Morita Masako, Nakamura Jun, and Ueno Akiko. Susan Kwilecki helped with the proofreading and the preparation of the index. George M. Thomas was responsible for running the computer analysis of my questionnaire. J. G. Bell of Stanford University Press and my colleagues in the Department of Religious Studies at Stanford were most generous in their support and encouragement of this project. Before I left Japan, I remarked to Yoshida Sensei that my university friends would laugh at me when I told them about the World of Miracles. "Don't worry," he assured me. "Just raise your hand over a dead goldfish and bring it back to life. Then they'll stop laughing!" Fortunately, my colleagues have been too polite to put me to the test.

My wife, Linda, deserves special thanks for the long hours she invested in typing this book and in preparing its illustrations and statistical tables. Finally, I must also thank our little boy, Colin, for letting his father have the time to put this book together. I told him that I was writing a book about people and ghosts. That *is* the long and the short of the matter.

This book was made possible by a fellowship from the National Endowment for the Humanities and by grants from the Japan Fund of Stanford University.

W.D.

---

*The word Sensei is a title of respect widely used in Japan for schoolteachers, college professors, physicians, masters of the occult, and other worthies.

Contents

Tables

Figures

DOJO

Magic and Exorcism in Modern Japan

1 Introduction

A Japanese *dōjō* is a building set aside for the nurture of various spiritual disciplines. The word dojo is said to correspond to the Sanskrit word *bodhimaṇḍa*, which means a place where a Buddha attains enlightenment, and is sometimes used as the equivalent of our English word seminary. In Japanese, the word is written with characters meaning a "place" (*jō*) for practicing "the Way" (*dō*, the equivalent of Tao in Chinese). Since the *Sōniryō* (Rules and regulations for monks and nuns) of the Nara period (A.D. 710–84) the word dojo has been used for unauthorized temples and for private religious gatherings that did not have the blessing of the government. Thus the popular chapels of the new Buddhist sects of the Kamakura period (1192–1333) were often called dojos in contrast to the established temples (*otera* or *jiin*) of the day. Today dojos are not only used for Zen meditation and the ritual recitation of the name of Amida Buddha. They are also places for practicing *jūdō*, *aikidō*, *kyūdō*, and other martial arts. Because a dojo is a holy place, people are expected to bow when they enter and leave. Even dojos used for the martial arts enshrine a Shinto altar in a conspicuous place.

A dojo is a "practical" kind of place, used not only to foster lofty ideas, but to realize them in some physical or at least palpable way. Since Japanese religion is more concerned with practice, discipline, and training (*shugyō*) than with theological erudition (*kyō*), one naturally associates dojos with a very "Japanese" kind of spirituality. They are appropriate places for developing *Yamato-damashii*, the Japanese spirit. To this day, dojos used for the martial arts are suffused with the ethos of the medieval warrior and *bushidō*, his idealized code of conduct. Whether a dojo is used for archery, for meditation, or for Buddhist ordinations, it is a place for "polishing the soul" and achieving spiritual excellence.

The dojo that gives its name to this book is heir to neither the high culture of the medieval warrior nor the great tradition of Japanese Buddhism. As a manifestation of popular, indeed folk religion, our dojo is closer to the Little Tradition of the so-called common man. It is a place devoted to the exorcism of evil spirits, the performance of miracles, and the building of the "Kingdom of God Civilization of the Holy Twenty-First Century."

The True-Light Supra-Religious Organization (Sūkyō Mahikari) is made up of over 150 dojos in Japan and has several missionary outposts in Europe, the Americas, and North Africa. Although Mahikari is evasive about its membership figures, by 1970 as many as 400,000 people had received its wonder-working amulet. Best estimates place the sect somewhere among Japan's middle-size New Religions.[1]

As with other messianic religions, the history of Sukyo Mahikari begins with a humble nativity legend. In Tokyo, in the year 1901, the wife of an officer in the imperial army was about to give birth. Shortly before her baby was born, the mother had a revelatory dream in which a rat from the Grand Shrine of Izumo, a magnificent creature with gold and white fur, bit the big toe of her left foot. Now, to appreciate the significance of this omen, much later developments must be anticipated. In the sect that her son was to found, it is believed that the left side of the body is the "spirit side," and is therefore the side of the body that ancestral and evil spirits are most likely to use (by inflicting illness and accidents) to send warnings and messages from the astral world. From this it was clear that the child that was about to be born would be no ordinary baby. When the vision came to an end, the mother opened her eyes and painlessly brought forth a son. Soon after the baby was born, the big toe on the mother's left foot began to hurt, as though the rat in her dream had actually bitten her. Because of his mother's mysterious experience, the son would always have a special reverence for the Izumo Shrine.

Okada Yoshikazu (later Kōtama), founder of Sukyo Mahikari, was born into a samurai family. His grandfather had been a tutor to the feudal lords of Nakayama castle. His father continued the family profession until the Meiji restoration (1868), when he joined the new imperial army and rose to the rank of major general. In his will he directed his son, Yoshikazu, to follow the hereditary occupation of his forebears. The young man accordingly entered a military academy called the Rikugun Shikan Gakkō and, after graduation, served in the imperial guards of the Taishō and Shōwa emperors.

During the Pacific War, Okada fell from his horse while serving in Indochina, seriously injuring his back. When he returned to Japan for medical treatment, physicians found that he had tuberculosis of the spine and predicted that he had only three more years to live. This was Okada's first encounter with the limitations of Western medicine. After his release from the hospital, he resolved that he would devote the short time remaining to him "to the service of God and mankind." To carry out his vow, he invested all his savings in four factories manufacturing military aircraft for the Japanese air force. When these plants were gutted by the firebombing of Tokyo in 1945, the future Savior was plunged into destitution. Like others in similar straits, Okada turned to religion, becoming a staunch member of the Church of World Messianity (Sekai Kyūsei Kyō).[2] Founded by Okada Mokichi (no relation to Mahikari's Savior), Messianity taught that sickness and misfortune are caused by the "dust" that accumulates on the surface of the soul. By purchasing an amulet a person could dispel this dust simply by raising his hand over another's forehead. The amulet, a transmitter of heavenly "spirit rays," was credited with miracles beyond number.

By 1959, Okada Yoshikazu had finally paid off the last of his creditors. On February 22 of that year he developed a high fever and became unconscious. Suddenly he found himself transported to the astral world, where he saw an old man with white hair standing in a white cloud and washing clothes in a golden tub. Later, Okada

Okada Kotama, founder of Sukyo Mahikari

interpreted this vision as a revelation of Su-god (the Lord God) *
and of the cleansing mission that was about to be entrusted to him.
Five days after the vision, on his birthday, Okada was awakened
at five o'clock in the morning by a divine voice saying, "Get up.
Change your name to Kotama (Jewel of Light). Raise your hand.
Trials and tribulation are coming!"

Except for his boundless interest in evil spirits, there was little
to distinguish Okada's gospel from that of Messianity. The first to
be healed by the new Savior was a dog. "At least a dog won't laugh
at me when I raise my hand," he thought. Gradually he began to
make converts, his earliest disciples being neighborhood bargirls.
On August 28, 1960, Okada officially launched his movement, first
called the L. H. (Lucky and Healthy) Sunshine Children and later
changed to the Church of the World True-Light Civilization (Sekai
Mahikari Bunmei Kyōdan). For the next ten years he vigorously
preached his gospel to all sorts of people, until Mahikari had become a nationwide movement. His following increased dramatically after a successful demonstration of his "purification" method
on the television program "Afternoon Show" in November 1968.
So successful did he become that he was forced to turn over the
instruction and initiation of neophytes to his disciples and confine
himself to the preparation of amulets (*omitama*) and high-level
evangelism.

As the movement expanded, Okada's messianic consciousness •
grew deeper. Although he never claimed to be the equal of Su-god,
he regarded himself as the physical embodiment of the god Yoni-
masu-ō-amatsu and as God's earthly "Proxy, Carbon Copy, and
Robot." To the titles of Spiritual Leader or Master (Oshienushi-
sama) and Savior (Sukuinushi-sama) were added the names Messiah Number One and Sacred Phoenix. Throughout this period,
revelations continuously came to Okada during the night that he
jotted down in "automatic writing" with incredible speed. These
were later collected in a 486-page volume called the *Goseigenshū*,
the scriptures of Mahikari. Members regard all of the Savior's

---

* Although Su no kami-sama means, literally, Lord God in Japanese, the church
treats these words as a personal name: Su-god. It is a shortened version of Mioyamotosu Mahikari Ōmikami-sama, literally, Revered Parent Origin Lord True Light
Great God.

words, even those that have appeared in the *Mahikari* magazine, as part of his Holy Teachings, or Mioshie.

On February 17, 1972, Okada Kotama's career came to a climax when he was presented with the medallion of the Knight Commander of St. Denis by the American Academy of Arts. The year after, he went to Europe and was granted a private audience with Pope Paul VI. I am told by Mahikari stalwarts that as a result of their meeting, the Pope instructed all Roman Catholic priests to study the Mahikari Treatment.

In 1974 Okada became ill. On June 13, he called his daughter Sachiko to him and announced that it was Su-god's will that she succeed him as Spiritual Leader of the sect. "You will have complete authority," he told her. "From now on you can do anything, just like your father." Then, in the presence of Su-god, he presented her with his own amulet. This, at least, is the succession story told to new members in the training sessions of Sukyo Mahikari.

The story is actually more complicated, since there are presently two contenders for the title of Spiritual Leader. Sachiko's rival is a certain Sekiguchi Sakae, said to be the owner of a taxicab company and various other enterprises in Tokyo. According to Sekiguchi's story, Sachiko went to her father's room ten days before his death and asked him what they should do if something happened to him. "Ask Mr. Sekiguchi to become Spiritual Leader of the church," he said, and then gave Sachiko a special amulet to hand over to Sekiguchi. Accordingly, on July 13, just after the Savior's funeral, Sekiguchi was publicly installed as Leader of the church.

Shortly after this, however, a mysterious "revelation memo" appeared in Sachiko's faction that said, "Take my amulet and give it to my daughter." Even these words were ambiguous, since Okada had two others daughters and Sachiko herself was adopted. Nevertheless, Sachiko (now taking the religious name Keiju) and three other leaders interpreted this to mean that she, and not Mr. Sekiguchi, was her father's rightful heir. The Keiju group was able to wrest control of the sect's main shrine and other properties from Sekiguchi, leaving him with no recourse but the courts. In 1978, after five years of litigation, the Supreme Court of Japan left standing lower court decisions to the effect that, at least in the eyes of the law, Sekiguchi Sakae was to be Mahikari's Spiritual Leader.

After the high court's decision, Sekiguchi quickly moved to oust the Keiju group from the sect's headquarters. Keiju changed the name of the organization from the Church of the World True-Light Civilization to the True-Light Supra-Religious Organization (Sukyo Mahikari) and moved her headquarters to Kanagawa Prefecture.* Since the court could not compel dojos built with local funds to change their allegiance, Okada Keiju still commands the loyalty of the majority of her father's followers. Keiju herself is a pleasant middle-aged woman who is said to spend most of her time inscribing amulets and interceding with Su-god on behalf of her followers. Although she seems rather uncharismatic to outsiders, the faithful believe that the spirit rays between her and Su-god are extremely "thick," and that she can read minds. Some have told me that she is half god and claim that they have a sense of security in her presence.

Today Mahikari is largely an urban movement. Only in a few places such as Hokuriku on the Japan Sea does it have a significant rural following. Because the Savior lived in Tokyo, even nowadays his followers are most numerous in the capital area. The church also has followers in Brazil, Belgium, France, Italy, Switzerland, Morocco, and the United States, many of them Japanese emigrants and their relatives. It is difficult to say how large the church is today. According to some reports, there were 300,000 to 400,000 members in 1970. Because each sect has its own way of defining and counting members, statistics on the membership of the New Religions are notoriously unreliable. Some, like Mahikari, seem determined to keep the exact size of their following a secret and refuse to submit reports of their membership to the government. I would estimate that although as many as one million amulets have probably been distributed to new members, the de facto membership probably numbers about 100,000 to 200,000 or even less. Extrapolating from some credible figures given to me by leaders in the Osaka area, I estimate that, excluding dormant members (*tō-*

---

* Okada Kotama insisted that the Japanese word for religion (*shūkyō*) should not be used by his followers because of its associations with "secondary deities" and established religions. In its place, he recommended his own neologism, *sūkyō* or supra-religion. In this book, I shall follow the common practice of members and refer to the organization simply as Mahikari. The words church and sect will be used interchangeably and without the connotations they have in the Christian world.

min kumite), the church may have as few as 50,000—75,000 truly active supporters. Mahikari therefore is far smaller than such gargantuan New Religions as Sōka Gakkai and Risshō Kōseikai and probably ranks somewhat below middle-sized movements like Ōmoto-Kyō. I must emphasize, however, that because Mahikari officials in Tokyo would not be specific about membership statistics, I present these figures only as rough estimates.

From this brief outline, readers familiar with contemporary Japan will quickly recognize the typical lineaments of a "New Religion." For those unfamiliar with these organizations, the following description by Joseph M. Kitagawa can serve as an introduction:

These new religions present nothing new, as far as their religious contents are concerned. Many of them derived their doctrines from Shinto, Confucianism, Buddhism, or Christianity. Their teachings are eclectic and not well systematized, but their simple, direct, and practical beliefs and practices appeal to the masses who do not feel at home with the complex doctrines of established religions. It is important to note, however, that they make full use of group psychology by offering both informal small group meetings and elaborate mass assemblies. Most of them are highly centralized in their organizational structure, utilizing cell group systems as well as incentive plans. A few of them have semimilitaristic disciplines. All of them use modern mass media of communication and have efficient methods of tithing or its equivalent. What gives each of these new religions its distinctive character is the personality of the founder or organizer. Many of these boast unusual spiritual powers in divination, sorcery, incantation, fortunetelling, and healing, which betray the shamanistic roots of their religious orientations. They also have the capacity to attract and maintain rapport with a large number of followers. For the most part, these new religions draw their adherents from the lower middle class, especially middle-aged and older women, although a few of them claim to have some followers among the upper middle class and young people as well.[3]

Beginning in the nineteenth century and continuing through the postwar period, the New Religions have had a dramatic impact on Japanese religious life. The earlier ones appeared in parts of the country undergoing rapid social and economic change and can be linked to the breakdown of social relations within the traditional rural community. The deterioration of the cohesiveness of the local *Gemeinschaft* lowered the usual resistance to infiltration by religious forces (gods, buddhas, and missionaries) from outside. The most spectacular time of growth of the New Religions has been the postwar period. Their rapid expansion has been explained by most scholars as a result of the immiseration of the population, the humiliation of military defeat, and the anxiety that resulted from the radical demographic dislocations of the period. Traditional Buddhist temples and Shinto parishes were both spiritually and sociologically ill-equipped to cope with problems of this magnitude. Under these circumstances, the New Religions alone seemed to offer real succor to the depressed, the disoriented, the sick, and the poor.

This study is not intended as an addition to the already existing battery of theories concerning the rise of the New Religions. There is little to question in the prevalent viewpoint that these movements have largely addressed themselves to the lower classes of Japanese society, to the sick and the needy. Although their period of greatest growth seems to be over, their continuing strength in the relatively prosperous 1960's and 1970's indicates that they do more than anesthetize the pain of social and economic exploitation. They also deal with the pathos of the human condition.

In this book I am not really interested in Mahikari as a New Religion. That is to say, my primary concern is not what is typical or untypical about it vis-à-vis other New Religions. I shall begin by freely admitting that it *is* typical of the lot. If there is any one shortcoming in books on the New Religions, it is their tendency to treat the members of these groups—the sick, the poor, the uneducated, the alienated—as one homogeneous lump of frustrated humanity. One of the major goals of this book is to take this lump apart and show the variety of specific needs that an organization like Mahikari creates and responds to. I shall be concerned therefore with the "insides" of this religion: how new religious ideas and behavior patterns become established in members' lives, how people change as a result of their participation in the sect, and how social, religious, and magical criteria determine status within the group. Although I shall begin by focusing on "the nature of personal experiencing" (Goffman) within the sect, my final goal is to relate the worldview of the sect to the cognitive orientation of the mainstream of Japanese society.[4] By studying how Mahikari members construct and maintain their "world-of-meaning," I hope to come to a better understanding of the function of cognitive deviance in modern society. Whereas most of the chapters that follow are concerned with the sociology and social psychology of a particular religion, this book is actually intended as a modest contribution to the sociology of "industrial consciousness." That is, I am interested not only in the generation of a specific mode of consciousness, but in its distribution and function in contemporary Japanese life.

Conventional wisdom has it that religion is dying out in the modern world. This notion—let us call it the dogma of secularization —can be traced back to the founders of modern social thought: to Comte, Spencer, Durkheim, Marx, and Weber. Expert opinion assures us that what Weber called *Entgötterung* (secularization) and *die Entzauberung der Welt* (the disenchantment, or literally, the decline of magic in the world) are *necessary* features of the modern world. Recent scholarship, however, including works by Thomas Luckmann, Mary Douglas, Talcott Parsons, and Robert Bellah, is less sanguine about the alleged inevitability of the decline of the supernatural. For scholars of this persuasion, the watchword of modern religious history is not decline but transformation.

A large number of religious movements have emerged in recent decades that give us pause when tempted to pronounce glibly on the universal decline of the sacred. The New Religions in Japan, not to mention the Neo-Evangelical movement, astrology, occultism, and youth cults in the United States, are typical examples. These and kindred movements seem to suggest that religion, like the proverbial phoenix, simply refuses to die. But the problem of secularization becomes more difficult when we turn to magic. If there is one characteristic that is universally associated with modernity, it is rationality. Per contra, if there is any attitude that is universally regarded as irrational and anti-modern, it is the outlook of the magician. The conflict between the magician and the secularist is every bit as intense as the struggle Sir James George Frazer depicted between the magician and the priest of old. Not only theologians, but sociologists and intellectual historians seem convinced that this *must* be a battle to the finish.

This book is about a magical religion. To cite Kitagawa again: "In essence, the new religions are antiintellectual and antimodern. . . . What they present as a positive goal for the future is a peculiar mixture of naive utopianism, traditionalism, *magic*, and promises of mundane satisfactions and benefits."[5] Mahikari describes its work as miracles (*kiseki*) and not magic. But what are miracles if not the bridge between religion and magic? Indeed, Durkheim's opinion to the contrary notwithstanding, Mahikari and other New Religions could rightly be characterized as "churches of magic."* Mahikari's members claim to be able to heal all kinds of diseases, repair broken appliances, improve the taste of food, open the eyes of the dead (or cause froth to appear on their lips), resurrect dead goldfish—all by raising their hands. Understandably, outsiders are bound to wonder how "churches of magic" like this can possibly exist in a *modern* society.

There are several ways to answer this question. One could, for example, simply regard these magicians as victims of a prolonged cultural lag. In that case, one would expect that insofar as they are able to function in modern society at all, they would have to compartmentalize their neolithic notions to keep them from interfering with everyday life. On the other hand, it has been suggested that the reason why these individuals are on the bottom of the social barrel is precisely because they harbor such antiquated ideas and practices. If it were not for their wishful thinking, they might "get ahead" in the world. In short, we are told that in the modern world, magic must be sequestered or else it will cause the maladjustment of individuals or the dysfunction of the entire social organism.

An alternative is to take a more critical look at the question itself. Is modern society, in fact, antithetical to a "thaumaturgical response to the world?"† Is it possible that magic, like religion, *reinforces* the institutions and values of industrial society? The an-

---

* Emile Durkheim believed that because magicians collect clienteles without creating among them the lasting bonds of a moral community, "*there is no Church of magic.*" In other words, he recognized the diffuse, but not the institutional character of magic. Without speculating about the role of magic in primitive society, it is my contention in this book that industrial society is not only compatible with, but actually encourages the institutionalization of magic in churches. See Emile Durkheim, *The Elementary Forms of the Religious Life* (New York, 1965), p. 60.

† My discussion of Mahikari as a form of magic is closely related to Bryan R. Wilson's description of "thaumaturgical responses to the world" in his book *Magic and the Millennium: A Sociological Study of Religious Movements of Protest Among Tribal and Third-World Peoples* (New York, 1973), pp. 24–25. The thaumaturgical response is based on an "essentially particularistic conception of salvation.... The individual's concern is relief from present and specific ills by special dispensations. The demand for supernatural help is personal and local; its operation is magical. ... The evils feared are all highly specific, and it is from their particular incidence (not from their universal operation) that salvation is sought."

swer to these questions will naturally depend, in large measure, on what we mean by modern, and where within the modern we locate contemporary believers and magicians. Perhaps the safest, if not the most adventuresome definition of modernization identifies it with industrialization. Around this core definition, one can go on to depict a penumbra of concomitant transformations that, collectively, can be regarded as a kind of loose (that is, variable) syndrome of historical change.

The dilemma of modernization theory is that it is always being trapped between saying too much and saying too little. When it says too much it tends to treat mere contingencies as though they were predetermined sequences of events. When it says too little, it fails to go beyond idiographic modes of scholarship. But it is the theories that say too much that are especially troublesome. Their greatest fault is their tendency to universalize the particular. For example, they make secularization, which obviously does occur in some quarters of some societies, into an iron rule of history. Most modernization theory seems to equate the "modernization process" with the diffusion throughout all levels of society of life-styles previously associated with the elite. This is especially true of scholars who emphasize the uniqueness of "modern consciousness." As they see it, modernization is virtually the trickling down to the masses of the controlling rationality, the "hypothetical" cognitive style, the achievement-orientation, the capacity for social and emotional distance, and the polite, but attenuated religious experiences of the ruling and owning classes. As production industry turns into service and knowledge industries, as class consciousness evolves into occupational and status awareness, in short, as modern man becomes "post-modern," this modern temper becomes the property of the entire society. This could be called the trickle-down theory of modernization. But there are difficulties with this approach.

The process of "post-modernization" fails to account for large segments of the working population left untouched in their "modern," or even "pre-modern" condition. Movements like Mahikari can be understood only in the context of today's "*pre*-post-industrial" society. Primarily a religion of unskilled blue-collar and lower-level white-collar workers, its worldview seems hardly to have caught up to the modern world. But the trickle-down theory fails to explain the general as well as the particular. Such theories of modernization and post-modernization, although elegant in their handling of secularization, are generally unable to explain the persistence of traditional religions, let alone the growth of new ones. The spread of magic, astrology, and other occult or ecstatic practices even among the middle and upper social strata can be especially vexing for the theory.

Although I part company with Max Weber on the question of the general "disenchantment of the world," his analysis of the function of religion in modern society is crucial for this study. Judged even by Hegelian or Marxist standards, Weber's concept of religion is profoundly dialectical. More than other sociologists, he has demonstrated the rationalizing effects of the most irrational aspects of religion. By some "cunning of reason," movements that, to judge from their theological content, are quite other-worldly can have a deep impact on the ordering and systematizing of this world. Thus we shall see that in Mahikari the elevation of a believer's "spirit level" through exorcism and magic can have a decisively rationalizing effect on his life. Far from contradicting the practical achievement-orientation of industrial Japan, the practices of Mahikari seem to increase the capacity of its lower-class members for responsibility, self-denial, and toil.

Weber was fully aware of the undertow of magic in the "rational" economic ocean that surrounds us. But he never seems to have reconciled its persistence with his conviction that the world was becoming increasingly disenchanted. Perhaps this oversight was due to the primacy he assigned to teleological rationality in his analysis of social conduct. In fact, his entire sociological corpus is based upon a hierarchical continuum of ideal-typical action, ranging from the most habitual and traditional to the most rational, calculating, goal-oriented conduct (*Zweckrationalität*). In this scheme, each mode of conduct is assigned its place according to the type of motivation or obligation lying behind it.

An adequate sociology of consciousness calls not only for a typology of the intentionality of human conduct. It also requires an understanding of the scope or distribution of the various forms of awareness. To be sure, Weber also pioneered in this area of research. Because of his methodological relativism, he strictly avoided questions about the truth of any group's worldview. And since his own concept of material or substantive rationality finally reduces to a kind of formal rationality, Weber is left without any way of discriminating between true and false consciousness. Sociological insight of this sort would, of course, presuppose considerable philosophical virtuosity. Without embroiling myself in this quagmire of speculation, in the concluding chapter I turn from Weber to Mannheim's analysis of substantial and functional reason. This will enable us to move from questions about the form of social conduct to questions about the relative degree of actual discernment associated with the various elements of an industrial society. The kind of penetrating or substantial rationality that Mannheim associated with elites is not equally distributed throughout society. On the contrary, much of the material prosperity and cultural poverty of industrial society as we know it seems predicated on limiting the scope of the rationality of the lower working classes to finite operations in the service of pre-established economic or military goals. The irony of all this is that the reason embodied in the elite strata of society continues systematically to generate the most monstrous irrationalities, whereas the religious delirium of the lower classes often has surprisingly rational effects. Collective illusions of the latter sort tend to ritualize optimism and reason alike. Churches of magic, such as Japan's New Religions, shepherd the lost sheep of the world into their industrial pens and keep them there, alive and well. Thus magic, like reason itself, has its "cunning."

In contemporary scholarship, it is assumed that scientists and philosophers are concerned with true ideas, whereas psychiatrists, criminologists, and students of religion deal with false ones. This, at least, could be alleged as an excuse for dealing at such great length with the ways in which Mahikari puts together its cognitive and practical world. Because this book is an essay in sociology, it will be concerned not so much with the truth value of Mahikari's gospel as with the relationships between the religious experiences of the faithful and their concrete life-situations and personal needs. Admittedly, many discussions of the role of need in the genesis of religious belief have been reductionistic. Such theories seem to say that religion is "nothing but" a projection or reflection of bodily need, economic deprivation, or sexual frustration. But the problem of reductionism is not solved by posting No Trespassing signs around the Elysian fields. Such phenomenological bracketing, as it is called nowadays, serves to inhibit research and limit one's understanding of the dynamic interaction between religion and the social world.

On the other hand, the models that dominate religious studies today tend to shift attention from the old-fashioned stress on need to a new cybernetic emphasis on man's capacity for imposing order on an otherwise chaotic world. Theorists and fieldworkers alike have been much taken, even bewitched, by such notions as Geertz's "general order of existence," Tillich's "ultimate concern," and Berger's "sacred canopy." My purpose here is not to deny the importance of the drive to posit meaning in life. In fact, I would agree with Weber that a person who is religious may be motivated by "the metaphysical needs of the human mind as it is driven to reflect on ethical and religious questions, driven not by material need but by an inner compulsion to understand the world as a meaningful cosmos and to take a position toward it." [6] Nevertheless, the further one moves from the privileged elements of society, the less disinterested this inner compulsion seems to become. Indeed, even the higher social strata have traditionally related religion to their own practical needs, using it, for example, to satisfy their deep craving for civility, order, and legitimation. All of the world's "great religions" have rushed to provide their high-class patrons with such metaphysical conveniences. Ironically, by turning with such gusto to the grandiose formulas of Geertz, Tillich, Berger, and others, sociologists of religion (together with theologians who "do" theology in the same academic berth) may actually be perpetuating religion's traditional ideological service to the social establishment. Religions, and with them their purveyors, devotees, and academic sympathizers, thereby continue to be legitimated by the order and exotic beauty of the sacred.

Readers immersed in this genteel scholarly tradition may be disappointed when they find that neither the subject matter nor the approach adopted in this book comes up to their own theoretical ideals. If I seem to give undue stress to the role of human need in the genesis of religious experience—and the need-generating function of religion itself—it is not merely in order to counterbalance what I see as an overly idealistic tendency in contemporary religious scholarship. It is also because the people who join Mahikari and related groups have described themselves to me as people in need. We shall see how this need, combined with a long tradition of folk religion, fosters a magical response to the world. We shall also see how this magical prehension of the world makes the world more manageable. By getting cleaned up, as they put it, followers of Mahikari seem to be able to perform better and achieve more. If their religion fails to instill in them the substantial or controlling rationality of their social betters, it indisputably helps them to cope with an industrial society as they see it—a world filled with evil spirits and loitering ghosts.

2 A Lady in White Comes to the Door

It was in mid-June of 1976 that I first heard about Mahikari. It was a beautiful day in Nakayama City. Recent rains had scrubbed the sky blue, leaving the air sweet and clean. On such a day only the most hardened realist would believe, or want to remember, that the sky's true color is photochemical gray. Since it was Sunday, I had decided to take the day off. I was just beginning to wonder why we had made no plans for the day when the doorbell rang. When I opened the door I found a lady dressed rather quaintly in a white bonnet and a matching summer dress. "I have come to tell you about a really *marvelous* religion," she began. "A Messiah just like Jesus Christ has appeared, and all sorts of miracles are taking place!" She concluded her little set speech by inviting me to a public demonstration to be held that afternoon from one o'clock to five.

After my visitor left, I quickly read through the tracts she had given me.

THE WORLD OF MIRACLES!

Here's something hard to believe. We have the solution to family problems, children's diseases, traffic accidents, mysterious illnesses, heart trouble, asthma, financial worries, and all kinds of unhappiness! See for yourself proof of the existence of invisible spirits! A demonstration of the Mahikari (True Light) Treatment.

Having never learned to curb my interest in the exotic, I felt like a moth drawn to fire. I quickly phoned my friend Mrs. Ōta, and we made arrangements to attend the meeting together.

The demonstration was held in a public hall near the railroad tracks. It was a humble place consisting of one large room, its walls and roof covered with rusted corrugated steel. At the corner of the street, we were met by devotees of the sect who showed us to the door. We entered, took off our shoes, and stepped onto the red carpet that covered the floor. As we walked to the middle of the room, the creaking floorboards seemed to sink under our weight. We sat down and waited.

Around us, about twenty people were sitting, Japanese-style, on the floor. The group was divided into couples facing each other. Some people had their eyes closed, their hands held palm against palm as though in prayer. Others, facing them, held their hands above their partners' foreheads, sometimes intoning a chant. Still others were receiving what seemed to be the same Treatment while lying on their backs or stomachs. In spite of the summer heat, all of these people had heavy towels wrapped around their legs.

In the front of the room a woman registered newcomers. Next to her a television set played a videotape of a scene that seemed similar to the scene in the hall, though perhaps a bit wilder. On the television, an Indonesian man was sitting opposite a Japanese woman. As she raised her hand over his head, he went into what appeared to be a fit or seizure. Since he spoke in his native language, we could not understand what was going on. At one point, he began to make the familiar Muslim prostrations and called out the name of Allah. The Japanese who received the Treatment on the program were also acting in a bizarre fashion, swaying back and forth like charmed cobras, writhing as though in agony, shouting, shaking their heads violently, waving their arms, and making strange motions with their hands. This was a kind of behavior I had never seen before in Japan. As a matter of fact, before this day I would have regarded such activity as quite "un-Japanese."

Two friendly young women materialized and offered to demonstrate what the Treatment was all about. We were asked to place our hands and feet together, the left thumb covering the right, the

The Mahikari Treatment (okiyome). Detail of Mahikari poster showing how spirit rays emitted from the hand expel sickness, poverty, conflict, and misfortune, and fill a person's life with health, peace, and riches.

big toe of our left foot over the big toe of our right. We were told that the Treatment would take about ten minutes. We closed our eyes, and the young ladies, now sitting opposite us, clapped their hands three times and began to recite what sounded like a Shinto incantation. After this, nothing seemed to happen. I presumed that they were holding their hands over us. I opened my eyes slightly and peeked. Yes, they were. Around me, I could hear others intoning the same chant, clapping their hands, or chatting with newcomers. From the snatches of conversation I could hear throughout the room, people seemed to be talking about various kinds of sickness and misfortune.

The young woman in front of me quietly began to sing a slow and soothing song that sounded like a melancholy folksong. At first I thought she was singing to me. But no. I suddenly realized that she was addressing "spirits" inside me:

Comrade spirits! Cast off all earthly attachments;
Perform your ascetic discipline [*shugyō*] in the spirit world.

If you leave sin and impurities behind you in this world,
In the astral world you will suffer all the more.

Painful as it is, every time you rid yourself of attachment
You get one step closer to paradise.

If, because of your attachment to this world, you possess someone's body,
You will be punished for the sin of escaping from the astral world.

There is no road to hell as terrible as that of attachment;
Behold the dawning of the spirit world and serve God!

If you do not get rid of your attachments to this world,
Repeated cycles of death and rebirth will be your fate until you fall into hell.

For the happiness of the lovely wife and child you left behind,
Devote yourself to fulfilling your obligations in the other world.

Within the hearts of your surviving family,
Create the desire to serve God's Mahikari faith.

Know that God has a prayer for saving
Hopeless lives and incurable diseases.

After the song was over, my partner was quiet for a few minutes. Then, in a loud, authoritative voice she pronounced the word *oshizumari* (Peace, be still!) three times, each time raising her hands over my head and lowering them along the sides of my body. Then she tapped lightly on my knee. "You may open your eyes now," she said. "Can you see clearly? Are you dizzy? Did you feel anything?" To please her, I said that I had had a rather peaceful feeling, as though I had been meditating.

Then she had me turn around and sit tailor-fashion in front of her. After gently feeling the vertebrae in the back of my neck, she raised her hand behind me and held it above me for about two minutes. Then she did the same thing to the other side of my neck. After this, she asked me to lie down on my stomach. Skillfully she examined the anatomy of my back until she came to what I supposed were my kidneys. Again, she raised her hand over one side

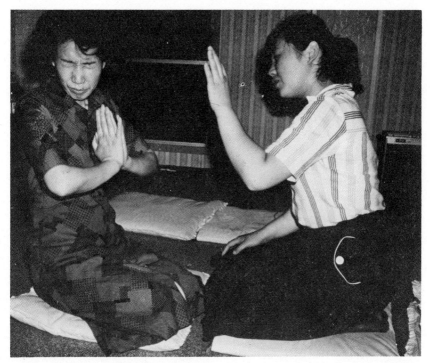

Giving okiyome to the primary soul

Giving okiyome to the body

and then the other. As she did so, she began to explain some of the group's ideas.

"Mahikari tries to prove the reality of God's existence by demonstrating his miracles in the most direct and concrete way possible. The purpose of the church is not just to perform miracles, but to make people aware of Mahikari, the True Light, or God."

"How are miracles performed?," I asked.

"All you need to do is raise your hand over people and the spirit rays [*reihasen*] from Mahikari will enter their bodies, purify them, and expel all the impurities and toxins inside. We begin by purifying the primary soul [*shukon*], a tiny point ten centimeters behind the forehead. Spirit rays entering the primary soul first attract and then expel the evil spirits that have become attached to our bodies causing illness and unhappiness." It was the movement of evil spirits that had convulsed the Indonesian man on the videotape, she explained.

She asked whether I had any particular illnesses. When I told her that I sometimes have trouble with my stomach, she had me roll over on my back. Holding her hand over my abdomen, she continued her explanation.

"There are various critical points along the body that we must focus on when we give a person the Treatment. The practitioner first has to feel around to find these places. Then he lifts his hand over the spot so that the hand can act as a lens to focus the spirit rays directly upon the afflicted area. This is the best way to 'melt' the toxins that have accumulated in our bodies from food additives, pollution, and above all, medicine. Medicine is poison," she said in a matter-of-fact tone of voice.

By this time my mind was reeling with questions. Sensing this, and perhaps hoping to make a new convert, the girls offered to take us to their dojo to meet their local leader, Yoshida Sensei. I readily agreed, and my friend Mrs. Ota, though uninterested herself, consented to come along. A five-minute walk along the side of the railroad tracks brought us to the dojo.

At this point I should pause to say a word about Nakayama City. The capital of a conservative, largely agricultural prefecture, the city has a population of about 600,000. Like so many other Japanese cities of its sort, it combines the worst elements of provincialism and rapid industrial growth. Too close to Osaka to develop its own cultural attractions, the city draws few foreign tourists. Those who do appear quickly change trains and head for the scenic spots in the southern part of the prefecture. To the north, on the other side of the Nakayama River, there are a number of steel mills and petrochemical factories that contribute both to the city's economy and to its environmental woes. Aside from the absence of anything positive about the city, visitors are also annoyed by the mephitic stench of the sluggish black rivers that run like clogged arteries through its heart. While we were in Nakayama, scientists put some fish into the oily water of these rivers and watched them die—in less than three minutes. It may not be a pleasant place, but Nakayama, I soon learned, was an ideal spot for breeding evil spirits.

The dojo is located in an unpretentious section bordering on Shinba, the quarter of town where the Eta, or Burakumin (Japan's outcastes), live. The unpleasant odor of the Shinba tanneries drifts as far as the dojo. The immediate neighborhood, though not as unpleasant as Shinba, is nondescript, as only Japanese cities can be. Surrounded by modest homes, a small sake factory, a burlap-bag supplier, small lumber yards, and a few tiny restaurants, the dojo is, literally, as gray as the rest of the neighborhood. A modest two-story building, it could easily be mistaken for the office of a construction company, were it not for the bright green canvas covering the staircase to the second floor. There, in large orange letters, are written the words:

TRUE-LIGHT SUPRA-RELIGIOUS ORGANIZATION
NAKAYAMA INTERMEDIARY DOJO

Beneath, in smaller letters, is the older name of the sect:

The Friendly Association of the
Lucky and Healthy Sunshine Children

We walked up the stairs to the second floor and went in. There the scene was similar to the one we had just left. People were sitting in twos facing each other, or holding their hands over others who were lying on the gray carpet discreetly covered with bathtowels. The room was quiet. Mounted above the walls, covered by yellow, gray, and white striped wallpaper, the blue plastic blades of eleven

electric fans moved slowly back and forth, impartially distributing
the hot summer air. In the front of the room was an altar made of
plain Japanese cypress and an altar scroll inscribed with the name
of the main deity of the sect: Mioyamotosu Mahikari Ōmikami. On
the left side of the altar, standing on a pedestal, was a small metal-
lic statue of Daikoku, one of the most popular gods of wealth in
Japan. One of Japan's Seven Gods of Luck, Daikoku was wearing
his customary flat cap, and was carrying a bag over his left shoulder
and a magic mallet (*uchide no kozuchi*) in his right hand.* On the
wall to the left of the altar was a photograph of the founder of the
sect.

We sat down and were introduced to a charming young woman
of eighteen, the Reverend Takagi, one of the ministers sent to the
dojo from the sect's headquarters in Tokyo. She asked if we would
like to receive the Treatment again. We said yes. The same proce-
dure was followed, but this time the minister first bowed before the
altar scroll enshrined in the front of the room, the statue of Daikoku, and the portrait of the founder. As I lay on my stomach receiving the Treatment, I tried to continue the conversation.

"We are surrounded by poisons," the Reverend Takagi began,
"by PCB, AF2, DDT, and others. Medicine itself is poison. All of
these toxins enter the body and become trapped. Once inside the
body, they coagulate and form spirit occlusions [*reishō*]. These in
turn lodge in the chromosomes and cause birth defects and cancer."
She went on to remind me of all of the stories about environmental
pollution that fill Japan's daily newspapers. "We get sick when we
eat poisoned food. But the reason we eat such food in the first place
is because evil spirits are possessing us. Eighty to 100 percent of
our sicknesses are caused by evil spirits," she informed me.

---

* Because wealth was traditionally measured in terms of good harvest, Daikoku
has usually been pictured standing on two or three bales of rice while a mouse,
his messenger, scampers about in search of fallen grains. In rural Japan, Daikoku
became a deity of the rice paddies. Because of his connection with food, he was
often enshrined in kitchens or dining rooms. In the Kyoto area, belief in Daikoku
goes back at least to the Muromachi period (1336–1573). Under the influence of
the Tendai and Shingon sects of Buddhism, his worship was fused with the cult of
the Shinto deity, Ōkuninushi. Mahikari has preserved this syncretistic tie, maintaining that Daikoku, or (Ōkunitama)-Ōkuninushi, is the symbol of the secondary, or
materialistic, deities.

The Nakayama dojo

"How do you know that?," I asked.

"You can tell by the way people's hands move when they are given the Treatment. The hands of a person being possessed by a snake spirit move this way." She pressed her hands together and began to make twisting, serpentine motions. "A badger spirit will move like this." She clenched her fists and rolled them together. "A fox goes like this." She intertwined her fingers and moved her hands in small circles. "When we are possessed by a human spirit, such as an ancestral ghost, our hands shake up and down. The spirit of a dead bird moves like this." She flapped her arms pretending they were wings. "When a spirit finally is exorcised and leaves the body, a person's hand or shoulder automatically rises towards the ceiling. Once a young girl came to our dojo and was possessed by a snake spirit that decided to leave her body by going out her leg. Since she was wearing a miniskirt that day, it was quite embarrassing," she said with a laugh.

By this time, Yoshida Sensei had come into the room. He was a slightly built man of about forty, balding, with a kind smile and bright, somewhat mischievous eyes. Chain-smoking as we talked, Sensei radiated the self-assurance of one who knows the answers to many questions and the remedies for all sorts of ills. He took over where the minister had left off.

"Su-god is really a remarkable deity," Yoshida Sensei began. "We have seen all sorts of miracles take place here. The oldest evil spirit we have exorcised died 1,500 years ago. The Savior once exorcised a spirit that had gone to the astral world some 4,000 years ago! Let me show you what I mean."

He summoned a young girl about seventeen years old and whispered something in her ear. He then turned back to me and introduced the girl as Wakimoto Kanako. "This girl's whole family has been possessed by evil spirits," he said. "Her father has stomach cancer, but thanks to Su-god, his color has already improved. Her aunt also developed cancer, and died because she did not join Mahikari. Her father's uncle, who now lives in Brazil, has been operated on twice for cancer of the bladder. Three years ago Kanako developed severe headaches. Her parents took her to several doctors, but no organic cause could be found. The headaches finally became so severe that she had to drop out of school. Recently, after her father became ill and the family joined the dojo, her headaches returned. She has been receiving the Treatment regularly and, thanks to our spirit investigations [*reisa*], she has learned that the spirit of a samurai who died some 400 years ago has been possessing her and causing this illness. Nowadays, after only ten minutes of the Treatment, her headaches go away. Watch this."

Sensei and the young girl prostrated themselves before the altar scroll, the statue of Daikoku, and the Savior's picture. Facing the girl, Sensei clapped his hands three times and began to intone the Exorcist's Prayer (Amatsu Norigoto).* After he had silently held his

---

* Because of the arcane wording of this prayer, I am reluctant to attempt a translation. Instead, let me cite an ancient Jewish-Christian exorcism that has nearly

hand over her forehead for a few minutes, the girl's hands began to shake. Her head shook slowly from side to side. Yoshida Sensei turned to me and explained that the spirit possessing her was trying to escape from the Light coming from his hand. From what the Reverend Takagi had just told me, I judged that the ghost of a human being was about to appear. Yoshida Sensei began his spirit investigation.

Talking softly to the ghost, he inquired, "Are you a human spirit?"

The girl, as though in a trance, nodded slowly. Yes, the spirit possessing the girl was formerly a human being.

"How long ago did you die?," Sensei continued. "Twenty years ago?"

The girl shook her head, her long, glossy black hair completely covering her face. "No. Before that."

"Fifty years ago?"

"No."

"One hundred years ago?"

"No."

"Longer still? Two hundred?"

"No."

"Three hundred?"

"No."

"Four hundred?"

The girl nodded her head in assent.

"What kind of person were you? A samurai?"

"Yes," said the girl on behalf of the spirit.

"Why did you possess Kanako? Were you in love with her?"

"No," the spirit answered.

"Did you bear a grudge against her?"

---

all of the flavor, power, and word magic, and even some of the symbolism of the Japanese prayer: "I conjure thee by the God of the Hebrews, Jesus, Jaba, Jae, Abraoth, Aia, Thoth, Ele, Elo, Aeo, Eu, Jiibaech, Abarmas, Jabarau, Abelbel, Lona, Abra, Maroia, Arm, appearing in fire, thou Tannetis, in the midst of plains, and snow, and mists; let thine inexorable angel descend and put into safe keeping the wandering demon of this creature whom God has created in his holy Paradise. For I pray to the Holy God, putting my reliance in Ammonipsentancho." A. Deissmann, *Licht vom Osten*, 3d ed. (Tübingen, 1909), pp. 192ff, cited in T. K. Oesterreich, *Possession Demoniacal and Other Among Primitive Races, in Antiquity, the Middle Ages, and Modern Times* (London, 1930), p. 101.

"Yes."

"Why did you bear a grudge against her? Did she do something bad to you in a previous life?"

"No."

"Why then are you angry with her?"

The girl began to write something on the floor with her finger.

Sensei turned to me. "This is automatic writing," he said. "Sometimes the evil spirits talk through the mouth of the person they are possessing. Sometimes they answer by making the person's head move. In other cases, they cause the person to do automatic writing on the floor. Even pre-school children who don't know Chinese characters write very complicated words when they are given a spirit investigation."

Turning back to the girl, he made out from the invisible characters she had traced on the floor that in her previous life she had been married to this samurai. When she was reborn in this world before him, the warrior's spirit became jealous and began to possess her.

"This is the cause of her headaches," Sensei concluded aloud.

Then, in a soft voice, as though he were speaking to a naughty child, Yoshida Sensei began to scold the spirit.

"Honorable Spirit, what you are doing is bad. If you leave the astral world to possess Kanako you are just postponing the discipline you have to go through before being reborn. Go back to the other world and leave her in peace."

After the spirit investigation and the scolding were finished, Sensei lifted his hands over the girl, now lying exhausted and inert on the carpet before him, and pronounced the benediction: "Oshizumari! Oshizumari! Oshizumari!" The spirit of the vengeful samurai went back to the astral world whence it had come. Sensei tapped the girl on the knee.

"Are you all right? Are you dizzy?"

She was in good shape. We thanked her, and she bounced off to join her friends.

By this time it had grown late. I began to worry that the bakery would close before I could pick up the cake I had ordered for our son's birthday party. When I asked how I could learn more about Mahikari, Sensei replied that an elementary training course was going to be given that weekend. If I took the course I could be presented an amulet (*omitama*) and would be able to perform miracles "just like Buddha and Jesus Christ."

Without a second thought, I agreed to take the course. After jotting down the details, we thanked Yoshida Sensei and the others and took our leave. Outside, I jokingly asked Mrs. Ota if she was ready to join Mahikari. "Not I!," she said with a laugh. After some pleasantries, I dashed off to the baker's.

So began six months of miracles and exorcism among the Lucky and Healthy Sunshine Children of Nakayama City.

3   *Learning Mioshie*

When I arrived at the dojo at ten o'clock on Friday morning, about forty people had assembled to register for the course. Several members were on hand to take orders for lunch, register neophytes, and take the $42.00 registration fee. I recognized Miss Watanabe, the young lady who had first given me the Treatment, the Reverend Takagi, and, of course, Yoshida Sensei. I noticed that Wakimoto Kanako, the girl possessed by the samurai spirit, was also present. We took our places on the tatami mats, sitting behind low writing desks, and waited for the morning lecture to begin. In the corner, a tape recorder played military marches and finally Tchaikovsky's "Swan Lake." At last someone turned the music off, and Yoshida Sensei walked to the front of the room. After brief prayers to Su-god, Daikoku, and the founder, the lecture began:

Your ancestors and guardian spirits have brought you to this training course. On Sunday you will receive your amulets and will be able to perform all sorts of miracles. Many people will be healed on the first day of the course. Some of you will experience strange bodily sensations. Some will feel mysteriously hot. Others will shake with cold. If you're possessed by a spirit from a cold hell, you'll be cold. But if the spirit comes from a hot hell, you'll become hot. Others are going to have diarrhea or will pass blood. Some will begin to vomit or spit up impurities. You may suddenly begin to cry without knowing why. Don't be surprised. The spirit rays from Su-god are already beginning to purify your bodies and make you ready to receive your amulet.

From now on you must lay aside your egoism. You must get rid of the idea that science is everything and get ready to believe in the unseen. Science can't explain the miracles that you are going to see. Receive the Teachings [Mioshie] with a humble, unquestioning heart.

Next Yoshida Sensei turned his attention to the subject of religion, miracles, and the uncanny world of spirits.

Mahikari aims at the renewal of the world* and the salvation of people both in this world *and* in the astral world [*yūkai*]. It does not ask members to give up their other religious affiliations. It simply says, try the Treatment [*okiyome*]† and see. We are critical only of religions that perform no miracles. Both Jesus and the Buddha performed miracles by means of the Mahikari Treatment. Gradually, however, the religions established in their names have turned into mere philosophy and speculation. Today, thanks to Mahikari, anyone can perform miracles and become a little Jesus or Buddha!

The World of Spirits: The Proof

In order to prove the existence of spirits, evil and benign, Yoshida Sensei began to discourse at length about spiritual phenomena in general. Like occult movements in the West, Mahikari stresses the importance of the aura. The pioneer researcher in this area was Dr. Uchida Hideo, once a research scientist in the field of electrical engineering, who since 1963 has devoted himself to writing science fiction. While studying the problem of interference in television and radio transmission, Uchida discovered that the human body itself gives off electromagnetic waves. He became interested in astrology and once even beheld his mother's astral spirit. He then invented a meter that allegedly enabled him to detect and study auras. Yoshida Sensei cited Uchida's findings:

---

* "Renewal of the world" (*yonaoshi*). World renewal was an orgiastic and eschatological theme often associated with faith in Maitreya, the Buddha of the Future. World renewal was a common feature in both the agricultural rites and the peasant uprisings of the nineteenth century. An important part of yonaoshi was the exorcism of evil spirits. See Miyata Noboru, "'Yonaoshi' to Miroku shinkō: Nihon ni okeru 'yonaoshi' no minzokuteki imi" (World renewal and faith in Maitreya: The folkloric meaning of world renewal in Japan), *Minzokugaku kenkyū*, 33, No. 1 (1968), pp. 32–44. See also Chapter 13, pp. 294f, below.

† Mahikari's therapeutic ritual is referred to variously as okiyome (purification), *Mahikari no waza* (the Mahikari Treatment), and *tekazashi* (raising the hand). Its function is the purification (*misogi*) and exorcism (*harai*) of body and soul(s) alike. Members also refer to the effect of okiyome as *kurīningu* (a Japanese-English word generally used for *dry*-cleaning!)

The healthy body gives off negative electromagnetic energy, whereas the sick body radiates positive energy. All bodies are surrounded with an aura, but there are three basic shapes named by Uchida after the type of halos found on traditional statues of the Buddha. The Amida Nyorai aura is a circular halo, the bottom of which comes down to a person's knees or shins. The Kannon (Avalokiteśvara) aura has an elongated turnip shape, which comes to rest on the ground around one's feet. The Fudō Myōō aura, like the Kannon aura, rests on the ground but has no fixed end point above the person's head. On the aura meter, it looks like a tornado. A pregnant woman has two auras—a separate one for the fetus—and a woman who has had an abortion will have an aura peppered with small dark spots.

Auras come in a variety of colors: yellow, cream, purple, dark gray, and black. Illness and pain show up as dark spots on the aura meter. Auras, Dr. Uchida believed, are inherited, lending credence to Mahikari's teachings about ancestral karma.* Ancestral spirits can be picked up on the aura meter on the anniversary of the ancestor's death. Generally, the spirit of a deceased child or a spirit related to one's father appears on the right of the aura, and a spirit on one's mother's side of the family will show up on the left.

Dr. Uchida also discovered that religious people with a grateful, polite attitude have auras that are thicker in front, protecting them from various mishaps. A selfish, unreligious person, however, has an aura that trails along behind, leaving him unprotected from oncoming dangers.

Although Uchida proved that the soul [reikon] itself is composed of weak positive electricity, research is still going on to show why this energy gives off an aura around the body. He reasoned that the soul energy probably ionizes the surrounding air and then radiates outward from the body in the manner of infrared, ultraviolet, or X rays. The aura meter has shown that people with supernatural psychic powers do indeed have what in Yoga is called the Third Eye. Uchida discovered this in the middle of the forehead—right where Mahikari's founder discovered man's primary soul [shukon]. Uchida was able to demonstrate aura beams coming from this Eye. These findings, all approved by the founder, are incorporated into Mioshie. The more people receive the Mahikari Treatment, the wider and more protective their auras become.[1]

Yoshida Sensei rounded off his remarks about the reality of spirit phenomena with some tales about statues of Jesus and Mary in various churches around the world. "Statues of the Virgin Mary

---

* There is no clear-cut distinction in Mahikari between the "sins and pollutions" (zaie) a person has accumulated in his past lives and those of his ancestors. He is made to suffer for both. This obfuscation between these two logically separable kinds of karma runs throughout popular Japanese religion and can be traced back to similar tendencies in Chinese religion since the Sung dynasty (960–1279).

A lecture during the elementary training course

Illustration of possessing spirits. From left to right, top row: ancestors; fox, badger, and snake; vengeful spirit. Bottom row: Tengu (heavenly dog) and Ryujin (dragon god); lustful spirits (the cause of "sexual karma" possession).

have been known to shed tears. Here is a picture of a statue of Jesus with blood running from the hands," he went on, holding up a newspaper clipping. "A professor in Akita Prefecture identified the blood as Type B. Mary and Jesus are showing their distress over the warfare between Christians in Northern Ireland—and over the fact that Christians no longer perform miracles," he declared. "Wherever you look, there are strange things happening! In the dojo we have seen all sorts of spirits appear. Ancestral ghosts, badgers, snakes, birds, men from outer space, ancient warriors and the wretched peasants they slaughtered, *tengu* [demonic tricksters with long noses], and foxes."

Cosmology

The next step in Sensei's proof of the existence of the spirit world was a discussion of the Fundamental Principles of the Structure of the Universe. Beginning with the Buddhist notion that all things are filled with nothingness (*shikizoku zeikū*), he went on to demonstrate that the entire material universe was created from spirit:

God is light, the Bible says. From research done by scientists at the University of Chicago we know that the "universal rays" from outer space continually invade the earth, where they are transformed into protons, electrons, neutrons, mesons, photons, and finally matter itself. But the Fundamental Principles of the Structure of the Universe are best understood according to the Miroku Principle.

At this point Sensei referred us to a list of triadic relationships in our textbooks:

Divine World	Astral World	Earthly World
Fire	Water	Earth
Proton	Electron	Meson
Ancestor	Self	Descendant
Parent	Child	Grandchild
Heart	Lungs	Stomach
Ruler	People	Land
Capital	Labor	Raw Materials

The Miroku Principle, actually a set of oppositions and transformations based on the archaic notion of yin and yang, is introduced to members in the elementary training course and is dealt with at greater length in advanced courses as the Principle of the Cubic Cross Civilization. Having little talent for arcane exposition myself, I shall turn briefly from Yoshida Sensei's lecture to the Savior's own writings in order to illuminate this idea. The following passage may sound like gibberish and may even cost me a few readers, but I have decided to include it here not only because it helps unravel the mystery of the Miroku Principle, but because it is a good example of the Savior's occult mode of theological exposition.

The "boss" of the tutelary shrines found throughout Japan is the creator god Ōkunitama Ōkuninushi, symbolized by the statue of Daikoku in the dojo. All the people of the world recognize him—even the Jews and the Egyptians. The festivals held in these Japanese shrines can be divided into those of spring (= fire), summer (= water), and autumn (= earth). The numbers corresponding to fire, water, and earth are, respectively, 5, 6, and 7. Now, according to ancient records from Japan's Age of the Gods, the festivals of fire, water, and earth are celebrations of the god Miroku. (The Buddhist deity Maitreya is merely a lower manifestation of this Shinto god.) The name of this god can be spelled 5-6-7. Because man cannot live, or be saved, without the fire, water, and earth that make up the world, the Miroku Principle is the paradigm for the normative order of both the world and human society. All things must be reduced to the "cross"—a coincidence of opposites.

Going beyond yin and yang, the Savior insisted that the three oppositions must be merged in a final synthesis. The cross that does not falter has three axes and forms a three-dimensional mandala. When the true cross turns around, it becomes a sphere or a triple cross (the Miroku Principle). Thus fire, water, and earth form a trinity and result in the globe itself. The Divine World, the Astral World, and the Present World constitute the universe. The sun, the moon, and the earth give us the solar system. Jewish medicine (which is purely materialistic), American mentalistic medicine, and the purely spiritual therapies of Japan must be combined so that men can find true health. The atom itself is built out of the proton, electron, and meson. The family is based on ancestors, self, and posterity. In the same way, when capitalists, workers, and raw materials form one harmonious economy, a nation will get ahead in international competition. In Japan the emperor, his subjects, and the land form a perfect whole; otherwise Japan would fall apart. Likewise, we find other natural trinities throughout nature and society: the head, the torso, and the limbs; gases, liquids, and solids; and so on. All of these homologizations follow the principle "spirit first, heart second, body third" (*rei-shu, shin-jū, tai-zoku*).[2]

Healing

After his exposition of the Principles of the Universe, Yoshida Sensei turned to the problem of sickness and medicine:

From God's point of view, there is no such thing as sickness. What we call sickness is merely God's way of purifying the toxins that have accumulated in our bodies. The Treatment serves to focus the Light or spirit rays upon these toxins so that they can be melted and expelled from the body more quickly. Vomit, excrement, and urine are the natural way to get rid of poisons and get cleaned up. When a woman has a baby, she gets rid of a lot of poisons. Likewise, it is good for us to work, since working makes us sweat. This is God's present to us. Sweat and you won't get sick! Try to sweat as much as possible! In the old days, you used to see kids going around with runny noses, . . . usually wiping them on their sleeves. That was *good* for them! By getting rid of impurities they cleaned out their heads. Kids nowadays aren't as smart as they used to be because their noses don't run as much.

Today, book after book is being written on the diseases caused by medicine itself. And every day doctors are being sued for malpractice. People have been known to drop over dead after being given a simple flu shot. Many schools have given up mandatory inoculation programs because of their side effects. The truth is: *medicine is poison*! Medicines, like food additives, accumulate in the body, become hard, and turn into tumors.

When a surgeon makes an incision in the body, he also cuts through the spirit body [*reitai*]. The pain caused by the surgeon's knife will last 150 years after you enter the astral world. Cutting the body is a sin. A regional leader of the church in Brazil writes in the *Mahikari* magazine that the high rate of meningitis in that country is due to the many tonsilectomies performed there.

During the lunch break, Yoshida Sensei invited me into his office to share some watermelon. This gave me a chance to ask a few questions about the lecture.

"Are there any circumstances under which a member can go to a doctor? For example, can tooth decay be cured by okiyome?"

"In the case of cavities or broken bones, it is best to get medical help. Okiyome won't be of any help, either, in curing cancers that have already been treated with cobalt. Cobalt destroys both the spirit cells [*reibō*] and the astral cells [*yūbō*] of the body. In this case, okiyome has nothing to work on, since it cures the physical body by first purifying the spirit body. Okiyome is also useless in treating leprosy, since this affliction is sent as a punishment by Su-god.

"Sometimes we do go to the doctor for X rays. For example, some members have gone to the doctor for an X ray and have been told that they have a tumor of some sort. Then they come to the dojo and receive okiyome for a few months and later go back to the doctor for more X rays. By comparing the X rays, they can see how the tumor has melted and shrunk. X rays help to prove our miracles!"

"Western medicine tells us that sickness is caused by bacteria and viruses," I said. "Is this wrong?"

"It isn't wrong. It's just not a complete explanation. Suppose we ingest germs and become ill. The question remains, why did we pick up the germs in the first place? That can be explained only by the presence of evil spirits in our bodies that cause us to eat infected food. Most people talk about being lucky or unlucky. That is an unscientific explanation. Spirit possession explains *why* people are lucky or unlucky in the first place."

"If illness is God's way of 'cleaning us up,' why does it have to hurt so much?"

"Pain is caused by an evil spirit expanding within the body. For example, take gastritis. There are two kinds: one accompanied by fever, the other without. Gastritis without fever is invariably caused by spirits. For example, take Watanabe Mariko, the girl who gave you okiyome the other day. She came to the dojo in perfect health but suffered excruciating abdominal pains when she received okiyome. Spirit investigations showed that she was being possessed by foxes."

The lunch break passed quickly, and the lecture began again.

Sensei now turned his attention to the body's twenty-seven vital spots (*kyūsho*).

The Mahikari Treatment will be most effective when directed toward the appropriate vital spots. The poisons in our system cause a hardening of the skin and muscles around these points, which can be felt by the hand. The minimum Treatment must include a purification of the primary soul, the lower neck, and the kidneys. When the kidneys are working well, the individual will have a slim waist. Malfunctioning kidneys cause the body to fill up with urine as far as the fourth vital spot, the lungs. This is why some people, especially foreigners, are fat or have a square body shape.

Some cures are surprising. Bed wetting can be corrected by purifying the child's temples. A cough is often cured by purifying the groin. Stomach cancer caused by physical influences should be treated by giving okiyome to the stomach itself. But if it is learned through spirit investigations that the cause of the cancer is an evil spirit, the following organs must be purified: the primary soul, the hindbrain, the lower neck, the kidneys, the front and back of the stomach, and the pancreas. For asthma, the individual should try to spit up as much phlegm as possible. Then his primary soul, hindbrain, lower neck, kidneys, stomach, pancreas, backside of the heart, and groin should all be purified. This disease is generally caused by spirit obstructions, and calls for more attention to the worship of one's ancestors.

To cure neuroses, purify the primary soul, the hindbrain, the lower neck, and the kidneys. One hundred percent of our neuroses are caused by spirit obstructions! Facial neuralgia is caused by spirits who have been killed in traffic accidents. Purify the primary soul. Angina pectoris is caused by spirits bearing a grudge. Purify the primary soul and the lower neck. Buzzing in the ears is caused by the flow of poisons inside the ear. Purify the side of the neck and the area just below the ears. Menstrual problems are brought about by the sexual lust of ancestral spirits. Purify the primary soul, the lower neck, and the uterus. Uterine tumors are caused by the coagulation of injections and drugs. Purify the front and backside of the uterus.

In a similar fashion, we were taught how to treat liver ailments, rheumatism, ulcers, dyspepsia, heartburn, gastroptosis, colds, irregular heartbeats, cerebral hemorrhage, concussions (in this case the person should not be moved and a doctor should be called), headache, nearsightedness, inflammation of the ear, ozena, throat cancer, polio, and color blindness. Finally, we were warned not to advertise that we could cure diseases or make diagnoses, since according to Japanese law only doctors can perform these functions.

In order to stay clear of the law and the wrath of the medical profession, Sensei suggested that we should offer only to *purify* souls and bodies.

The Nature of Man and Spirit

After his discussion of the healing powers of okiyome, Yoshida Sensei turned his attention to the nature of man:

According to Mioshie, man has two souls: the primary soul [*shukon*] in the forehead and a secondary soul [*fukkon*], which lies five centimeters behind and below the navel. The former is the seat of conscience, reason, and right desires, and is planted in us from the moment of our conception by the "strict" or "fire" deities. The secondary soul, however, is the locus of material, evil desires and is implanted in the fifth month of a fetus's existence by the "secondary" or "water" deities. The character for man in Japanese corresponds to the proper relationship between these souls.

He drew the following diagram to illustrate his point:

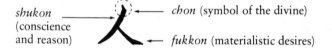

shukon ——— chon (symbol of the divine)
(conscience
and reason) ——— *fukkon* (materialistic desires)

The upright stroke symbolizes the primary soul under God's rule (the *chon* symbol). The small stroke stands for the secondary soul. If the secondary soul becomes too large the result is bad and has to be crossed out:*

The human body is a trinity composed of the physical body [*nikutai*], the spirit body [*reitai*], and the astral body [*yūtai*]. The first is shed when a person dies and becomes a corpse. Then the spirit and astral bodies (which give off spirit and astral rays, respectively) leave for the other world. There the individual must perform various austerities in order to purify himself from the "sins and impurities" [*zaie*] or bad karma of the past. As punish-

---

* I present this ideograph as a simple example of the way in which Mahikari uses Chinese characters and occult etymologies to "prove" its theological assertions. Although many of the points made in the lectures and in the Savior's writings are elaborated in terms of etymologies of this sort, I have omitted them in this book because of their complexity and tedium for Western readers (and at least one Western writer).

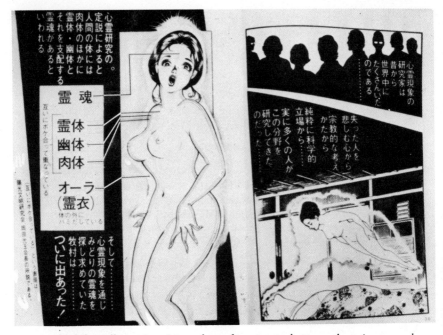

Mahikari illustration. Lines show, from top to bottom, the primary soul (forehead), the spiritual, astral, and physical bodies, and the body's surrounding aura.

ment for his wrongdoings, a person is sometimes transformed into the spirit of an animal. Or men may be changed into women. It is not uncommon for an ancestral spirit to take the shape of an animal when it possesses a person. The reason why spirits try to leave the astral world prematurely (that is, before they are ready to be reincarnated) is that the austerities they must undergo there are so painful and severe. Possessing a person in this world is a way spirits have of shirking their obligations in the astral world. Unfortunately, such an escape only prolongs their days of torment.

In the other world we continue to suffer from the illnesses that caused our death in this world. Members of Mahikari, however, have a way to avoid this. When a member dies, his family and friends gather around the coffin for the wake and give okiyome to his corpse. This cleans up the source of his disease and will make his burden lighter in the astral world.

The Butsudan

Whereas okiyome is the primary weapon against spirit possession, the worship of ancestral spirits at the Buddhist memorial altar
(*butsudan*) is also important. Knowing how to feed and worship
the spirits of one's ancestors has been the key to health and happiness for many Mahikari followers. Ancestors do send warnings or
omens to their families if their graves are neglected or if their tomb-
stones fall over, but making offerings (*kuyō*) to them at the grave
itself is not very efficacious. Most ancestral possession is caused by
"mistakes" in their descendants' ritual behavior; they may, for example, arrange the memorial tablets in the butsudan incorrectly, or
fail to make the proper kind of offerings. Ancestral spirits, when
interrogated, often admit that they possessed certain individuals
because they were hungry and hoped to get a meal, or because they
were miffed about the condition or placement of their memorial
tablets in the butsudan.

The care of the butsudan and its tablets (*ihai*) is a popular topic
in Mahikari study groups. I once attended such a meeting, during
which the fine points of the butsudan cult were discussed for over
two hours. Questions such as these were discussed:

QUESTION: Should I place flowers so that they face the butsudan itself, or
should they face the people in the room?
ANSWER: Flowers must face the memorial tablets, since they are an offering to the ancestors. They should be colored flowers, and if
they are not sweet-smelling, a dash of perfume will make them
really *hai-kārā* [high-collar, that is, classy]. Make sure the
flowers in the butsudan do not wilt and offend the ancestors.
QUESTION: Should the flowers be placed on the left or the right side?

No one seemed to know the answer to this question. Mr. Yama-
giwa, who happened to be a butsudan repairman, said he had heard
that flowers should always be placed on the left-hand side, though
he was not sure why. No one could remember any definitive answer
in Mioshie to this question, so the group decided that Mr. Yama-
giwa was probably right.

Yoshida Sensei's long discussion of the butsudan and its rules can
be summarized as follows:

(1) The butsudan must always be placed above eye level and never below a staircase or on a wobbly chest of drawers. *Example*: Once a junior high school principal came to the dojo because his son was constantly getting into trouble. When he was given oki-yome, an ancestral spirit appeared to complain that the family's butsudan had been shoved under the stairs. Since the ancestor resented being trampled on by the family, he decided to make his resentment known by possessing the child, causing him to misbehave. The butsudan was moved and, for the first time, the child became well mannered.

Nothing should be placed on top of the butsudan. If the house has two stories, the butsudan should be put upstairs. If you live in an apartment building with other families living upstairs, do not worry; even if they walk over your butsudan every day, that is no insult to your ancestors. Since each family has its own spirit level (*reisō*), the spirit rays coming from different butsudans will not get mixed up. The butsudan should face the light. Other than this, the direction in which it faces does not matter. A small light should be installed inside to give the ancestors a "taste of Eden." Members of the family should not sleep with their feet toward the butsudan. This would be an insult to the ancestors.

(2) The memorial tablets should be painted with black lacquer and trimmed in gold. Tablets of this sort make the best contact with spirit rays and are therefore the easiest for spirits to dwell in. Make sure the gold lettering does not fade. Plain, unpainted tablets or paper ones simply will not do. Putting such tablets in your butsudan is like building a shack for your ancestors. You should never use the thin kind of tablets that are stacked together in a bundle. With tablets like this, only the ancestors on the outside of the bundle ever get to eat.

(3) The tablets of those who died more than thirty years ago should be incinerated on a new steel grill or sent to the family's Buddhist temple for safekeeping.* The spirits of these ancestors

---

* When a family joins Mahikari its members do not give up their traditional affiliation with their family temple (*dannadera*). Although they come together for the wake in order to give the corpse its last okiyome, the funeral itself is regularly entrusted to a Buddhist priest. Mahikari's attitude is that the dead (i.e., the priest, a devotee of a "secondary deity") should bury the dead.

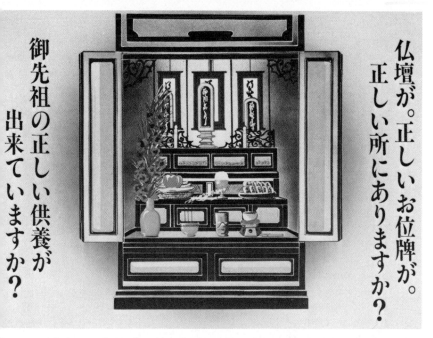

仏壇が。正しいお位牌が。正しい所にありますか？

御先祖の正しい供養が出来ていますか？

A memorial altar, or butsudan. Detail of Mahikari poster asking "Are your butsudan and memorial tablets arranged correctly?" and "Do you know the right way to present offerings to your ancestors?"

Butsudan enshrined in a member's home above a crucifix, praying angels, a statue of the Virgin Mary, a British soldier, a monkey, and miscellaneous bric-a-brac

should then be induced to move into the tallest tablet in the butsudan, which is placed behind all the others. This is the most prestigious position in the butsudan and is reserved for the oldest spirits
in the family. The other tablets (each bearing the posthumous name
of the deceased) are arranged in strict hierarchical order according
to the person's date of birth (not death). The younger the spirit,
the shorter the tablet and the farther toward the front of the butsudan it is placed. In the case of grandparents, both posthumous
names may be written on the same tablet, since they would naturally be at the same spirit level. (In Mahikari, it is believed that
people always marry individuals at the same spirit level.) Only if
Grandma and Grandpa used to quarrel a lot should you give them
separate tablets! No pictures should be placed in the butsudan.
Since Amida Buddha has gone back to the divine world, you should
remove any of his statues from the butsudan. When rearranging the
butsudan, the leader of the family should face the tablets and say
to the ancestors, "Those of you who died thirty years or before
please move to the large family tablet in the center. All others,
please take your places in your respective tablets." Someone then
reads both the posthumous name and the secular name of the deceased so that each spirit knows where to go. If a new tablet is
being set up, the deceased is asked to take up his residence in it.
Then appropriate hymns from the prayer book are sung, but not
the Exorcist's Prayer. The family must apologize to the ancestors
for any neglect or mistakes they have made in their worship, and
should inform the ancestors that their descendants are now living
in the Age of the Baptism of Fire and that the ancestors should no
longer be attached to this world or try to perform austerities here.

(4) Once a day, present food offerings before the butsudan. Serve
the ancestors exactly the same food you have had for dinner. Bow,
ring the bell in the butsudan twice, and say, "All ancestors, please
come to eat!" When offering fruits or candies, take the offerings
out of their boxes and wrappers before presenting them to the ancestors. Peel all apples and other fruit, cutting them into small
pieces, and leave a fork with them. Otherwise, serve food with
chopsticks. Do not offer a whole cluster of bananas—half will do.
Always give an ancestor a special treat on the anniversary of his or
her death. When presenting your paycheck before the ancestors,

thank them sincerely and say, "Please use the spirit value of this money." You should always announce important things to your ancestors, such as a pay raise. Other than this, you should not pray before the butsudan, since this might bother the ancestors and interrupt the austerities they are performing in the astral world. If you *must* pray before the butsudan, *never* ring the bell. This will really upset them, since they will think it is dinner time! In the evening you should say goodnight to them, turn out their light, and close the doors of the butsudan. In the morning, open the doors, say good morning, and turn the light on again.

(5) When dusting the butsudan, divide your dustcloth into three parts. Use one part to dust the outside, the second to dust the upper part (the head) of the memorial tablet, and the third to dust the base. When dusting the tablets, always hold them by the base because it would be rude to pick them up by the head. When you touch the tablet, say "Excuse me, I'm going to clean up."

(6) Never give okiyome to the tablets for more than two or three minutes. Yoshida Sensei recommends not purifying them at all, since that might attract the ancestors back to this world.

(7) Each nuclear family should have a butsudan for the ancestors of the husband's family. It is not necessary for the wife to have one for her own ancestors because, after her marriage, she is incorporated into her husband's family and assumes its religious obligations. If she wishes to worship her own ancestors as well, she must use a separate butsudan and place it in a less honorable part of the room.

Although Mahikari's concern about ancestors may sound strange, and over-meticulous to Western ears, the proper veneration of one's forebears is of perennial importance to the Japanese and is a fundamental ingredient of their religions, old and new alike. I noticed that participants in the elementary training sessions showed more interest in the lecture on the butsudan than in any other part of the three-day course. This was the only time people ventured to ask questions.

The first day's lecture came to an end promptly at 6:00 P.M. Weary with the revelations of the day, I was eager to go home. But Sensei prevailed on all of us to stay a little longer to receive okiyome. At seven, just as I was finally about to make my escape, there occurred the most violent and dramatic spirit seizure that I witnessed during my six months in the dojo. A young man who had received his amulet only one month earlier suddenly fell to the floor while receiving okiyome. Yoshida Sensei rushed to his side and immediately began a spirit investigation. Suddenly the man, sweating and shaking violently but still entranced, jumped to his feet and begged for water. "Some thirsty soul in hell must be possessing him," Sensei said. Finally the man lay down on the floor again, and Sensei continued to interrogate the spirit possessing him. It turned out that the man had once been driving his car along the road when a vehicle in front of him ran over a cat. He stopped his car and got out to look at the dead animal. Out of pity, he had made the sign of the cross over the body of the cat, even though he was not a Christian himself. Now, three years later, the spirit of the cat, thinking that he was a "soft touch," possessed him in order to "get saved." Yoshida Sensei politely addressed the cat's spirit and told it to go back to the astral world to finish its penance and become, as he put it, "a good animal." Sensei pronounced the benediction over the trembling body of the young man, and the spirit disappeared. After he stopped twitching, the young man thanked Sensei, bid all a goodnight, and took his leave. Finally, I too went home. As I walked through the labyrinth of narrow, crooked streets, I pondered how I could ever make sense of what I had heard and seen that day.

Deity

By ten o'clock the next morning we had assembled at the dojo for the second day's lecture. Only a few of the forty people taking the course failed to show up. After the usual prayers and prostrations, the lecture began.

Yoshida Sensei first explained the nature of deity and the great changes that have taken place in heaven since the world began. Examining the etymologies of the divine names and words Amaterasu, Dainichi Nyorai, Amida, Gotama, Avalokiteśvara, Allah, and Amen, he valiantly demonstrated that the nature of God is light and that his real name is Su:

Originally Su-god was one. Later he created the god Miroku (Maitreya) and the forty-eight deities who are associated with the forty-eight characters of the Japanese syllabary.* Through these deities, forty-eight types of men came into existence. Because the sounds of the Japanese language have evolved under their guidance, Japanese is a divine language spoken by gods and spirits alike. Only the Japanese language has words with automatic potency [*kotodama*].† Spirit investigations, even if conducted in Paris, London, or San Francisco, must therefore be given in Japanese because evil spirits in the astral world understand no other language. Because they are filled with kotodama, prayers such as the Exorcist's Prayer cannot be translated into other languages.

The universe is arranged in a hierarchy of approximately 200 levels, ranging from the lowest hell to the highest heaven, where Su-god himself resides. The higher one moves, the hotter the temperature of each level becomes. Above mankind are ranged all of the guardian spirits [*shugo-rei*], who are actually ancestral spirits. These spirits, connected to us by "thick spirit rays," are especially valuable in helping to ward off bad luck. For example, a man once developed a bad toothache and decided not to go to work. The train he usually took was derailed, and many people were killed. That he was saved was the work of his guardian spirits.

Above the guardian spirits are the ancestral spirits in general. Still one level above them come the "spirit-governing gods" [*reitōshi*], the tutelary gods [*ubusunagami*], the clan deities [*ujigami*] of the typical Japanese village, and, finally, the forty-eight gods themselves. The individual is joined to all of these divinities by invisible spirit rays or cords.

The gods are divided into two camps. The strict or fire deities are directly under the control of Su-god. We have seen that these are the gods who create our primary souls. In addition, there are the easy-going "water gods," or "secondary deities," who are the sponsors of material wealth and desires. These gods have implanted secondary (material) souls in us. The established religions—Buddhism, Shinto, Christianity, and so on—worship secondary deities exclusively.

According to Sensei, the Savior associated the strict deities with the yang principle, masculinity, and Eastern civilization. They are

---

* The leader of these forty-eight deities is Kuniyorozu Tsukurinushi Ōkami, ancestor of Ōkuninushi in the *Kojiki* (A.D. 712, a compilation of ancient myths and legends).

† Kotodama in the Shinto tradition is actually a kind of word magic. Mioshie is filled with discussions of kotodama and *kazudama* (numerologies). The Savior's use of spiritual etymologies as a method of theological exposition rests on his conviction that Japanese and the characters with which it is written are pregnant with divine meanings. Thus he believed that the word *kanji* (character or ideograph) should be written with characters meaning "divine letter" and not, as is usual, "Chinese character."

therefore related to those peoples who practice ancestor worship and put a high value on loyalty and patriotism (*chūkun aikoku*). The lenient gods, on the other hand, he connected with the materialistic cultures of the West, with the yin, or feminine principle. The strict deities can be symbolized by a red vertical axis, the lenient deities by a blue horizontal line. When the two groups are working together in harmony they form a cross.

The gods first created the divine world and then the world of spirits. After this, they created man, first his spirit and then his body. At first man was ruled by his primary soul and obeyed his divine Parent faithfully. In those days, Sensei noted, there were no quarrels, sickness, or pollution. Mankind was ruled by a theocracy that unified religion and government (*saisei-itchi*). Then, in order to advance man's material civilization more rapidly, Su-god and the strict deities decided to retire and let the worldly water gods take over. Man's primordial unity (the Perfect Cross Civilization) came undone, and the world entered the Age of Division (*Hodoke no Yo*). Because the auxiliary water deities have now withdrawn, there are no real gods in the Shinto shrines or living Buddhas in the temples.

If you have a Shinto god-shelf [*kamidana*] in your home [Sensei continued], it is empty. You may make offerings in front of it, but it is foxes that carry the food away, thinking to themselves, "What fools they are to think that there are gods here!" The Heian Shrine in Kyoto caught fire in 1976 because there were no gods living there. It is because of the retirement of the easygoing gods that we no longer need a statue of Amida Buddha in our butsudan. Amida has returned to the divine world.

At first, the gods' plan to retire seemed to work. Man's appetite for material things increased, and with it his wealth, science, technology, and general well-being. But finally things got out of hand. Strife, warfare, and immorality increased together with man's material possessions. The strict gods, concerned about this unforeseen turn of events, held a conference and decided to send messengers—prophets and holy men—"to put the brakes on." And so the next age was called the Age of the Brakes [Bureeki Jidai]. Moses, the Buddha, Jesus, Mohammed, Confucius, Lao Tzu, Mencius, Zoroaster, and Nostradamus made their appearance. All of these prophets performed miracles merely by raising their hands. Later on, the five great world religions that were founded by the saints and prophets in the Age of the Brakes degenerated into mere philosophy. The art of miracles was lost.

Finally we come to the present, the Latter Days, or Mappō as it is called in Buddhism. Mankind has nearly forgotten God and knows little, if anything, about spirits. Religion itself has become a "corpse." Great cataclysms have shaken the world, but man has yet to repent and return to God. Realizing that man's material civilization had now progressed too far, Su-god caused the water gods to retire and put the strict deities back in power. This began in January 1962. At that time, a photographer with Japan's *Yomiuri* newspaper happened to take a picture of Mount Fuji that by chance caught in it the face of the god Kuniyorozu Tsukurinushi, leader of the forty-eight fire deities, spread out over the side of the mountain. A specialist at Sophia University, a Catholic university in Tokyo, allegedly identified this as the face of Yahweh himself, obviously a strict deity. The Savior took this as sure proof that the Eschaton, the Age of the Baptism by Fire, had begun.

Recent climatic and geological changes in the earth are symptomatic of this Great Change in heaven. The atmosphere has become hotter as a result of the return of the fire gods. In 1963 the speed of the rotation of the earth was accelerated suddenly by 3/10,000 kilometer per hour. Scientists still do not realize the importance of this fact. Throughout the world the weather has become unpredictable. In India in 1972 there was a heat wave of 50° C. The Mississippi River has flooded. In Peru and Chile there have been extraordinary rainfalls. In Bangladesh there have been windstorms, rain, and tornadoes. The Sahara Desert is slowly making its way into the central part of Africa. The ice in the Arctic Ocean is melting. There have been volcanic eruptions in the seas and an increase in the number of butane gas explosions in cities. The Japanese islands themselves are now threatened with submersion under the waters of the Pacific Ocean.*

Throughout the world men are hungry for sexual pleasure and money. Even in Japan, people have been infected with the spirit of individualism, liberalism, and democracy! From now on things will become worse. Eventually, only one-tenth of the world's population will remain. Of these, members of Mahikari will form the "top class." Those not lucky enough to die soon will perish as though they were doing the "twist" in a frying pan. Various mysterious diseases will combine with pneumonia to create incurable epidemics. Hospitals will spring up everywhere but will not be able to handle the droves of patients. People will finally become so miserable that they will die insane. In the end, there will be lines of people before the homes of Mahikari members waiting to receive okiyome. Members will be notified by the dojo through a telephone chain when the Age of the Baptism by Fire reaches its climax. Already our ministers have special knapsacks packed and are ready for any emergency.†

---

* Since the publication of the two-volume novel *Nippon Chinbotsu*, by Komatsu Sakyō (translated by Michael Gallagher as *Japan Sinks*; New York, 1976), the idea that the country, convulsed with earthquakes and erupting volcanoes, might some day sink under the Pacific seems to have become a highly entertaining nightmare in Japan, at least for readers of books of this sort.

† The Reverend Takagi told me that in her knapsack, which bears the Mahikari emblem, she keeps salt, a towel, matches, candles, a rope, and other emergency equipment (except, of course, medicine).

After mankind has been sufficiently purified through the Baptism by Fire (and the Storm of Raruro), the strict and lenient deities will once again be united. The material and spiritual civilizations that have evolved throughout the course of history's several dispensations will be rejoined to form the Perfect Cross Civilization, or what our textbook called "the sacred age of the non-confrontational love and harmony Civilization of the Kingdom of God." Once again the "unity of religion and government" will be established on earth. Japan will finally be recognized as the spiritual center of the world, the Japanese as the dominant, chosen race. Man will then reach the level of divinity and will live according to the teachings of the Sacred Phoenix, Okada Kotama. Those who are members of Mahikari today are purifying themselves in order to become the "Seed-People" of the glorious theocratic society of the future.

Such was the gist of the elementary training course that I attended in Nakayama City. What does not come across in this summary of the lectures is their anecdotal and rambling style. Each lecture was salted with dozens of stories about miraculous healings, escapes, coincidences, and windfalls. For example, immediately after a woman took the elementary training course, her goldfish died. She took it out of its bowl, put it in another bowl filled with fresh water, and gave it okiyome for ten minutes. The fish returned to life. In another case, robbers broke into the home of a Mahikari member. The wife, who was alone in the house at the time, hid and chanted the Exorcist's Prayer under her breath. The men were later arrested and the stolen goods returned. In other instances, members allegedly repaired broken television sets, radios, automobiles, air conditioners, and wristwatches simply by "raising their hands." As one might expect, nearly every imaginable disease was touched upon, from simple acne to brain cancer. Housewives improved the taste of rice by giving it okiyome. In the same way, members of the Mahikari Youth Corps have made wine, noodles, and rice more tasty. Smokers have been able to remove the coal tar from their cigarettes, and concerned consumers have dispelled dangerous food additives in a matter of minutes. Wherever a Mahikari altar scroll (*goshintai*) has been enshrined, people have noticed a decrease in the number of traffic accidents. Typhoons inevitably avoid dojos wherever they are built. (Yoshida Sensei had no sooner said this than a typhoon struck Nakayama City, but no one seemed to register the contradiction or irony of the situation.)

By noon on Sunday we had been sufficiently instructed in Mioshie and cleaned up through okiyome to receive our amulets. Our group was arranged in rows before the altar. Yoshida Masako, Sensei's wife—and the president of the dojo—called each person to the front of the dojo and put the amulet, a small golden locket, over his head. Inside the locket (which one is not supposed to open) is a piece of paper with a simple wedgelike mark (the chon, symbol of Su-god). After receiving our amulets we sat down, carefully wrapped them in a plastic wrapping material, and put them into their knitted pouches. The men were instructed to pin these pouches to the inside of their undershirts, the women theirs to their brassieres. After one more hour of practice and review, we were ready to cast out evil spirits, heal diseases, and improve the general happiness and well-being of the human race.

4 The Spirit History of the Yoshida Family

During the lectures, Yoshida Sensei told us about his own conversion to Mahikari. In the following pages, I have put these remarks together with what I learned from him and his wife on many other, less formal occasions. The spirit history of this family is, I think, a valuable example of the kind of family experience and personal motivation that brings people into Mahikari, and of the way in which evil spirits are thought to possess and harass entire families.

The Yoshidas live on the north side of Nakayama, in an old but comfortable farmhouse inherited from Sensei's father. Although large apartment buildings now encircle the area, a few of the rice paddies and fields of the original farm still remain. A couple of blocks away is a small Shinto shrine. Although its festivals were discontinued after the war, the shrine buildings and the surrounding grove are a reminder of the days when the area was still a village under the protection of its own deity (ujigami).

Sensei and his wife are in their middle forties. They were married in 1955 and are actually first cousins—nothing unusual in Japan. Their common ancestors, the Fujimotos, originally were lance masters under the feudal lords of Nakayama castle. Because the Savior's ancestors served under the same lord, Sensei likes to think that there is a karmic relationship between the two families. Before the Yoshida family moved to Nakayama Prefecture, they are believed to have served as priests at the Grand Shrine at Ise. In recent times, however, neither side of the family has been unduly religious.

Sensei remembers his father as a reticent, hardworking penny-pincher. In addition to amassing a good deal of the farmland in the area, the old man also ran a lacquerware company. After the war, when raw materials could no longer be imported from China, he was forced to give the company up. As Nakayama City spread northward, the price of the farmland skyrocketed, so that the Yoshidas became quite well-to-do. Sensei, who never liked farming, sold most of the property, went to college, and became an elementary school teacher. After spending several years in the classroom, he was promoted to a position with the Department of Education in Osaka where, among his other responsibilities, he helped prepare college entrance examinations. In his free time, he travels about Japan giving lectures to parents and nurses on "human relations," often under the aegis of the Red Cross. In 1978, he accepted the principalship of a large elementary school between Nakayama City and Osaka.

Sensei's mother was a warmhearted and generous woman who was especially devoted to the worship of Jizō-sama, the patron of mothers and children. The Yoshida family belonged to a Jōdo Shin-shū temple. Sensei fondly remembers his mother visiting temples here and there. When the children were sick, she sometimes consulted mediums about the cause of their illnesses. Because of their different temperaments, Sensei's parents frequently quarreled, though not so loudly that the neighbors could hear.

In 1957, Sensei's father became seriously ill with gout and was taken to a large hospital in the city, where doctors decided that they would have to amputate his leg as soon as his general condition improved. In spite of countless pills and injections, he grew weaker. Believing that his time had come, he made up his mind to return home to die. The doctors warned Sensei that his father's condition was so critical that he might die in the car on the way home. While Sensei was still pondering what to do, his father suddenly passed away. Sensei recalls with remorse that he himself was not at the hospital at the time. In gratitude for all that his father had done for him—and left to him—Sensei built a large grave. To keep out the weeds, he paved the whole gravesite with cement.

In 1964, the Yoshidas' daughter, their third child, suddenly became ill with an intestinal disorder. Mrs. Yoshida took the child to a local clinic to be examined. The doctor incorrectly diagnosed the case, and the child grew worse. When Mrs. Yoshida took her to the clinic again, the doctor realized that the problem was beyond his own competence and sent them to a specialist in the city. Strangely enough, the hospital where the doctor sent them was the very one in which Sensei's father had died—a place where the Yoshidas had vowed they would never again set foot. When Mrs. Yoshida realized where the doctor had sent them she fainted, only to come to her senses in the very room where her father-in-law had died! It was soon discovered that the daughter was suffering from a twisted colon and needed an operation at once. Three days later, the child was dead from "complications."

Not long after, in 1967, Sensei's mother became ill with stomach cancer. After her doctors had given up all hope, Sensei began to drive her around the countryside to visit various mediums (*kitōshi* or *ogamiyasan*) and a religious masseur (*okaji*) who was a devotee of "Odaishi-sama" (Kōbō Daishi), founder of Shingon Buddhism. When they first consulted the masseur, even before they could put their questions to him he said, "Someone in your family has just died with a distended stomach."

Sensei's mother's body was now beginning to take on the same dreadful shape as his daughter's. Sensei noticed, however, that even though his mother constantly had diarrhea, she was never bothered when she was being taken to one of these mediums. One of them gave her an herbal concoction and worshiped the family's ancestors for them. He also told Sensei that the kind of concrete grave he had built for his father was "improper" and would have to be rebuilt if his mother was to be saved. Although the grave was changed, the mother's condition grew worse. Fearing that the end was near, Sensei's wife went by herself to the medium's house. "Tonight is a dangerous time," the medium warned her. "Be careful." That night the old woman died. Sensei built her a fitting grave on Mount Koya, as she had requested. It was only later, after the family had joined

Mahikari, that they realized the cause of her cancer was the medicine she had been taking.

At about the same time, Sensei began to have trouble with his stomach. Every year he went to a doctor friend for a complete examination, including stomach X rays. Sensei believes that people with too much stomach acidity get ulcers, whereas those with low acidity get stomach cancer. "In my family there is practically no acidity at all!," he lamented. Fearing that he too was about to get cancer, he took medicine six times a day for his "sagging stomach" and soon became quite emaciated. It bothered him even to smoke. To function at all he needed eight hours of sleep—something he felt was abnormal. In the meantime, Mrs. Yoshida also began to have stomach troubles and was told by her doctor that if she was not careful she would develop a duodenal ulcer. By this time, both husband and wife had begun to suspect that their whole family had fallen under some kind of curse. In their distress, they worshiped first one *kami* (god) and then another, and paid more attention to their butsudan.

In 1969, while Sensei was giving one of his "human relations" lectures, he heard about Mahikari. That weekend, one of the men in the audience developed a toothache that caused his whole cheek to become swollen. A member of Mahikari who happened to be in the same group gave the man okiyome, and the swelling immediately went down. Still skeptical, Yoshida Sensei nevertheless determined to look into this for himself. Not long after, Sensei attended a training session at the Osaka dojo and became a member of Mahikari.

Although he estimates that he has received okiyome over a thousand times since he joined the church, Sensei has never had any spirit movements or seizures. Once, about two years after he received his amulet, he did have the feeling that he was walking on clouds when he was being purified. He pointed out to me that according to Mioshie, very humble people are most likely to have spirit movements and seizures. "I'm too tricky and stubborn," he confessed with a laugh. "Stubborn people seldom have spirit movements because the stubborn spirits that are possessing them refuse to show themselves." He speculates that he has been possessed by one of these intransigent ghosts since he was a child.

Although Sensei has had no dramatic spirit experiences, his wife has been a veritable fountain of revelation. Through her experiences while receiving okiyome from her husband, the spirit history of the family has been constructed. After Sensei received his amulet, he began to give his wife okiyome regularly. As the spirit rays entered her body and began to dispel the toxins and evil spirits within, she could feel a fist-sized lump in her stomach begin to move about throughout her whole body, as though it were trying to flee from the Light. When she took the training course, she was bothered for the whole three days by a dreadful cold sensation in her hips and had to sit through the lectures surrounded by pillows just to keep warm. As soon as she had received her amulet, the cold feeling went away. On their way home from the ceremony, her nose began to run, though she had not caught cold. And when they got home, she found that she had soiled her underwear. "These are sure signs that Su-god is beginning to clean me up," she told herself. The next day, she developed a rash where her amulet touched her chest, and an evil-smelling pus began to develop from the sores. The more she gave herself okiyome, the more pus appeared. Since this was further evidence of her cleansing (kuriningu), she gave thanks to God for both the rash and the pus. Finally, when the rash did not go away, her faith wavered, and she used a little talcum powder on it, which, unfortunately, made it all the worse. Only after she apologized to God for her lack of trust did the rash go away. Since that time the Yoshidas have not used medicine of any sort.

Not long after this, while Sensei was out of town on business, their son's foot became paralyzed. Not knowing what to do, Mrs. Yoshida finally took him to a doctor, who diagnosed the case as polio and said that the boy would need six months of electrotherapy. When Sensei returned home, they called the Osaka dojo for help. The minister there suggested that the affliction was probably a warning from their ancestors to move their butsudan to a new place. (It had been stored on top of a filing cabinet.) They gave their son's foot okiyome in three different places, and soon he was completely cured. The disease had obviously been caused by their ancestors, who were vexed by the clatter of drawers constantly opening and closing beneath their memorial tablets.

When Sensei first gave his wife okiyome, her hands began to

move in small circles, a sign that she was being possessed by the spirit of a badger. When he questioned the spirit, he discovered that the badger was really the ghost of Mrs. Yoshida's uncle. Shortly after he had entered middle school, this uncle had committed suicide by jumping from a train at Uchida Station in the city. Afterward, his spirit continued to loiter around the station (as a *jibakurei*), causing all sorts of accidents and misfortune. Because the uncle's spirit had already taken several human lives by the time it appeared to Mrs. Yoshida, it had developed into the form of a badger. As such, it continued to possess her for more than a year, making an appearance every time she received okiyome. Finally, Sensei's wife went to the head of the Osaka dojo to be purified. This man interrogated the spirit and told Mrs. Yoshida that to get rid of the spirit once and for all, the Yoshidas would have to go to the spot where her uncle had died and make offerings to his spirit. Accordingly, Sensei and his wife made a box lunch, bought some candy, and cut some flowers—all to be used as offerings—and took the train to the Uchida Station. There they asked the stationmaster for permission to pass through the wicket and make offerings next to the tracks. The suicide had taken place fifty years before, so no one knew exactly where they should make the offerings. The stationmaster showed them the two main junctions and suggested that they go to one of them to worship. With his permission, the couple began to make their offerings. Then they intoned the Chōrei Hymn and lifted their hands to purify the area around the tracks.

The next day when they arrived at the station—for they were determined to carry on like this for the whole week—the stationmaster had strange news. For years, a certain old man had passed by the Uchida Station. That morning, the stationmaster asked him whether he could remember the boy's suicide and where it had occurred. The old man not only remembered the incident; it was in his arms that the boy had died! The stationmaster pointed out the place where the old man said the suicide had occurred. For the rest of the week, the Yoshidas went there to make their offerings and raise their hands. Mrs. Yoshida also visited her parents' home to beseech the ancestors in the butsudan there to take (invisible) food offerings to the station to feed her uncle's spirit.

Later that week, when Sensei was giving his wife okiyome, the uncle's spirit once again appeared. Thanks to their offerings, he no longer took the shape of a badger, but appeared as a real human spirit. He confessed that he had once tried to kill Mrs. Yoshida by causing her to become dizzy while riding her bicycle over a high bridge. Mrs. Yoshida reasoned that the spirit had tried to kill her by causing her to fall because he himself had died by falling from a train.* He had also caused her grandfather to get cancer. Finally, with tears of joy, the uncle repented and, after thanking them all profusely, disappeared into the astral world once and for all.

Other ancestral spirits began to invade Mrs. Yoshida's body. Because the Fujimotos had been lance masters, many had died violently, and in their abode in the astral world, continued to bear grudges against humanity. Most had died so long ago that Sensei was unable to recognize them. One that he did recognize was his own great-great-grandfather, Kikue, who had died in the late Tokugawa or early Meiji period. Even in those days the Yoshida family had been quite well-to-do, and had many servants and maids living in their home. Kikue had an illegitimate child by one of these maids and, realizing that to marry a mere housemaid was out of the question, put the infant to death. In the astral world, the child became a "malicious ghost" and returned periodically to take the lives of eight members of the family, the last being Sensei's father. When the infant's spirit appeared to Mrs. Yoshida, it threatened to kill her too, "in order to make Yoshida Sensei suffer." Fortunately, the family had already joined Mahikari, and the spirit was unable to carry out its threat.

The spirit of Sensei's own father also possessed Mrs. Yoshida. Like her uncle's ghost, this spirit appeared in the form of a badger. Speaking through Mrs. Yoshida's mouth, the spirit told his son, "You have done something very bad to me. I wanted to return home to die, but you let me die in the hospital. It was I who took the life of your daughter. I knew it was wrong to make her sick, but in the other world I was lonely and in agony . . ." It now became clear to the Yoshidas that it was the spirit of their daughter's own grandfather who had tricked them into returning to the hospital where he himself had died. The spirit also voiced displeasure at his

---

* We shall later refer to this kind of experience as homeopathic possession.

son for selling off the land that he had worked so hard to acquire. Sensei then recalled that all along he had had trouble selling this property. Again and again, deals had been made, only to fall through. His father's spirit had clearly been behind these financial problems too.

After hearing his father out, Sensei began to teach him Mioshie. "After you die, you must forget the things of this life. This is part of your discipline in the astral world. Su-god doesn't want you to fret about the property you bought when you were alive. Taking people's lives is a great evil. So apologize to God and return to the astral world to continue your austerities." After Sensei explained to the ghost that he could no longer farm the land with apartment buildings springing up around the neighborhood, the spirit agreed that Sensei could sell some of the land, provided that he would buy up other land as a hedge against inflation. When the spirit heard Mioshie from his son, he "repented in tears." After this, the spirit movements in Mrs. Yoshida's hands began to be directed by a human spirit, indicating that her father-in-law's spirit had moved up in the hierarchy of the astral world. "You've found a wonderful kami," the spirit declared. "If you want anything from me or your other ancestors, treat this deity with care."

When the okiyome was finished, Sensei called his two elder sisters to tell them that their father's spirit had appeared to him. "If you want to meet him, come on over," he said. The next day the two sisters and their children came to the Yoshidas' home. The spirit appeared in Mrs. Yoshida's body once again, and again Sensei explained Mioshie to him and begged him not to bother the living any longer but to return at once to the astral world. After the benediction, the spirit went away.

Some time later, the Yoshidas determined that they would set up a Mahikari Purification Center in honor of Sensei's father. To that end, they borrowed $2,300 and rented a building not far from Nakayama castle. The center was a complete success. People in the neighborhood noticed that after it had been set up the number of traffic accidents in the area seemed to decline. Even typhoons avoided the city. Before long, so many people had become members that there was not enough room to accommodate all who came to the monthly worship services. And so they decided to build a new

dojo. Yoshida Sensei sold some land valued at $16,000 and bor-
rowed $11,000 against his pension fund. He used the money to buy
the lot for the dojo. Then he sold more land and raised the $66,660
that was needed to put up the building.

Although most of the spirits that possessed Mrs. Yoshida were
Sensei's ancestors, other sorts of apparitions also made their appearance. Once, for example, the Yoshidas had been planting onion
seeds. No sooner were the seeds in the ground than birds came to
eat them. To get rid of these pests, they sowed poisoned rice seed
among the onions. Mrs. Yoshida laughed to recall how she once
was possessed by a whole flock of poisoned birds.

It was not a laughing matter, however, when Mrs. Yoshida
started to be possessed by the ancestral spirits of other families in
their neighborhood. Whenever a message came to her from one of
these spirits, Mrs. Yoshida would go to the family and say, "Uncle
so-and-so appeared to me and said that he needs a new memorial
tablet" or "Grandfather so-and-so wants his butsudan changed in
such-and-such a way." At first the neighbors seemed happy to receive these communications from the other world and did whatever
the Yoshidas suggested. But gradually they began to resent the messages as intrusions into their families' private affairs. Finally, four
or five neighbors got together at the house of the Hiratas and decided that as a group they would snub and isolate the Yoshidas, a
practice called *mura hachibu* by rural Japanese. One of the neighbors telephoned Mrs. Yoshida's parents and begged them to put
pressure on the Yoshidas to give up their bizarre trafficking with
the dead. They even called the Department of Education in Osaka
to complain that a public servant like Yoshida Sensei should not be
allowed to have a second job as a religious leader.* For six months,
the neighbors refused to speak to the Yoshidas.

During those lonely days, it was a comfort to have the ghost of
Sensei's father appear to them and say, "I know you are having a
hard time. But don't give up!"

"Where are you now, Father?," Sensei inquired.

---

* In fact, this was illegal, and Sensei was finally forced to turn over the presidency
of the dojo to his wife. Although she presides over ceremonies and presents amulets
to new members, he (at least until his recent appointment as principal of an elementary school) continued to give all lectures and to act as the de facto leader.

"Thanks to the new dojo you've built, I've now gone up to a beautiful place—to paradise, in fact. Here, there are souls dancing, beautiful flowers, and birds forever singing. People can do whatever they want to do. If you want to read a book, you can read a book. . . . I have you to thank for all of this. Keep it up and don't give in to your neighbors!"

In the sixth month of their isolation, an ancestor of their arch-enemies, the Hiratas, possessed Mrs. Yoshida while she was receiving okiyome. Sensei could not hide his anger from the ghost and began to reproach it for causing his family so much grief.

"Get out of here and go back to hell," he ordered. This outburst was quite unlike Sensei, who always speaks gently and respectfully to spirits, even when scolding them.

"I am sorry," said the spirit. "I only came to apologize. Today, twenty of us ancestors are disowning the Hiratas. We have asked God to let us take up our residence in *your* altar scroll and serve *you* from now on. Tomorrow, I will make Mrs. Hirata sick and make her whole family apologize to you. Mrs. Hirata's nose and chest will suddenly become all clogged up so that she can't breathe," the spirit foretold.

Sensei, unable to control himself, shouted, "Go to it! Go right to it! But don't kill anybody!"

The next day, their neighbor, Mrs. Hirata Haruko, went to work as usual. Suddenly she experienced the very symptoms that, unbeknownst to her, her own ancestor's spirit had predicted to the Yoshidas. A neighborhood friend took her to a nearby doctor, who could find nothing wrong with her. Puzzled by the case, the doctor sent the woman to an eye, ear, nose, and throat specialist. But the specialist was also baffled. That evening, the Hiratas held a family conference. A disease that doctors cannot figure out has to be a curse, they reasoned. Knowing that the Yoshidas—crazy as they were—had a powerful kami enshrined in their house, the family decided to eat humble pie and send Mrs. Hirata to them to ask for help. The next day, somewhat sheepishly, Mrs. Hirata went to the Yoshidas' house to implore Su-god to save her from her mysterious illness. Sensei happened to be home at the time. He reminded her, coldly, of all the trouble the Hiratas had brought on his family.

"First you put us in a quarantine. Then you called my employer to complain about me. And finally you even called our relatives to try to get them to make us give up our center," he scolded.

In spite of her husband's tirade, Mrs. Yoshida agreed to give okiyome to Mrs. Hirata. Her affliction soon disappeared, and the two families patched up their differences. Thanks to the miracle, the Yoshidas' mura hachibu came to an end. The Hiratas even joined Mahikari, though they never practiced okiyome very much. Finally, about a year after they took the training course, they dropped out. But to this day they continue to be on good terms with the Yoshidas.

As time went by, Mrs. Yoshida's spirit seizures became less frequent. By the time she became the president of the dojo in 1974 she had been completely cleaned up. In December 1976, after a dry spell of three or four years, she once again had an important spirit experience. In that month, her father developed cancer of the stomach. When Sensei gave his wife okiyome in her father's presence, her grandmother appeared to them and announced that she had attacked her own son because she was not being properly worshiped. After the benediction, Mrs. Yoshida's father begged them to go to his house and check his butsudan for him. This they did, only to find several "mistakes" in the arrangement of the memorial tablets. When he was operated on later in the month, two small malignant tumors (caused by his mother's ghost) were removed from his stomach. But his doctors gave him a good chance for complete recovery, and the old man resolved to take the Mahikari training course as soon as possible.

Now that her husband has a more demanding job, Mrs. Yoshida (also called Sensei by members) has assumed more responsibility for running the dojo. There she spends a good part of every day, raising her hand over members, listening to their problems, and investigating evil spirits that appear. A kind and gracious woman whose face glows with maternal concern, Mrs. Yoshida is just as effective as her husband in dealing with members. When people come to the dojo to inquire about Mahikari she is quite persuasive. Her mind, like her husband's, is well stocked in spirit lore. As lovely as she is when she puts on her pink kimono to preside over official ceremonies, it is in daily counseling that Mrs. Yoshida is most inspiring.

The Yoshidas have three lively but well-behaved children: two daughters, Toshiko and Akiko, and a son, Hiroshi. Toshiko had always been close to her grandmother Yoshida. Once, when Sensei was giving his wife okiyome, the old woman's spirit appeared. Although she had done much good in this life, she told them that her soul had fallen into agony in the other world. The grandmother asked them to tell the girl to be good, to study hard, and to stay well. Since the child was still awake, her parents called her into the living room and told her what her grandmother had said. At that time Toshiko was in the fourth grade. After she received her amulet, Toshiko at first had no spirit experiences. But about a year later, a spirit caused her to fall down on her side when she was receiving okiyome. Since the spirit refused to speak, the family does not know what sort it was. The Yoshidas' son, Hiroshi, once had occasional spirit seizures; for example, he was possessed by a dog that he used to pass on his way to school. Since he has been cleaned up, he no longer has these experiences. The children are busy with schoolwork, and there is little time for them to go to the dojo. Twice a week, Toshiko gives okiyome at the Yoshida home to people who drop in to their Purification Center. Hiroshi usually stops by the dojo about once a week on his way home from school. The youngest child, Akiko, recently took the training course. Sensei likes to say that he would give half his fortune if only the children would come to understand the Savior's Teachings.

5 *The Lost Continent of Mu and Other Revelations*

Shortly after I received my amulet I had the opportunity to take the intermediate training course held in Osaka. Because the advanced training course was not given until after I had left Japan, I cannot claim to have mastered all of Mioshie. But I was able to attend some advanced study sessions in Tokyo and was given the textbook for the advanced course and various magazines published by the church. This chapter is based on these sources and can be regarded as a sampling of Mahikari's deeper mysteries.

Eight other members of the local dojo in Nakayama City took the intermediate training course when I did. We all boarded the super-express at Nakayama Station and arrived at Osaka in an hour and twenty minutes. As we walked from the station to the lecture hall, we were greeted at every corner by members of the Mahikari Youth Corps, dressed in their familiar green and white uniforms. A short walk brought us to the auditorium that the church had rented to accommodate the crowd of over 500, drawn from all parts of Japan. As we waited for the doors to open, several people gave themselves okiyome. Some of the women held their hands in front of them as if to purify their breasts. Another gave okiyome to her husband's back. One old woman sat with her hand raised over a large, disfiguring growth on her throat.

We registered and put on our headbands,* and soon the meeting began. The lecturer, a short man dressed in a conservative black double-breasted suit, was given a rousing welcome. The lectures proceeded with the same kind of etiquette I had noticed in Naka-yama. Now and then young women materialized to refresh the speaker with iced tea or coffee. They walked to the platform in measured, ritualistic steps, lifting their trays slightly above eye level as though making an offering to a god. At one side of the black-board, a member of the Mahikari Youth Corps sat stiffly at atten-tion, waiting for periodic signals from the lecturer to erase the board. In mid-morning the group paused in order to perform a familiar Japanese ritual, group calisthenics.

The advanced courses go well beyond the elementary course in their coverage of the sect's cosmology and cosmogony. The uni-verse is now explained in terms of seven dimensions, or levels, rang-ing from the first—a state of mud and chaos—up to the seventh, the divine world of Su-god himself. The world we inhabit is the Third Dimension, a world where gods and spirits can see us, but where we cannot see them. The Fourth Dimension is the astral world, where spirits are reborn after death. Above that, in the Fifth and Sixth Dimensions (the God-Spirit World), there are gods with only spiritual bodies. The Seventh Dimension consists of pure spirit and thought, and is the realm of the forty-eight deities, Maitreya, clan deities, tutelary gods, the "spirit-governing gods," and, of course, Su. Trainees are instructed in the names of some of the sect's lesser-known deities and of the emperors of Japan who ruled before Jimmu. (Whereas the traditional mythology of the *Kojiki* regards Jimmu as the first emperor, Mahikari claims that the Japanese im-perial throne is older by several millennia.) Most of these names are ridiculously long. Even polite members could not help chuckling when the speaker, understandably, twisted his tongue on such names as Amehinomotoashikabikiminushi Mihikari Ōkami Su-

---

*The Japanese often put on cotton headbands (*hachimaki*) when engaged in activities regarded as especially important, sacred, burdensome, or sweaty. In Shinto festivals, the young men who carry the palanquins of the gods almost invariably wear a hachimaki. The headband is therefore used to symbolize an individual or a group set apart in a special state or condition.

mera Mikoto. Considerable time was spent on this divine and imperial nomenclature.

To describe the demonic nature of the present age, the speaker referred us to a diagram in the textbook (see Fig. 1), which he then explained. The creature's right side is disfigured by the overdevelopment of material desire and represents man's worldly progress, which the Savior taught was the cause of the divisiveness of our age. His right eye, bulging from the socket, can no longer work with the

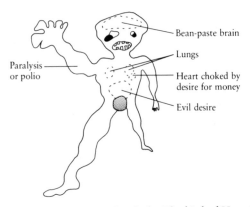

Bean-paste brain

Lungs

Paralysis or polio

Heart choked by desire for money

Evil desire

FIG. 1. *Modern Man Trying to Catch the Bluebird of Happiness. Illustration from Mahikari textbook.*

left or focus properly. Because it refuses to cooperate with the spiritual eye, the right eye always seems to be sneering at the world; it stands for our insatiable hedonism. The right hand is swollen with the desire for money and material possessions, and the arm to which it is attached is paralyzed by polio, a paralysis stemming from identifying freedom with social disorder. More specifically, the paralysis is manifested in the conflicts between (1) science, religion, politics, and education; (2) spiritual and material civilization; (3) government and the people; (4) students and teachers; and (5) capital and labor. The brain of this unhappy fellow, although it seems to be filled with bean paste (*miso*), is actually hollow and withered up—a symptom of the "cerebral anemia of the human race." His small left eye stands for the general atrophy of our spiritual awareness. His hideous mouth reminds us that, "thanks to freedom of speech," we spend our days carping and criticizing everything. His lungs are afflicted with the "tuberculosis of thought." In an age when such creatures roam the earth, even "culture vultures" and "crippled intellectuals" are not immune from sickness, poverty, and natural disasters. The only way in which this wretched man has advanced beyond his ancestors is in his ability to excrete —poisons. That such a miscreant could ever catch the bluebird of happiness and be satisfied with life is clearly an idle fancy. Thus the Savior used to say that in the "culture of lies" (*itsuwari no bunmei*) in which we live, high and low alike are "caught in the poisonous negligee of the witch Materialism."

According to Mioshie, Japan was once part of a continent called Mu, which now lies hidden beneath the waters of the Pacific Ocean. Japan, the oldest country in the world, will once again become the spiritual center of the human race.

In ancient times, dinosaurs swaggered about Japan; others, the size of an American F-4 fighter jet, darkened the skies. (These winged monsters were a manifestation of the dragon god, Ryūjin, discussed in the next chapter.) "Ancient documents" reveal that thousands of these creatures died at the foot of Mount Tsukuba during the great geological cataclysm that took place in Japan 100,000,000–100,050,000 years ago. At that time, lava flows covered their bones, so that today the Japanese have no dinosaur skeletons of their own to put in museums. In those days, Japan also boasted mountains that were higher than the Himalayas or the Alps. As the glaciers of the Ice Age moved down over Mu, elephants and other animals, including man, migrated to the south where the weather was less severe. The South Sea Islanders are the descendants of these migrants. The Savior maintained that the "academic theory" that the Japanese are the descendants of these southern peoples is an out-and-out lie.

According to the Savior's research and revelations, Mu was a landmass extending from Japan to Easter Island in the south and to Hawaii in the east. From east to west it measured 5,000 miles, and from north to south 3,000. It was in Mu, or ancient Japan, that

Su-god first drew up the spiritual "blueprints" (*hinagata*) that he used for the creation of the human race. In order to fulfill various functions, the first humans were created in five different colors: yellow, red, white, blue-green, and purple. The colored stripes on the Mahikari banner carried at all festivals are a reminder of the Five Colored Races of primordial times, whom Mahikari now aims to unite. Masks of these five original races can still be seen in a Shinto shrine in Kyushu. Of these races, the yellow was dominant. To be more accurate, the Japanese were dominant; the Chinese and Koreans, the lesser yellow races, were of a lower rank—but not quite as low as the other four.

Ancient Japan was the site of an enormously advanced civilization that ruled over the entire globe. In order to communicate with human beings, Su-god sent his descendant Sumera Mikoto to rule as emperor and high priest over the Japanese. Under his rule, the 2,400 different kinds of letters used by the peoples of Mu were invented. These "letters of the divine age" (*kamiyomoji* or *shindai-moji*) were the origin of all the ideographs, syllabaries, and alphabets in use today. Thus all the languages of the human race originated in Japan.

Sumera Mikoto, to hold together his farflung empire, dispatched fifteen Japanese princes and one princess to various parts of the world. The most illustrious were put in charge of the ancient civilizations of Mesopotamia, Egypt, India, and the Incan and Canadian empires. This divine nobility—confused by the Chinese with the sixteen disciples of the Buddha—first taught mankind how to hunt, fish, build ships, weave cloth, and make paper.

Relics of the ancient civilizations they established, Mioshie tells us, yield valuable insights into the life of the peoples of Motherland Mu. For example, in Egypt the chrysanthemum, symbol of the Japanese prince Tutankhamen (and still the flower of the Japanese imperial family), has been found, together with many artifacts from Japan that he deposited in the pyramids. These pyramids were in fact monuments set up to honor his "stem family" in Japan. The Savior taught that the pyramids were first built in Japan. This can be seen, he said, from the etymology of the word *piramidō*, which should be written with the characters "sun-coming-spirit-hall." According to Mioshie, the ancient name for Japan, Yamato, means "nation at the top of the pyramid."

The inhabitants of Mu originally worshiped one god called the Heavenly King, but, not daring to use his real name, they referred to him simply as kami, or God. Open-air temples made of stone were built to worship this deity and his symbol, the sun. In addition to the chrysanthemum, the pyramids, and the sun, the official symbols of ancient Japan were the cross, the snake, the swastika (a symbol of the "order of the universe"), and a three-cornered crown. The scriptures of Mu, which were carried by colonists to all parts of the world, later showed up in Polynesian legends, in Chinese texts, and in the writings of Plato. The Old Testament is a Hebrew translation by the Japanese prince Moses of Zoroaster's *Zend Avesta*. The Zoroastrian scriptures were originally brought to the ancient Near East from Mu by way of India and Burma.

According to Mioshie, Israel and Japan have always had a close relationship. "Records" still preserved in Japan show that Moses once visited Japan in his capacity as king of the Jews appointed by Japan's ninety-fourth emperor. The Kōso Kōtai Shrine in Ibaraki Prefecture has preserved a stone on which Moses engraved the Ten Commandments. The Hebrew language was a gift of the Japanese emperor to the Jewish people. Documents owned by the same shrine prove that Jesus Christ came to Japan at the age of eighteen in order to study and perform austerities. At twenty-three he returned to his own country with a seal of kingship conferred on him by Emperor Suinin. A picture in the shrine shows him wearing a robe with three imperial chrysanthemums embroidered on the front. Once back in Israel, Jesus got into trouble and just barely escaped crucifixion: his younger brother was executed in his place. After this narrow escape, Jesus returned to Japan, where he died at the age of one hundred and eighteen. A statue that he made of out of the bones of Mary and Joseph is still in the possession of the shrine.

Okada Kotama also believed that the original Hebrews were called Eda (branch) peoples, a Japanese word from which we get the word Jew. The word Israel comes from a corruption of Isuzu, the sacred river that flows through the Ise shrines in Japan's Mie

Prefecture. Once, when some of the Jews returned to Japan, the country's rulers declared that they could not intermarry with the local inhabitants. The Tokugawa family in particular was afraid that if a Jewish emperor were to come to power in Japan, the shogunate's authority would be shaken. This political discrimination was the origin of the Eta (Eda), Japan's outcastes.

Under the hegemony of ancient Japan, Mu flourished. Shrine records show that not only Moses and Jesus, but also Mohammed, Confucius, Mencius, Lao-tzu, and the Buddha all visited Japan. The Buddha, for example, came to the country at the age of two and was enlightened when he met the Sun God. To understand the teachings of the Buddha one must therefore first master Japan's *Kannagara no michi* (that is, Shinto).

In those days there was no racial discrimination among the Five Colored Races. The country was filled with music and wealth. Science, technology, and scholarship abounded. Airplanes and spaceships soared through the skies. The Muvians' telephones worked better than our own. Large underground cities were built. According to "records" later discovered in Tibet, the capital of Mu, Hiranipura, was especially impressive. The various districts of the capital were separated by canals and joined by bridges surmounted with large turrets and golden gates. The palace was a towering edifice of red, white, black, and speckled stone. The emperor's chambers had an ivory ceiling and walls made of gold, silver, copper, and other metals that gave off a mysterious, soft glow. Merchantmen from Hiranipura plied the seas of the world. In its harbor, countless ships lay at anchor, waiting to unload rich cargoes from Japan's distant colonies.

Among the denizens of Mu, no trace of barbarism could be found. Because the people were close to God, they had a supernatural kind of knowledge and a Third Eye with which they could see into the future and move material objects simply by thinking. (A blind man was recently found in Samoa who allegedly had the ability to "see" through his skin. Although scientists at first dismissed the story with customary scorn, it was later verified by the Paris edition of the *New York World*. This man evidently had preserved the ancient power of the Third Eye now lost by modern men. Significantly, his miraculous eye was found in the middle of his forehead, the very place where the Savior located our primary soul.)

The people of ancient Mu lived longer than we do. We know, for example, that Moses lived to the age of one hundred and twenty, the Buddha to one hundred and sixteen, Jesus to one hundred and eighteen, and Methuselah to nine hundred and sixty-nine. It is therefore quite possible that the inhabitants of Mu reached the age of a thousand. As though to drive home the point conclusively, the advanced textbook points out that the California sequoia lives to be over two thousand years old, the camel to a hundred, the elephant to a hundred and fifty, and certain tortoises and the Greenland whale to four hundred.

In spite of all of these material and spiritual blessings, the people of Mu became proud and materialistic. Shortly before the destruction of the continent, the ancestors of the Sun Tribes (Taiyōzoku) intermarried with the ancestors of the Moon, or Water, Tribes (Mayazoku). This primordial miscegenation divided the Five Colored Races so that nuclear warfare broke out between Mu and its rivals in Atlantis. Many of the evil spirits that haunt the world today are the souls of those who fell in these battles. Various cataclysms—beginning with the fall of the Tower of Babel—were sent by Su-god as a warning to mankind. The last king of Mu, named Ra Mu, finally prophesied to the Five Colored Races, "If the Water Tribes continue to indulge themselves in extravagance, Su will cause our empire to sink beneath the sea!"

Some time after this, about 15,000 years ago, an earthquake rocked the southern part of the continent. This was followed by the eruption of volcanoes and by gigantic tidal waves. After the lava from the volcanoes stopped flowing, the people tried to rebuild their cities. But again the earth was seized with convulsions, and a pillar of fire five kilometers tall filled the sky. The whole empire echoed with the cries of the dying. As the flames flickered out, night fell and lightning filled the skies. The people, still dressed in all their finery, rushed into the temples and cried out to Ra Mu, their priest-king, to save them. Instead, Ra Mu addressed them with words of rebuke. "Did I not predict that this would come to pass? Yet out of the ashes of this kingdom other peoples will arise.

If they too forget that it is better to give than to receive, a similar fate will overtake them!" Suddenly, leaping flames and black smoke put an end to the king's speech. At midnight, the entire continent and its 64,000,000 inhabitants sank beneath the waters of the Pacific.

Even after the disappearance of Mu, the descendants of the Motherland (peoples who had migrated, forming colonies throughout the world) continued to disregard the will of Su. Consequently, the earth was repeatedly visited by catastrophe. It took 55,000 years for the earth to recover after the great cataclysm of Noah's Flood. The seventh and last of these great upheavals—the Baptism of Fire and the Storm of Raruro—now threatens to destroy the human race. Only if the Five Colored Races are reunited under the Japanese emperor and the teachings of the Sacred Phoenix, Okada Kotama, is there any hope for mankind. If this mission is not carried out, the miracles that are taking place will cease.

The Savior, who is said to have been an authority on geology and ancient history, was highly critical of the shortsightedness of Japanese scholars. In many fields, such as parapsychology and archeology, he believed that foreign scholars had taken the lead. Thanks to them we now know, for example, that Japanese civilization is the oldest in the world. Because of their pioneering research we have learned that, whereas Mesopotamian culture goes back 7,000 or 8,000 years and Indian civilization 4,000 or 5,000 years, Japan's Stone Age reaches back a full 20,000 or 30,000 years. Geologists, paleontologists, anthropologists, and zoologists at last are getting together and making these facts known. Unfortunately, the Japanese Teachers Union, a Communist-dominated organization, is trying to repress the true story about Japan's ancient history.

At the conclusion of the three-day intermediate course, the trainees received their new amulets. Most of the members from Nakayama felt that they now had a better understanding of the teachings of their church. When I asked one woman what significance the story of Mu and the other revelations had for her, she said very simply, "Why, it helps me understand the World of Miracles!"

6   *Gospel Sources*

Messiahs are seldom original thinkers. Their gospels are usually filled with spiritual tidbits gleaned from this source and that. My purpose in this chapter is to trace the origins of Mioshie, the Mahikari gospel. To do this, we must look both at the two religions from which the sect originated historically and at the much broader tradition of popular or folk religion from which it draws its deeper inspiration. Finally, we shall see that in addition to folk religion, folk customs and folktales help to give shape and content to the spirit experiences of Mahikari members.

The Sectarian Movement

Sukyo Mahikari is but one of a number of movements that grew out of the Ōmoto sect, founded in 1892 by a peasant woman named Deguchi Nao (1836–1918).[1] The Omoto movement reached the apex of its popularity under the dramatic leadership of Nao's adopted son, Deguchi Onisaburō (1871–1948), a shamanistic messiah who boasted of countless adventures in the spirit world.[2] Fearing that Onisaburo was about to begin a millenarian rebellion, the government arrested him briefly in 1921 and again in 1935. At the time of his second arrest (together with his wife and fifty other followers), the government destroyed the headquarters of the movement. Only in 1942 was Onisaburo allowed to go free. This violent encounter with the government cost Omoto thousands of members. At the peak of its popularity in the period between the two world wars, its adherents numbered nearly two million. Recent statistics indicate that its membership has now dropped to about 144,000. Without going further into the history of this fascinating movement, I shall mention here only those elements borrowed and elaborated by Okada Kotama in his own revelations. The most important of these was a healing technique called *miteshiro* (honorable hand-substitute).

When I first witnessed miteshiro in an Omoto church in a suburb of Nakayama City, I was immediately struck by its similarity to okiyome. The minister of the church bowed before a Shinto altar, clapped his hands, and intoned a prayer (the Amatsu-goto). After this a "salvation song" (*sukui no uta*) was sung, then another that recited the story of the creation of the world (*Ama no kazu uta*). Like the Exorcist's Prayer in Mahikari, both songs were replete with powerful word magic (kotodama). The minister asked the supplicant (my obliging research assistant) his name, address, age, and the nature of his affliction; he then turned and reported these facts to the deity. Finally, the minister took a rice ladle (*oshakushi* or *shamoji*) wrapped in a red folder and moved it slowly around the patient's body, as though it were an X ray scanner searching his body for hidden lesions.

Later, I learned from the minister that Deguchi Onisaburo got the inspiration for this healing ritual while watching a quarter moon during Tanabata, the Festival of the Two Stars, which takes place annually on July 7. The crescent shape of the moon suddenly reminded him of a rice ladle. Could not a ladle that is used to scoop up (*sukū*) rice be used to save (*sukū*) people, he wondered. And so he began literally to ladle out divine spirit (*shinki* or *reiki*) in a spoon in order to exorcise evil spirits and drive out disease and misfortune. Whenever an evil spirit became violent, he found that he could pacify it by reciting prayers and spells.

In addition to the obvious similarities between miteshiro and okiyome, various other ideas originating in Omoto have found their way into Mahikari. For example, Omoto, like Mahikari, talks about the "retirement" or "eclipse" of the gods. Both religions elaborately describe the spirit world, the Kingdom of Heaven (or the Kingdom of Maitreya), the renewal of the world (yonaoshi), and the need to wipe away the "clouds" of sin piled on the soul by one's ancestors. Omoto still has an ambivalent attitude toward medical science and is opposed to the use of chemical fertilizers.

Influenced by Honda Chikaatsu's book on occult etymology called *Kami no Mokuji*, Onisaburo took a deep interest in "spiritual word studies." Omoto's pantheon, like Mahikari's, includes forty-eight tutelary spirits associated with the Japanese syllabary. It also teaches that the world is now under the influence of evil spirits, corrupt religions, and materialism, but that someday it will be united under a "single spiritual sovereign." The notions of karma and spirit levels are common to both religions. But what is most important is an apocalyptic Plan that, mutatis mutandis, is found in nearly all the sects that originated in the Omoto movement: the imminent destruction of the world, the coming of a messiah, and the founding of an earthly paradise.[3]

When we turn to Sekai Kyūsei Kyō, or the Church of World Messianity, the parallels with Mahikari become more obvious still. Okiyome, for example, is nearly identical with Messianity's ritual of *jōrei*, or spirit cleaning. Since Okada Kotama was once a follower of this sect,[4] he was naturally familiar with jorei and with the general teachings of Messianity before he launched his own movement.[5]

Sekai Kyusei Kyo was founded by Okada Mokichi (1882–1955), no relation to the founder of Mahikari. Until 1934, Okada was a teacher in an Omoto church in Tokyo. In that year, for some reason, he refused to continue using the sect's official rice ladle for healing and started to use a fan instead. This heresy led to his expulsion and to the founding of his own group.[6] As time went on, he discovered he could heal diseases simply by touching a person's body with a piece of paper on which he had written the word Light (*hikari*). When he found that he could infuse his own charisma into paper amulets, enclose the amulets in golden lockets, and sell them for 2,000 yen apiece, Okada was on his way to fame and fortune as a new messiah. Success, however, is never without pitfalls, and in 1950 he was jailed for evading 80,000,000 yen in income taxes.[7] Today, Sekai Kyusei Kyo uses its amulet (called *oma-mori-sama* or *hōshu*) in much the same way that Mahikari uses the omitama. Like the omitama, which it resembles, the omamori-sama is said to work miracles of all sorts by means of spiritual cords that bind people to the other world. As in Mahikari, this amulet is presented to neophytes after a three-day training course.

Both sects recognize the importance of the spirit world. According to Okada Mokichi, spirits are constantly on the move throughout the universe. "They can expand or shrink at will, pass through tiny crevices in walls or keyholes, travel vast distances with astonishing speed."[8] The world of spirits is a three-storied cosmos in which the better sort of spirits, having higher vibrations, can hover closer to the Light without being burned up. Evil spirits, on the other hand, are condemned to live in the freezing cold of the lower regions. As in Mahikari, if the evil spirits work hard, they can improve their lot in the other world and gradually move upward. These beings influence people in this world by acting upon the spiritual cords connected to their "secondary" souls. Good spirits, however, affect the individual's "primary" soul.

In Messianity, it is believed that, by acting directly on the clouds covering the spiritual body, jorei can get rid of the toxins in the physical body. Disease is thought to be nature's way of purifying the body. Fevers, for example, liquefy the toxins in the body and flush them out. Hence the importance of "discharges of nasal mucous, phlegm, perspiration, and so on" in the nosology of both religions.[9] Although Okada Mokichi recognized the existence of evil spirits and stressed the value of his amulets in expelling them, jorei seems far more subdued than Mahikari's practice of okiyome. The omamori-sama does not seem to produce the kind of stereotyped hand movements or violent spirit seizures that one commonly sees in a Mahikari dojo. Since there are no specific "vital spots" toward which jorei is directed, the ritual appears to be oriented toward the individual's general well-being.

In both religions one finds two sets of deities and principles (fire/water, east/west, spiritual/material, male/female) joined by the cross. Both messiahs described in detail the origins of Japan in the primordial past. Both shared similar eschatological expectations, though Okada Kotama's visions were spelled out in more lurid detail. Nevertheless, the founder of Messianity also taught that an Age of Daylight would appear only after the world had passed through an apocalyptic period of chaos, during which incurable diseases would spread over the world. Mahikari's Savior also seems to have learned from Okada Mokichi that the temporary advance of material civilization at the expense of the things of the spirit was part of the Divine Plan.[10] Both religions teach the existence of the aura, the transmigration of the soul, the existence of spiritual vibrations and cords. Like Okada Kotama, Okada Mokichi taught that there is a law of spiritual attraction between couples at the same spirit level that causes them to marry. Sexual frustrations and fears can be carried over from one life to the next. This idea, also borrowed by Okada Kotama, continues to exert enormous influence on Mahikari's young single members.

Compared with Mahikari, Sekai Kyusei Kyo is a far more successful and better-established religion. With several "paradises" now completed—the one in Atami being the best known—the sect currently numbers about 670,000 believers. When I visited one of its churches near Nakayama University, it appeared that members of this sect were possibly of a somewhat higher socioeconomic background than my friends in Mahikari. Although members gave testimonies about the miracles they had experienced, their reports were no match for the emotional outbursts I had become used to at the dojo. The minister's sermon even included helpful suggestions on how to handle a husband who watches television during dinner or forgets to say goodbye to his wife in the morning. In short, the sect, or at least the branch I visited, seems to have evolved into a more "respectable" middle-class movement in which evil spirits and their shenanigans would be embarrassing and probably unwelcome. Another indication of the sect's comparative refinement is its emphasis on the importance of art in religious life. This theme, taken over from Omoto, is conspicuously absent in Sukyo Mahikari.

It should be clear by now that the religious thought and activities of our three messiahs, Deguchi Onisaburo, Okada Mokichi, and Okada Kotama, fall into one continuous historical tradition. Likewise, we must regard miteshiro, jorei, and okiyome, their respective spiritual therapies, as successive developments of basically the same healing ritual.

Apart from this direct historical descent, I should point out that there is a much broader, less formal, diffusion of thaumaturgical manual healing in Japan.[11] The most important of these non-sectarian thaumaturgical manual healing schools was founded by Eguchi Toshihiro. Eguchi Sensei turned to the study of the traditional healing arts when doctors trained in Western medicine were unable to cure his son's pleurisy. After studying some 300 types of folk medicine he finally came upon the "laying on of hands" (*te no hira ryōji*) method. His son-in-law, Miyazaki Gorō, later published a book called *The Hand and Its Miracles*, in which the principles of this art are elaborated.[12]

According to Miyazaki, the practitioner should pray, then raise his hand. After that, he should leave everything to the hand itself. The hand can be placed directly on the patient's body, or it can be held a short distance away. The best way, however, is to raise the right hand over a patient while holding the left hand at one's hip, palm upward, in order to collect the radiant energy of the sun. The source of healing, however, is not the sun, but God himself. Radiation is emitted through the hand, which acts like an electrical wire conducting the healing energy. The patient's body functions as a transformer, which allows this energy to be absorbed. As in Mahikari, the patient's head is first radiated. This is followed by the kidneys and whatever parts of the body are afflicted. The electromagnetic wave energy that enters the body through the practitioner's fingertips penetrates the five organs (*zō*) and six viscera (*fu*), causing any stiffness in the body to "melt." According to Miyazaki, various miasmas (*jaki*) produce disharmony whenever they lodge in the body. Of these there are two sorts. The first are the subtle, biological miasmas produced by the movement of the body. These are the byproducts of life itself and are produced with carbon dioxide. Such miasmas cause disease only when they are not removed from the body in the normal way. The second sort are the pathological miasmas. These are described as "thick, heavy and slow." As long as there are no tumors on the nerves or lymph ducts, such impurities are also normally expelled from the body through the nostrils, ears, or mouth. Disease is caused when these passageways become clogged, thereby trapping the pathological miasmas in the body. Biological miasmas, on the other hand, are extremely "fine" and can pass even through obstructed channels.*

Miyazaki used to train people in this healing art once every month in a Shinto shrine in Nara. Although medicine is frowned on by the movement, many of his followers are willing to mix Western medicine with this folk therapy. "Natural" foods such as brown rice are also recommended. As in Mahikari, some people report feeling a hot sensation in the palm of the hand when giving the treatment.

I first came across this therapy in 1973, while studying a utopian community called Ittōen located in southeast Kyoto.[13] Although the laying on of hands is not an obligatory practice, about ten or twelve members of this community continue to practice the art, which they learned from Eguchi Sensei himself. An elderly member of Ittoen, Suzuki Gorō, has written a book on the subject, which covers about the same points discussed by Miyazaki.[14] He too claims to have healed a wide variety of diseases, from nearsightedness to cancer. Like Okada Kotama, Suzuki points out that this kind of manual healing was used by both Jesus Christ and the Buddha. His description of Eguchi's teaching sessions at Ittoen leaves little doubt about the religious nature of the treatment. On each of three successive days of the session, Eguchi had the members of the community sit in meditation for twenty minutes. Then, after reciting a poem by the Emperor Meiji, he went around the room laying his hands on all until their "life force" was stirred up. Prayer was also recommended as part of the therapy.[15]

---

* The notion of the five organs and the six viscera originated in the anatomical topography of traditional Chinese medicine. In this therapeutic tradition, disease is thought to occur whenever the energy flows between the organs and the viscera become obstructed. We have seen that in Mahikari, too, disease is regarded as an obstruction. Healing, on the other hand, is thought of as a "melting" of the body's lumps, toxins, stiffness, and obstructions. The difference between Mahikari and these other therapies lies in the source of the obstructions. For Mahikari, they are the result of the coagulation of medicines, food additives, and other pollutants in the body; the ultimate cause, however, is the evil spirits who like to live in such filth. Obstructions are therefore properly regarded as spirit-obstructions (reisho).

The Myth of Mu

To return to the direct historical influences on the shaping of the Mahikari gospel, it should now be obvious that most of the Savior's teachings were distilled from the revelations and practices of Omoto and Sekai Kyusei Kyo. What about the rest?

It too was borrowed. For example, let us take the story of the sunken continent. This is a theme popular among occult groups in the West, from the Rosicrucians to the Theosophists. The sunken continent is generally pictured as Eden, the Gardens of the Hesperides, or the Elysian fields. It was a primordial paradise and the original home of all later civilizations, material and spiritual cultures, alphabets, and races. As such, it has easily become—as in Mahikari—a prototype for the paradisal civilization of the future. In contrast to scientific archeology, which views man's history as a "rise" from a pre-civilized to a civilized state, the theosophical myths of the sunken continent tend to treat man's present condition as a degeneration of past civilizations. The Savior's primary source of information in these matters was the Anglo-American writer of historical fiction (or better, fictitious histories) Colonel James Churchward. Churchward's evidence for conditions in Mu came from such venerable sources as the Easter Island Tablets, Indian and Mayan Records, the Naacal Tablets, the Troano Manuscript, and the Lhasa Record, and from other evidence preserved "in Certain Monasteries in India and Tibet whose names are withheld by request." [16] That Churchward could decipher all of these "ancient records" is explained by his unique method for learning languages. He simply stared at words for a long time and let their meaning emerge in his inner consciousness.

According to Churchward, "savagery came out of civilization, not civilization out of savagery. . . . A savage, left to himself, does *not rise*. He has fallen to where he is and is still going down." Paleolithic men were therefore more civilized than Neolithic.[17] The original civilization of Mu was the source of all that was, and is, good in nature and society. His descriptions of this paradise leave little to the imagination.

Over the cool river, gaudy-winged butterflies hovered in the shade of trees, rising and falling in fairy-like movement, as if better to view their painted beauty in nature's mirror. Darting hither and thither from flower to flower, hummingbirds made their short flights, glistening like living jewels in the rays of the sun. Feathered songsters in bush and tree vied with each other in their sweet lays.[18]

There are, however, some rather revealing discrepancies between Churchward's account of Mu and the description of the sunken continent in Mahikari. Japan plays virtually no role in Churchward's account. In fact, he was rather vague about where to place the northwest boundary of the continent, deciding finally that it was somewhere around the Ladrones. On his own maps, the Japanese archipelago is therefore always drawn far to the north of Mu. In his book *The Children of Mu*, he does point out that in premodern Japan there were many artifacts that reflected conditions in Mu 15,000 years earlier. He was especially impressed by the Japanese flag, which he believed was one of the sacred symbols of the sunken Motherland. Unlike Okada Kotama, who believed that the yellow race (the Japanese) was the original and dominant people in Mu, Churchward speculated that the Japanese were merely the descendants of the "Quiche Mayas" of the Motherland. Furthermore, he disputed the Mongolian origins of the Japanese and insisted that they were originally a white race. Caucasian Churchward was fascinated by visions of colonists leaving Mu in boats manned by crews of "stalwart, young adventurers with milk-white skins, blue eyes and light, flaxen hair."[19] He was intrigued by reports that "in the dense forests of Honduras and Guatemala there still existed villages of *blond white Indians*." *

---

* James Churchward, *The Lost Continent of Mu* (New York, 1959; paperback), p. 19. Emphasis in the original. The writings of both Churchward and Okada Kotama are filled with the ethnocentrism that has so often blemished the myth of the sunken continent. Churchward, for example, believed that blacks originated in the southwest corner of Mu. Today their descendants are "pure Negroes and the worst savages among the islands of the Pacific Ocean" (p. 84). Likewise, Max Heindel in *The Rosicrucian Cosmo-Conception* (1929) traces Negroes "and the savage races with curly hair" back to Lemuria (Mu) and the Jews back to a later period on Atlantis when human beings were "governed more by . . . Cunning than by Reason." The most hilarious of these racist theories was put forward by Lewis Spence, a Scotsman who zealously promoted the story of Atlantis and believed that the Cro-Magnons, a race of pure Atlantian blood, were responsible for Europe's high culture. To this pure blood line "we owe the genius of Shakespeare and Burns, Massinger and Ben Johnson, Milton, Scott, and, to come to our own times, Mr. H. G. Wells and Mr. Galsworthy are almost purely Cro-Magnon." Cited in

The sixteen princes of Mu sent out to rule over the world (and extolled in Mahikari's advanced training courses) seem to be a Japanized version of the "root races" commonly found in the writings of the Theosophists.* Whereas Western occultists predict that history will culminate in the domination of the world by Slavs and Americans, Mahikari regards this as merely a penultimate stage in a cosmic and ethnic evolution in which the Japanese will finally triumph. Nevertheless, like Madame Blavatsky (*The Secret Doctrine*), A. P. Sinnett (*Esoteric Buddhism*), Claude Falls Wright (*Modern Theosophy*), Max Heindel (*The Rosicrucian Cosmo-Conception*), and Churchward (in his several books on Mu), Okada Kotama conceived of the history of the human race (the Five Colored Races) within the context of a Divine Plan. The effect was to remythologize Japan's history (which had been radically secularized after the surrender in 1945), giving his own followers the dominant place in the unfolding plot of the universe.

One obvious source of Okada's vision of "history" was the eschatology of the Bible. Since the time of the Shinto scholar Hirata Atsutane (1776–1843), the Bible and the Christian religion have had considerable influence on Japanese nativism, New Religions, and revitalization movements of all sorts. Even though Okada believed that he had successfully synthesized monotheism, polytheism, and pantheism, his emphasis on Su-god was actually a form of henotheism inspired by similar tendencies in Omoto, Sekai Kyusei Kyo, and other New Religions attentive to the religious traditions

---

Robert Wauchope, *Lost Tribes and Sunken Continents: Myth and Method in the Study of American Indians* (Chicago, 1962), p. 121. Churchward, however, believed that some of these European progenitors were merely "idiots and degenerates," as was "obvious from the abnormal shapes of their skulls" (p. 169).

* The picture the Theosophists painted of the Muvians was not altogether complimentary. Madame Blavatsky herself believed that some of them had four arms and an eye in the back of their heads that gave them psychic vision. Later, Annie Besant, W. Scott-Elliot, and Rudolf Steiner recorded their own "researches" on Lemuria. Scott-Elliot thought that the Third Eye of the Muvians had evolved into our pineal gland. Steiner, an Austrian who founded the Anthroposophical Society in 1907, wrote a book called *Cosmic History: Atlantis and Lemuria* (1923), in which he revealed that the Muvians were feebleminded. Originally, they were a race of egg-laying hermaphrodites who had but one eye; their vision improved only with their subsequent discovery of heterosexuality. How different were Okada Kotama's panegyrics on the ancient Nippono-Muvians!

of the West. Undoubtedly much of his knowledge of the Bible was gleaned from these sects and from such redoubtable sources as Colonel Churchward. This, at least, would help to explain some of his odd ideas about the Bible, such as his notion that Jesus worshiped a god called Christ. The stress on altruistic love, the ideas that all men are children of God and that God is Light, and so on, are either borrowed from or parallel to statements in the Bible. The sect's emphasis on the coming of the Messiah or Savior, the Baptism by Fire, the Apocalypse and Judgment, though modified to fit the Japanese context, are all ultimately of biblical provenance. The star of David, though given new allegorical meanings, decorates the entrance to the sect's headquarters in Tokyo's Den'enchōfu; like the cross and the swastika, it is thought to have been one of the mystical symbols of ancient Mu. The odd sloping roof of the edifice was designed by Okada to represent Noah's ark. The headquarters is also referred to as Eden.

Many of the ideas Okada wove into Churchward's account of Mu were taken from the "records" and "antiquities" said to be preserved by the Takenouchi family in a shrine in Ibaraki Prefecture. This information has been set forth by Yamae Kiku in a book called *The Authentic History of the World Secreted Away in Japan*.[20] It is from this book—which the Savior regarded as the last word on ancient history—that we learn that Jesus died in Japan, and that nearly all the other saints and holy men of the world at least visited the country.

The same book was one of the sources for Okada's idea that writing was discovered in Japan. I might add that the "letters of the divine age" (*shindaimoji*) were actually a bogus idea popular among Shinto nativists in the Tokugawa period, for example, in Hirata Atsutane's *Jinji nichibunden* and Ochiai Naozumi's *Nihon kodai monjikō*. Ban Nobutomo (1775–1846), however, disputed the authenticity of these characters, and by the turn of the twentieth century nearly all Japanese scholars had ceased to believe in them. In the ultra-nationalist period preceding World War II, the shindaimoji regained their popularity, especially in such patriotic and military circles as the Rikugun Shikan Gakkō, where the Savior was educated. The real significance of these letters was ideological. Modern linguists are convinced that the shindaimoji were merely

fabrications designed to compensate for the Japanese sense of inferiority vis-à-vis the language and literature of China and were
part of a nationalistic idealization of ancient Japan. As such, they
are another example of the nativism that runs through Mahikari's
gospel.

The Folk Tradition

Although Japan's New Religions and messiahs have borrowed
liberally from several of the world's Great Traditions—from Christianity as well as from Buddhism and Confucianism—their greatest
inspiration has been the Little Tradition of the common folk. Some,
such as Soka Gakkai and Rissho Kosei Kai, have leaned more toward Buddhism, and others, such as Konkokyo, Omoto, Sekai
Kyusei Kyo, and Mahikari, toward Shinto; but all are deeply influenced by the outlook, values, and practices of Japanese folk
religion, which is highly syncretistic. The clan gods of the local
community, nationally known shrines and temples, shamanistic asceticism, Taoist magic, Buddhist cosmology, and Confucian moral-
ity all contributed to this diffused, popular religiousness. Its values
and worldview are clear reflections of the interests of its clientele
—peasants, artisans, and merchants confronted with the daily, and
deadly serious, problems of survival. What the common man looks
for in religion is not metaphysics, but a kind of spiritual, or thaumaturgical, pragmatism. He wants his cow to calve, his wife to
bear, the drought to end, the plague to pass him by, and finally, an
easy death and rebirth in a better world. If, in addition to this,
he were finally to look down from Heaven or the Pure Land and see
his descendants prospering, he would know—as members of Mahikari are wont to say—that his was truly a "superb" religion.

The deep influence of folk religion on the lives of the followers of
Mahikari will become evident when we examine their experiences
of spirit possession in greater detail. Before they join the dojo, many
members consult palmists, mediums, diviners, and faith healers
about their personal problems. Others go on pilgrimages, perform
cold water ablutions in the middle of the winter, or seek to purify
themselves in other ways. Even after they join the dojo, these ideas
and practices continue to influence members' behavior.

The most important influences of the folk religion on Mahikari have to do with the notion of spirits, their fate, and how to contact and exorcise them. This set of ideas and practices falls under the general topic of shamanism, one of the most important ingredients in Japanese folk religion. Shamanism can be traced back to prehistoric customs originating in north-central and southeast Asia. Shamans were of various sorts: purveyors of good luck, mediums able to converse with the dead, and psychopomps who knew how to win happy rebirths, or even nirvana, for their followers. Some were wanderers who practiced religious disciplines and magical arts in the mountains. Others, especially after the Muromachi period (1338–1573), settled down in villages to act as priests and sedentary mediums. During the early Meiji period, many shamanistic practices were outlawed by the government. After the Pacific War and the guarantee of religious freedom, some Japanese became interested in reviving these ancient spiritual techniques.

In and around Nakayama City there are several mediums (*reibai* or *ogamiyasan*) still at work. On nearby Mount Koya, headquarters of the Shingon Buddhist sect, several faith healers and diviners continue to ply their esoteric crafts. A member of the Nakayama dojo was once a mountain ascetic himself. Another was a medium who could see spirits in his sleep. Still another joined the sect in order to acquire the powers of a seer. After joining Mahikari, however, members are supposed to shun mediums. Mediums often acquire their frightful skill by performing such austerities as standing under cold waterfalls in the fastness of the mountains. According to the Savior, animal spirits that loiter about these gloomy spots take possession of the ascetic in order to serve as his familiar. Whenever the medium is asked a question, the animal spirit rises up to his primary soul to give the answer. Mahikari also teaches that because of their trafficking with spirits, mediums, when they die, must do severe penance in the astral world.

As in other religions, what is forbidden is usually what is most tempting. Because the families that join Mahikari often consult mediums and faith healers, the church regards these masters of the occult as serious rivals. Nevertheless, the church shares many of the traditional seer's religious notions and techniques. Even the Savior's mission, to heal the living and save the spirits in the astral world, was not unlike the profession of the archaic shaman or the contemporary healer. His own vision of the old man with the white beard has been recorded among the visions of other Japanese clairvoyants.[21] Mahikari's emphasis on ascetic discipline (shugyo) is a common shamanistic idea. The sensations of heat and cold that members experience during training sessions and while giving and receiving okiyome might be traced back not only to Buddhist visions of hell, but ultimately to the ancient shamanistic motif of the mastery of fire. In both Mahikari and traditional shamanism, wide use is made of word magic (kotodama) and miraculous healing songs. The three-day training course might even be regarded as a kind of initiation during which the neophyte is not only instructed, but purified. Would it be far-fetched to suggest that the illnesses some people experience when they take these courses are a survival of those real or ritual maladies commonly suffered by the ancient shaman during his initiation?

Okiyome itself bears the imprint of mediumistic healing rites such as the traditional ritual called *yorigitō*. Yorigito is performed by two people, a medium who makes "contact" with the other world and an ascetic who controls and interprets the medium's behavior. The ritual is instigated, and paid for, by a client who approaches these specialists with some pressing problem, such as illness. The medium is first entranced by the ascetic and then becomes possessed either by a deity or by a vengeful ghost. In the latter case, the ascetic compels the spirit, now speaking through the medium, to identify itself and tell why it has caused such mischief. Finally, the ascetic scolds the spirit, reduces it to a state of obedience, and dispatches it to the other world. After this, supposing the ritual is successful, the misfortune or illness of the client will disappear. In short, yorigito is a kind of vicarious exorcism performed by the ascetic and medium on behalf of the client.*

* See Carmen Blacker, *The Catalpa Bow: A Study of Shamanistic Practices in Japan* (London, 1975), pp. 252–314. Similar shamanistic duets performed by the (active) ascetic and the (passive) medium go back to Japan's earliest recorded history, e.g. to the *Wei Chih* (ca. A.D. 297), the *Hou Han Shu* (ca. 445), and the *Sui Shu* (ca. 630). See Wm. Theodore de Bary, ed., *Sources of Japanese Tradition* (New York, 1967), I, pp. 3–10. The *Nihongi*, book 9, gives us a vivid account of such a duet in which the empress herself played the medium's role. See W. G. Aston,

Among the New Religions, a ritual that is closely related to these archaic shamanistic rituals, and to Mahikari's okiyome, is the exorcistic rite of the Salvation Cult, studied by Takie Sugiyama Lebra. In this ritual, a leader of the sect plays the ascetic's role (*chūkaisha*), and individual members assume the part of the medium (*bontai*). "The *chūkaisha* and *bontai* sit side by side in front of the altar and go through a spirit-inviting ritual, invoking the names of deities and buddhas and repeatedly bowing to the altar. The spirit's arrival is signaled by the sudden rapid movement of the *bontai*'s folded hands in which a special charm is held. Unless unusually resistant, the spirit identifies itself and conveys its message through the *bontai*'s mouth or hands (by tracing letters on the floor) in response to requests and questions by the *chūkaisha*."[22]

There are important similarities between okiyome and these mediumistic encounters. In yorigito, the ritual of the Salvation Cult, and okiyome alike, exorcism is performed as a duet. In the Mahikari sect, the person giving okiyome and performing the spirit investigation takes the active part of the ascetic or exorcist; the person on the receiving end plays the role of the medium. All of these rituals seem to follow the same basic pattern. The medium is first "entranced," producing various kinds of ecstatic or seemingly transrational behavior.* This is followed by the interrogation and scolding of the possessing spirits.[23] In Mahikari, some investigators are said to know what spirit is possessing a person even if there are no palpable spirit movements. By reading the person's mind, the investigator is able both to identify and to scold the evil spirit "in his heart." The result is a silent confrontation between the investigator and the evil spirit. In fact, according to the Savior, the best spirit investigations are silent. These wordless scoldings and investigations may be related to the shaman's clairvoyant eye (*gantsū*).[24]

---

trans., *Nihongi: Chronicles of Japan from the Earliest Times to A.D. 697* (Rutland, Vt., 1972), pp. 224–26. Generally, the medium was played by a woman, the ascetic by a man.

*In Mahikari, entrancement is induced by intoning the Exorcist's Prayer. I do not wish to suggest, though, that all who receive okiyome fall into an actual trance. By the use of "entrancement," I do not mean to make a judgment about the subject's actual state of mind. I shall use the word more objectively to refer to the dramatic or ritual posture assumed by the subject in this part of the exorcistic scenario.

Finally, the subject is disenchanted, and the spirits possessing him are pacified and sent back to the other world.

There are also some very important differences between these traditional shamanistic healing rituals and okiyome. In yorigito, both deities and evil spirits appear; in okiyome, one encounters only evil spirits. If a deity does appear, spirit investigations inevitably reveal that this apparition was only an evil spirit masquerading as a deity. The most important difference is that in Mahikari there are no specialists, virtuosi, or religious professionals. People therefore take turns playing the active role of the ascetic and the passive part of the medium. In this duet, clients become mediums and bring their problems to the séance themselves.* Like the ritual praxis of many other New Religions, okiyome can therefore be thought of as the democratization, or rather—bowing to the Savior's dislike of this word—the popular diffusion of a professional, mediumistic technique. "Anyone can do it."† Exorcists, to use the sociologist's jargon, constitute an "open stratum."

Folktales

Folk religion is not the only point of contact between the New Religions and the traditions of the common man. The folktale, both as a repository of stories about gods, buddhas, and demons and as a form of expression, is also of great importance. The "in the beginning" of classical mythology has never had the impact of the "once upon a time" of folktales on the religious imagination of the Japanese. Mythology, which has always been heavily larded with the ideology of the ruling elite, has never been as close to the common

---

* Vicarious okiyome also takes place in Mahikari. For example, the oracles Mrs. Yoshida received as a proxy for the ancestors of her neighbors show clearly how the Mahikari "medium" can intercede on behalf of others. In these family duets, Yoshida Sensei, who has never had any spirit movements or seizures himself, unknowingly played the classical role of the male ascetic. His wife, just as unwittingly, took the part female mediums have played for millennia in Japan. See Chapter 4, pp. 56–63 *passim*.

† Among Japan's traditional types of exorcism, perhaps the closest to okiyome is the possession scenario in the Ontake sect, in which the medium (*nakaza*) and the ascetic (*maeza*) simply change places after the ritual has been performed. See Percival Lowell, *Occult Japan or the Way of the Gods* (Boston, 1894), pp. 3–8, 130–36.

people as the tales passed on in legends, popular theater, and sermons.

The influence of the folktale is naturally strongest on those who by an ingenuous suspension of disbelief are able to forget that, after all, these stories are make-believe. Two examples will suffice to illustrate this attitude.

Mrs. Nakata Asako is well known in the Nakayama dojo as a person well read in spiritualist literature of all sorts and well versed in folktales in particular. Since I happened to be interested in tales about foxes, I asked her if she could tell me any. She obliged by telling the following story.

Once my father was eating his lunch in an open field when a young boy appeared in front of him. The boy first went dancing to the right and then, after a pause, to the left. Thinking this strange, Father looked to see if anybody else was around. There, sitting just a short distance away, was a fox. After watching the fox for a few minutes, Father noticed, much to his amazement, that whenever the fox's tail moved to the right, the boy automatically danced to the right. Likewise, when the fox twisted his tail to the left, the boy danced to the left. Father was so engrossed in this performance that he didn't notice the disappearance of his lunch box. The fox had a good meal that day!

Because her father had told her this story himself, Mrs. Nakata insisted that it was true. Furthermore, she recalled, when she was a girl, she had often heard foxes barking in the bamboo forest behind their home in the country. At night she sometimes saw as many as one hundred or two hundred foxes, lanterns in hand, on their way to a wedding.*

I first became aware of how literally folktales and ghost stories are taken by some Japanese one weekend when Yoshida Sensei invited my family to his summer home on the Inland Sea. As we drove along the rugged coastline, the highway passed through a number of long, dark tunnels. Coming to the longest of these, the Tanba tunnel, Sensei slowed the car and told us a story he had recently heard on the radio about this place. Several drivers had reported seeing a young woman dressed in white standing at the roadside in

---

* In Japan, the will-o'-the-wisp (*ignis fatuus*) is often described as lanterns carried by foxes on their way to a wedding (*kitsune no yomeiri*).

the middle of the tunnel. A number of people stopped and gave the woman a ride. After they let the mysterious passenger out of the car a wet spot was always found in the seat of the vehicle where she had been sitting. In every case, both the driver and his original passenger later became ill.

When I asked him if this was not just a ghost story, Sensei said he was sure it had actually happened. Furthermore, a friend of one of the dojo members had had this experience himself. Sensei went on to speculate, as is his wont, that in this case the woman in white was probably the spirit of some unfortunate person who had died by drowning; hence the wet spot on the seat. When, out of curiosity, I later told a Japanese friend about this story, he too assured me that such things do in fact happen. Incidentally, although this person was not a member of Mahikari, he, like Yoshida Sensei, was a teacher with a college education.

Stories told in lectures are, in effect, modern versions of traditional miracle and possession tales. Like the folktale, these stories are characterized by simple plots, suspense, and irony. They too are "once upon a time" tales that, according to the raconteur, "really happened." Their function in the lectures seems to be both to edify and to entertain. All, of course, are given a Mahikari denouement. The two following tales are good examples of Mahikari spirit lore and could even be styled "testimonial folktales."

The tale of how a factory was possessed by a snake spirit is one of the most celebrated stories in Mahikari. It seems that for some time an ironworks in the city of Nagoya had been plagued by accidents and threatened with bankruptcy. One of the workers in the plant, Mr. Umeyama, happened to become a member of Mahikari. Not long after, he hurt the middle finger of his left hand. Because this is thought to be the "spirit side" of the body, he immediately suspected there was something mysterious going on in the company. The next morning he went around to the various spots where accidents had occurred and gave them okiyome—much to the amusement of his fellow workers.

One morning while he was thus engaged, he came across a pile of new steel plates. On the topmost plate he noticed the yellowish-brown figure of a snake. He called nearby workers to take a look. One woman employee gasped when she saw the snake and said that during the previous year two snakes had appeared in the factory. A certain Mr. Yamashita, who worked in that part of the plant, had poured gasoline over them and set them on fire. The shape the two snakes took as they writhed in their death throes was the same as the snake image that had now appeared on the steel plate. Mr. Umeyama contacted his local dojo and asked for advice. Following his minister's suggestion, he built a small shrine on the spot and for five days worshiped the steel plate, offering raw eggs, rice, and water to the snake spirits. Miraculously, the fortunes of the steel-frame department, which had been in greatest financial trouble, began to improve. Mechanical breakdowns and accidents came to an end. In the meantime, Mr. Yamashita, who had killed the snakes, began to act strange and started to speak in a queer voice. Four days after the discovery of the mysterious plate, he disappeared and was never heard from again.

The second "testimonial folktale" relates how the spirits of a peasant couple possessed their own grandson and caused him all sorts of grief. There was once a bright and ambitious youth by the name of Tanaka, who, after graduating from Keiō University, entered a prestigious brokerage house in Tokyo and seemed to be in line to become the director of the firm. One day, the person directly above him was indicted for corruption, and the youth, because of his close relationship with this man, was also arrested. Unable to prove his innocence, he was fined an enormous sum of money. His father, the director of a different company, was forced to mortgage the family home and sell the car in order to pay the fine. After this, the youth went home to live with his parents.

One day, he discovered a car just like the one his parents had owned parked in front of the house. For old times' sake, he got into the car. No sooner had he done so than three of his former schoolmates from Keio happened to come strolling by. Noticing that the keys were in the ignition, they asked him to lend them his car. The youth, ashamed to admit that his family no longer owned a car, agreed to let them take it. Although he expected them to bring it back after a drive around the neighborhood, three days went by and his friends had not returned. In the meantime, the three Keio boys had driven down to the Izu Peninsula, where they had had an accident and wrecked the car. When they told the police they had borrowed the car from Tanaka, the authorities checked out their story, and naturally discovered that the car was registered under a different name. Thinking that Tanaka had stolen the car, they immediately called for his arrest.

The boy's mother, now at her wits' end, finally went to a dojo for help. When she received okiyome, the spirits of her husband's mother and father appeared to her. Before their death this couple had been tenant farmers. Once, when they were unable to pay their taxes because of a poor harvest, their landlord came with his henchmen and wrested away what little they had by force. In desperation, the old couple took their own lives. The spirits now confessed to their daughter-in-law that they had thought about taking out their wrath by killing their own son. Finally, however, they decided that would not be very "interesting." Instead they thought, "Let's bide our time, cause the family to prosper, and then take out our revenge on our grandson." Even a Keio diploma could not ward off the grandparents' revenge.

Other tales and anecdotes recounted in the lectures presuppose such familiarity with popular Japanese customs that I omitted them in my earlier description of the training course. One example will suffice. This story came up when Yoshida Sensei explained the "retirement" of the strict deities.

According to Mioshie, when the strict fire gods retired from the world they left "dragon bodies" behind them. This was the origin of the modern dragon. These divine dragons were later slain by men who first drove sharp holly leaves into their eyes and climaxed their sacrilege by ripping out the dragons' entrails (*zōmotsu*). This horrible deed was the origin of the Japanese New Year's dish, *ozōni*. The slaying of the dragons also explains the customs of the Setsubun Festival, a celebration marking the end of winter and the beginning of spring. During Setsubun, the Japanese go to Buddhist temples and throw handfuls of roasted beans to drive away evil spirits, shouting, "In with good luck; out with the devils!" (*fuku wa uchi, oni wa soto*). During this festival, some people place the head of a dried sardine and a branch of holly in the vestibule of their homes in order to ward off evil spirits and insects. Because the use of holly at Setsubun goes back to the slaying of the dragon bodies of the gods, Mahikari members are urged to have nothing to do with the custom. Nor should they take part in the bean-throwing ceremony at the temples. The custom of throwing beans can also be traced to the retirement of the fire gods. When they announced their forthcoming retirement, the gods asked when mankind would want them to return. In reply, our sinful ancestors threw roasted beans at them and told them to come back when the beans sprouted eyes. And so the custom of bean-throwing at Setsubun only reminds the gods of man's ancient affront.

Today the dragon god, Ryujin, continues to perform austerities in the forest. The reason woodcutters so often go deaf is that they cut down trees where Ryujin is at work. Also, there are reports every year of people who get lost in the forest and die. These are people who go into the forest to urinate, not realizing that it is Ryujin's territory. The moral of this story, Yoshida Sensei concluded, is that in order to avoid the god's wrath, one should always urinate in a place that Ryujin avoids, such as the side of a path, and never in the middle of the forest.

Testimonies at the dojo are literally ghost stories. They are also similar to traditional miracle tales, which relate how people triumphed over poverty, bad luck, disease, and family problems. Today they might be called success stories. But so much for their genre. More interesting is the way they come into being. Although a person may be possessed before he comes to the dojo, he is seldom aware of his condition until he receives a spirit investigation. The pace of the dialogue between the exorcist and the evil spirit is usually quite leisurely, especially since spirits only answer yes or no to questions put to them. After the benediction is pronounced, the subject consults briefly with his exorcist-partner. If the spirit's answers were ambiguous or weak, the exorcist may offer various suggestions that will help to clarify the experience: "You were probably possessed by an ancestral spirit" or "Perhaps this samurai spirit was in love with you" or "Your ancestors were probably killed in a war and did this to you in order to take revenge." Later, the subject mulls over these suggestions. Gradually, the exorcist's "probablys" and "maybes" are forgotten, and the spirit story begins to take shape. During the following weeks, the subject may continue to receive spirit investigations. More pieces are added to the nascent spirit story. In the meantime, his ailments go away and his luck improves. Finally, Yoshida Sensei or one of the local ministers invites him to give his testimony at the monthly worship service. This gives the person an opportunity to sit down and write out his story in full.

Testimonies that are especially vivid or entertaining become well known among members of the dojo. Although some are deeply moving and are read in a flood of tears, others are quite humorous. Some members earn a reputation for their comic style. Even before they reach the microphone, the congregation begins to twitter with anticipation. Although the more talented of these raconteurs deliver their accounts without notes, testimonies are expected to be written out and turned in to the staff after the meeting. Often they are published in the dojo's monthly broadside, "The Fountain of Miracles." Occasionally, testimonies from the local dojo are selected for publication, together with the writer's photograph, in *Mahikari*, the church's national magazine. Although skeptics believe that these published testimonies have been edited by the publications staff at the church headquarters, I am inclined to believe that most of the time all that is changed is mistaken characters or grammar. The most significant editing takes place in the person's own reflection on his experience.

The Logic of Gospel Bricolage

We have seen that Mahikari's gospel is a conglomeration of several different sources: Shinto deities, Buddhist hells, Christian eschatology, Japanese nativism, occultism, and the antiquarian research of Yamae Kiku and James Churchward, to name only a few. We have also discovered that most of the Savior's revelations were simply borrowed from Mahikari's parent sect, the Church of World Messianity, and its grandparent, Omoto. Westerners raised in a tradition predicated upon the Law of the Excluded Middle generally do not take kindly to syncretism of this sort. They tend to identify religious borrowing with a lack of integrity or authenticity. Looking at Mioshie, many would feel compelled to agree with Freud that "where questions of religion are concerned people are guilty of every possible kind of insincerity and intellectual misdemeanour."[25]

My purpose in these concluding remarks on the gospel sources is not to join the chorus condemning religious thought per se, but to explain some aspects of the theological *bricolage* that characterizes not only Mahikari, but most of the other New Religions as well.* What turns of language, thought, and emotion make possible such a generous reconciliation of diverse and even contradictory elements? Here I shall concentrate on four factors that seem to make this syncretism possible: etymological reasoning, homological reasoning, relentless induction, and something I shall call the "hothouse of emotion."

Okada Kotama relied heavily on logopneumatology (*kotodama-gaku*), or spiritual word studies, for the development of his ideas. Often he would quote a detailed definition of a word in Heibonsha's *Dictionary of Shinto*, only to dismiss it as academic humbug and sophistry; and then, declaring that the word should be written with entirely different ideographs, he would reveal its "true" meaning. By using this eisegetical method, he determined that scholarship (*gakumon*) really means "the suffering of self" (*ga-kumon*), or egotism. To take a more lively example, he once enumerated all the accidents and robberies that had occurred in Tokyo one Christmas. This he attributed to the unlucky name Santa Claus, which, he maintained, should be written with Chinese characters meaning "many disasters" (*san-ta*) and "undergo hardships" (*kurō suru*). From this he concluded that the Sunshine Children should receive their Christmas presents only from the lucky hammer of the god Daikoku, and not from San-ta Kuro-suru.

The muddle behind this etymological reasoning is simple enough. The origin of a word is easily confused with its real meaning, especially by those unfamiliar with the elementary principles of semantics. Because an etymology is based on words, nuances, and images already deeply implanted in our minds, it seems to be a natural way

---

*Bricolage is a French word referring to the activities of a jack-of-all-trades, or *bricoleur*. According to Claude Lévi-Strauss, mythical thought is a kind of intellectual bricolage. The bricoleur's "universe of instruments is closed and the rules of his game are always to make do with 'whatever is at hand.'" *The Savage Mind* (Chicago, 1966), p. 11.

to reveal the secret depths of the obvious. Ideographic languages such as Japanese and Chinese offer still greater temptations in this regard because words written in these languages can be taken apart and manipulated as though they were pieces of a jigsaw puzzle. Philosophers and messiahs can easily rewrite a word (without changing its sound) using different ideographs that automatically conjure up entirely different sets of images and associations. As we shall see later, etymological reasoning of this sort is closely related to Mahikari's magical response to the world.

The founders of the New Religions also conjoin disparate ideas and symbols by the simple assertion of what a secularist might regard as crude homologies and strained correspondences. In some cases, these homologies stem from a traditional association of ideas, such as the identity of physical, moral, and spiritual impurities in Shinto. Often the connecting links between the homologized elements are not entirely obvious, as, for example, when the training-course lecturer transports us from the Buddhist notion that all things are filled with nothingness (*shikizoku zeikū*) to the biblical words "God is light" and then on to the findings of modern physics, all in one fell swoop. Nevertheless, serious practical conclusions are drawn from this mode of argumentation. For example, we have already seen that the East is homologized with yang and fire, the West with yin and water. Now, Western medicine uses ice or cold water to relieve painful swellings in the body. But Mahikari teaches that in the Age of the Baptism by Fire, this Western or yin-based therapy must be abandoned. Only heat should be used in physical therapy. Symbolic homologies of this sort are also related to what I shall later call "homeopathic" spirit possessions. In both cases, like produces like, or, by the Law of Similarity, like is so closely associated with like that they ultimately become the same.

The third logical peculiarity that one notices about Mahikari and kindred faiths is their use of a relentless kind of induction. For example: to prove that there have been all sorts of climatic aberrations since the beginning of the Age of the Baptism by Fire, long lists of natural disasters, heat waves, and volcanic eruptions have been compiled. The cumulative effect of this massive "evidence" is to lull the mind into acquiescence. This effect is especially powerful since weather conditions before the Baptism by Fire began are not mentioned at all. Testimonies are another example. A stream of deeply emotional stories is constantly poured forth by the Mahikari press in order to prove that okiyome really works miracles. Not surprisingly, disconfirming evidence never gets into print. The aim of the "experiments" put on by the Mahikari Youth Corps in evangelistic rallies is to confirm miraculous experiences, not to falsify scientific hypotheses. The effect of relentless theological induction is therefore to confirm specific ideas or miracles without actually verifying the general claims of the church. Another consequence is the growth of a "cognitive situationalism" in the thinking of the faithful that dilates concrete experience with no regard to its broader context or logical consequences.

Unlike the three stimulants to syncretism already discussed, the fourth is not actually part of the logic that holds the gospel together. Rather, it describes the affective climate in which Mioshie is nourished. I call it simply the hothouse of emotion. Just as a hothouse is needed for the nurture of tender plants, a dojo is necessary for growing the Seed-People of the Holy Twenty-First Century.

In the sociology of religion it is widely recognized that even churches that have put miracles behind them must have their own high walls and stained-glass windows to preserve a sacred realm separate from the rest of reality. Like the curtain and stage of the theater, symbolic barriers of this sort are necessary for ensuring the integrity of the church's worldview and practices. If true for churches, this rule applies still more to movements not in the cultural mainstream, and to the so-called cults that have been alienated from the definition of reality imposed by the social elite. Peripheral groups of this sort not only have rejected the world and the churches that have compromised with it; they have given the world, and the churches, no alternative but to reject them in turn.

In Mahikari's case, nearly every aspect of the gospel is an instance of "cognitive deviance." It rejects medicine in favor of magic. It declares that members of the polite professions—priests, lawyers, and doctors—will burn in hell, and hints that philosophers will not fare much better. It scoffs at the version of history taught in the public schools as Communist-inspired. It belittles science in favor of a yet-to-be-seen spiritual science, and it discards psychology for parapsychology. Little wonder, then, that from the point of view of a secular Japanese, Mahikari is a ridiculous combination of magic, superstition, and irrationalism. The point not to be missed, however, is that although sects of this sort are rejected because of their deviant ideas and practices, their deviance itself has the function of maintaining the isolation and the emotional atmosphere needed if the World of Miracles is to prosper.

7 Why People Join the Dojo

When I interviewed members of the Nakayama dojo, I found that though most were quite frank about why they had joined, others seemed rather evasive. Occasionally, a husband and wife would give contradictory reasons for having joined the sect. Understandably, many people sought to disguise embarrassing personal needs under the mask of more objective, socially acceptable motivations. A number of young women, for example, claimed to have joined the church "out of curiosity" or because of some minor physical ailment; several of them, I accidentally found out later from third parties, had really joined because of trouble with a boyfriend or after an engagement had been broken. Some people seemed to find it hard to admit that they had joined because of their fear of sickness or death. Perhaps this is why Yoshida Sensei himself initially told me that he had joined "in order to scoff." In spite of these problems—inherent in any interviewing situation—why people join the dojo is no mystery.

The question why people join must be broken down into two more basic considerations: the *influences* that bring them to the religion and the *motives* they allege for joining. My statistical survey of the four dojos in the Osaka area gives an idea of both.*

* The text of the questionnaire and the description and basic results of the survey are presented in Appendix A.

Table 1. Sources of Influence on Members

Source of influence	Percent of responses
Recommended by a relative	39%
Newspapers and advertisements	23
Recommended by a friend	22
Recommended by a supervisor	7
Public testimonial meetings	6
Recommended by a stranger	6
Recommended by a person in the same place of work	5
Recommended by a person in the same line of work	2

NOTE: Percentages in this table and in others that follow may not add to 100 because of rounding and multiple responses. The number of cases will be given only when the total drops below 350.

Influences

Responses to the question "Why did you join Mahikari?" are given in Table 1. The relatively high percentage of members who were influenced by newspapers and advertisements bears out the importance of careful market analysis and mass distribution schemes —what Ikado Fujio calls the "Coca Cola method" of evangelism— in the spread of Japan's New Religions.[1] More important is the way the findings underscore the influence of families, friends, and neighbors in these movements. Compared with their influence, the proselytizing of bosses, strangers, and fellow workers is remarkably ineffectual.

Recruitment in Mahikari is strikingly different from the growth of established religious groups such as the "mainline denominations" in the United States. Sociologists have described recent arrivals in suburbia as individuals shopping for a new "church home" in a veritable supermarket of denominations. Peter L. Berger and Thomas Luckmann, for example, picture these religious consumers busily pushing their shopping carts through the aisles of spiritual products, comparing this one with that before "checking out" at the counter. The American mode of religious affiliations, they conclude, is based on a pluralistic religious market and a "population of voluntary consumers of religion."[2]

Neither Ikado's Coca Cola method nor the Berger-Luckmann supermarket model exhausts the means available to and actually used by religious groups in the distribution of their sacred wares. Although Japan, like America, has its own share of active religious consumers and a pluralistic market flooded by a vast array of marginally differentiated products—marginally differentiated because they are concocted from the same religious traditions and social values—there are religions in both countries that seek to attract the more passive consumers too, the people who do not like to "go shopping." Such organizations augment the Coca Cola method with what might be called the Avon (or in Japan, Pola) approach. The Avon approach makes use of an active door-to-door salesperson and presupposes a consumer who stays at home. The system works as well for religion as it does for cosmetics. Let us say, for example, that one day Aunt Betsy or the next-door neighbor drops by with the Good News about Messiah X. She tells the person what X has done for her and persuades our potential religious consumer to go with her to an evangelistic meeting. If the product she is promoting meets the person's needs, or strikes his fancy, Aunt Betsy may make a "sale."

In this Avon system of distribution, the consumer has relatively little opportunity to compare products. In this respect, the Avon method is quite different from the supermarket. This does not mean, however, that over the long run the consumer will limit his choice to one brand. In Mahikari, for example, almost a third of the present members once belonged to other New Religions. Judging from my interviews and survey, these people often join a religious group in search of a miraculous cure or some other concrete benefit. If the sect proves ineffective, they drop out until they are introduced to an alternative "thaumaturgical product" by another "ad," friend, or relative. Thus they go from product to product (or rather, from religion to religion), comparing the cost-benefit only in retrospect.[3]

Potential consumers are influenced, or programmed, for the product they will finally purchase by both tradition and circumstance. Even before they joined Mahikari, almost half of the present members already believed in parapsychology, the Fourth Dimension, UFOs, and similar occult phenomena stressed by the church.[4] Likewise, they were no strangers to the traditional Japanese butsudan cult. A little over half responded positively to the question "When you were a child, did your parents zealously tend their butsudan?" * Furthermore, many of the people who join Mahikari are the children of parents who themselves often visited mediums and religious healers in time of need.

In spite of these positive religious and occult influences, a large number of my informants denied that they had been particularly religious before joining Mahikari. Most would number themselves among that majority of the Japanese population that seems completely indifferent to religion. But this indifference, which shows up in numerous statistical surveys, should not be confused with a philosophical rejection of religion. When a Japanese describes himself as unreligious, he usually means that he is not currently committed to any specific religion or doing any particular shugyo. Religion —like ideology in general—is a situational and fluid sort of thing, especially in Japan. Mahikari members who characterize themselves as formerly indifferent to religion should therefore not be regarded as converted agnostics or atheists.[5]

Motives

We shall discuss the influence of sex, age, education, occupation, and income later; but first let us see what people say was their motive for joining the dojo. From the responses shown in Table 2, it is obvious that sickness is by far the most important reason for joining.† In the comparatively prosperous 1970's, poverty, which seemed to figure so prominently in the spread of the New Religions

---

* See Appendix A, Question 13. Because many branch and nuclear families do not enshrine their family butsudan in their own home, the 43 percent who replied negatively to this question were not necessarily saying that their parents were negligent in their religious duties.

† It has been estimated that 60–70 percent of those who join the New Religions do so for reasons of health. Clark Offner and Henry Van Straelen, *Modern Japanese Religions: With Special Emphasis Upon Their Doctrines of Healing* (New York, 1963), pp. 244–45. But some of the New Religions may appeal more to those suffering from interpersonal friction than to those who are ill. James W. White, *The Sōkagakkai and Mass Society* (Stanford, Calif., 1970), pp. 85–86. The motives for joining one or another of these movements may vary, and seem to change as the individual religion becomes established.

Table 2. Motives of Members for Joining Mahikari

Motive	Percent of responses
Sickness	52%
Interest in miracles	22
Interest in spirits	18
Interest in religion	11
Anxiety in the family	9
Anxiety over the impasses of society (politics, pollution, etc.)	6
Financial anxiety	4
Problems with people outside the family	4
Marital problems	2

immediately after the war, seems to be a negligible motive for joining Mahikari. Concern over such problems as pollution, politics, or the "impasses of society" in general moved only 6 percent to join. Even problems with "human relations" (anxiety in the family, problems with people outside the family, and marital problems) seem to be relatively minor issues.

Curiosity. From my own participation in the life of the dojo, I could have predicted that the majority of members had joined for reasons of health. Nor was I especially surprised to learn that more were interested in miracles or spirits than in religion per se. I was already quite familiar with the members' unquenchable thirst for the miraculous and the arcane. But who were these people who had joined out of "interest" in miracles, spirits, or religion? My interviews with members had already made me suspect that curiosity was not often a real motive for joining. Were the people who said they had joined because they were interested related to those who in interviews had professed mere curiosity?

Comparing people who said they joined out of "interest" in miracles, spirits, or religion with those who said they joined because of sickness, I found very little overlapping between the two groups. That is, the sick and the interested seem to be two distinct subgroups within the organization. The percentage of men who said they were "interested" was considerably higher than the percentage of women, indicating, perhaps, that being interested in things was regarded as a "masculine" kind of motivation. More significant, such motivations were most likely to be found among young people who came from comparatively well-to-do families and who had had some college education. This leads me to speculate that those who said they joined Mahikari because they were "interested" were primarily those who, lacking any more serious motivation (such as illness) yet wanting to give some plausible reason for their involvement, chose one of these responses *faute de mieux*.[6] After all, I had not allowed them the more realistic option, "To please my family." Those who responded to the survey question by saying they had joined Mahikari out of "interest" therefore do seem to be a group overlapping with those who, in interviews, claimed they had been motivated by mere curiosity. I suspect that many, if not most, of the interested are the children of members who joined for reasons of health or other personal difficulties. Thus we may assume that many of these young people were actually obligated, rather than genuinely motivated, to join the sect.

Not all interest and curiosity, of course, can be dismissed as a subterfuge for more urgent, but abashing, needs. For example, Mrs. Nakata Asako, aged sixty, the wife of a calligraphy teacher, has always been interested in spirits. It is she who told me the fox story related earlier. In the Nakayama dojo, Mrs. Nakata has a well-deserved reputation as a person well-versed in folklore, Western spiritualism, and the occult. Among her favorite books are tales of adventure in the astral world. Although she claims to have joined Mahikari out of sheer curiosity, she too had real needs. Her present husband is a *yoshi*, that is, a man who has taken his wife's family name in order to preserve her family's identity.[7] Unfortunately, the couple was unable to have a son who would carry on the Nakata name. Believing that the family was cursed, Mrs. Nakata consulted various mediums about the arrangement of her family's graves.* (In a low voice she added as she talked with me, "Yoshida Sensei himself is a grave-teacher [*ohaka no sensei*].")

But even though Mrs. Nakata was fastidious about visiting the family graves, no son was born. She began to go to a Christian

---

* Many Japanese believe that the direction in which a tombstone faces can be unlucky and can cause ancestral spirits to haunt and harm their own descendants.

church, but was disappointed because the pastor did nothing but talk about the Bible and history (*ohanashi bakari desu ne!*). Because no miracles took place, she soon lost interest in Christianity. She visited palmists and, at the suggestion of friends, various Buddhist temples. One day when she was on such a pilgrimage, she was about to write out the posthumous name of an ancestor on a wooden stick as a votive offering when she suddenly became possessed by a spirit, and her whole body began to shake.* An ascetic (*gyōja*) who happened to be nearby shook his rosary over her and drove out the spirit—which, he informed her, was actually her first husband, who had died during the war. After this, Mrs. Nakata began to wish that, like the ascetic, she could have the power to exorcise the possessed. Finally she read Okada Kotama's book *The World of Miracles* and joined Mahikari. Aside from miracles, one of the things that impressed her most about the sect was that its founder had spent a whole week in the astral world.

Mrs. Nakata's case is obviously not an example of pure curiosity about miracles, spirits, and religion. For her, as for many other Japanese women, it was longing for a child that sparked an interest in religion and the occult. Her interest in the supernatural grew until she began to seek mediumistic powers herself. Mrs. Nakata's interest in books on the occult is also typical of many other members. Yoshida Sensei, for example, is constantly picking up books on auras, the astral world, and psychic healing, many of which have nothing to do with Mahikari. On the shelves of another well-read member I found books like *Mediums Talk About the Riddles of the Sixth Dimension*; *Introduction to Para-Physics: Solution to the Riddles of the Fourth Dimension*; *New Ways to Eat: Freedom and Health Through Food*; *Medicines the Japanese Take* (an exposé); *Christ Died in Japan*; several volumes of James Churchward's works on the sunken continent of Mu; and the Bible. Films about occult subjects, such as the American movie *The Exorcist*, also pique the interest of members.

Illness. Over half of the people who join Mahikari do so for rea-

---

* In Japan, when a person dies it is customary to change his "worldly name" (*zokumyō*) to a posthumous "Buddhist name" (*kaimyō*) that is engraved on his tombstone and memorial tablet.

sons of ill health. Nineteen percent of those surveyed reported that in the two years before they joined, someone in their family had had cancer or some other incurable illness.[8] Many, like the Yoshidas themselves, had suffered repeated bereavements and misfortunes that had cast shadows of gloom and anxiety over their families for years. Although the illnesses that bring people to the dojo vary from pimples to cancer, the following cases are not untypical.

Shimizu Masao, aged fifty-seven, and his wife Masako, forty-two, live in a large, comfortable two-story home on the west side of Nakayama City. Before the war, Shimizu's parents were wealthy landlords who rented out as many as 300 homes in this part of town. During the American fire-bombing of the city in 1945, the family's real estate investments were completely wiped out. When the war came to an end, Mr. Shimizu returned home from the munitions factory where he had been stationed and began to rebuild the family fortune. "In those days I used to work from six in the morning to ten at night. I used to keep awake by drinking coffee all day long." Hard work did not entirely reverse his bad luck. Some of the buildings he rebuilt were expropriated by the government in order to make way for a new petroleum storage center. A new home that he had built for himself burned to the ground a month after it was finished. At present, his greatest single investment is a large office complex in front of City Station.

Today, Mr. Shimizu is a sallow-complected semi-invalid suffering from heart trouble and periodic kidney failure. His heart spells, which sometimes last for days on end, twice have brought him to the point of death. Although his doctor never said that his case was hopeless, Mr. Shimizu read several books on heart and kidney disorders and came to this conclusion himself. Certain that Western medicine could not help him, he stopped going to the doctor and turned to "natural" foods such as plankton, wheat germ, and powdered snails. He also developed a deep faith in Chinese herbal medicine.

By 1974, Mr. Shimizu had been bedridden for six years and was in critical condition. At that point, he turned to books about spiritual healing. One book, he recalls, was by a priest on Mount Hiei who claims to heal diseases by projecting an aura. Another was about the healing powers of Kōbō Daishi (Odaishi-sama, as people in Nakayama call him), the founder of the Shingon sect of Buddhism. This profoundly impressed him:

By performing very difficult austerities, Odaishi-sama was able to bring a cooked fish back to life merely by raising his hand over it. The fish immediately swam away. Unfortunately, Odaishi-sama's austerities were so severe that he was unable to teach these techniques to his disciples. Nevertheless, I was able to find a priest on Mount Koya who specializes in spiritual operations [*shinrei shijutsu*]. When I visited his home, I had become so sick they had to carry me in on a stretcher. While my wife waited in an adjoining room, the priest blindfolded me and took me into his operating room. First he examined my abdomen with his hands. As he did so, he uttered spells [*kiai*] in a deep voice that seemed to come from the bottom of his heart. Finally, he blew all over my body. After the treatment was over, I opened my eyes and saw nothing more than a small knife lying next to the operating table. The priest gave me some Chinese herbs to drink and an amulet with the name of Dainichi Nyorai [Mahavairocana, principal buddha of the Shingon sect] to enshrine in our butsudan. Thanks to this operation, I was able to walk back to the car. And when we arrived home, I even took a walk around the block.

Although this "operation" seemed to save Mr. Shimizu from a certain death, the cure was not permanent. One day, Mrs. Shimizu noticed an advertisement in the newspaper about Mahikari. Hoping to find a way to help her husband, she went to the Nakayama dojo to see for herself what the Mahikari Treatment was all about. The first time she received okiyome, a yellow light filled her eyes. "This must be a god," she thought to herself. After she took the elementary training course, she gave okiyome to her husband. To their amazement, his blood pressure went down. A few months later, Mr. Shimizu decided to take the course himself. Being of an empirical turn of mind (he had studied engineering and business management in college), he was determined to find out whether the course really had any beneficial effects. "I had heard that when people take the course, they suffer miraculous bouts of diarrhea, fever, coughing, and vomiting that purge the impurities in their bodies. And so I used a Western-style toilet and carefully examined my urine and stools. During the three days of the course, I noticed a remarkable improvement."

Although he has never responded to okiyome with any spirit movements of his own, Mr. Shimizu is convinced that it has improved his condition. "The Mahikari Treatment is superior to the spiritual operation I had on Mount Koya, since *anyone* can do it, even without performing austerities." Despite Mr. Shimizu's lack of spirit movements, Yoshida Sensei suggested to Mrs. Shimizu that her husband's illness and misfortune had been caused by a "big, bad spirit." Although she has discussed this possibility with her husband, Mr. Shimizu still insists that his illness is the result of long years of overwork. He admits, however, that the burning of his new home *might* have been the work of evil spirits. But even this seems farfetched to him.

In my interviews with members, I often asked whether they would use okiyome on an automobile that had broken down on the way to an important meeting. Although a few members told me they had in fact used okiyome on their cars, there is no specific mention of what I shall later call "thaumaturgical auto repair" in Mioshie itself. Because the church did not tell members what to believe in this matter, I hoped to fathom the depths of their belief in physical miracles by asking this question. Mr. Shimizu said that he would call a cab before he would give okiyome to his car. "If I were on a deserted road in the middle of a forest when the car broke down, I *might* try okiyome, but not otherwise." He was quite certain that okiyome could not fix a broken piston rod.

Another question I regularly asked members was, "Which do you think is the more serious cause of air pollution, people or evil spirits?" This was prompted by my knowledge that the Savior had received a revelation to the effect that pollution is the work of evil spirits. But Mr. Shimizu did not agree. He believes that pollution is caused by factories and cars and not by spirits. "In Nakayama City," he pointed out, "companies making fabric dyes pour their wastes into the river on weekends when the pollution controllers are not on the job. The best way to cut down on pollution is for government to take action and pass stricter laws. Okiyome itself will not do the job. If all offenders were converted to Mahikari, they might stop polluting. But the fact is they are not being converted." Although he has never tried to perform a physical miracle himself, Mr. Shimizu admits that he believes in them "up to a point." But not to the point where he bothers to give okiyome to his food before he eats, as many members do. I asked him whether he thought he could completely overcome his medical problems by using okiyome. Avoiding a direct answer, he admitted that his urine still had albumin in it, but that after receiving okiyome his kidneys felt "soft and relaxed."

Although Mrs. Shimizu joined the dojo only for her husband's sake, she has become quite active in the sect. She admits that before she joined she had had the typical Japanese attitude of "believing only when all else fails" (*kanawanu toki no kami da nomi*). She has been possessed by her husband's ancestors several times but has yet to be possessed by any of her own.* Asked about physical miracles and whether she would give okiyome to their car, Mrs. Shimizu said, "I always check the gasoline and the battery before taking the car out, and so it never stops on the road. If the car did break down, I would first call the garage. Only if the garage was far away would I give okiyome to the car." Every morning when she goes to the office, she goes into the room where the air conditioner is housed and gives it okiyome. "Much to the janitor's delight, it hasn't broken down once this year," she boasted. I learned from her husband that Mrs. Shimizu had once repaired their color television by "raising her hand" over it. Like her husband, Mrs. Shimizu believes that air pollution is the work of factories and not evil spirits. "The way to get rid of pollution," she said, "is for people to stop polluting. If okiyome were used by people all over the world, it might help solve the problem, but giving okiyome in just one country would accomplish nothing."

In order to let her wax philosophical, I asked Mrs. Shimizu what was the most important thing about Mahikari for her. Her answer was a mixture of earthy common sense and classical Buddhist wisdom. "Mahikari helps me become relaxed [*ki ga raku ni naru*] and get rid of desire [*yoku*], curiosity [*kōkishin*], and worldly thoughts [*zatsunen ga naku naru*]." With a laugh, she added that it

---

* Even though her husband has been adopted into her family, Mrs. Shimizu, like many of the women in the dojo, tends to be possessed by his ancestors more often than by her own. See Appendix A, Question 7.

might not be a good idea for young people to get rid of *their* desires, but that it certainly was good for *her.*

The interesting thing about this family is the degree to which they have harmonized the thaumaturgical practices of their religion with a secular and even skeptical attitude toward the use of magic in a technological society. Mr. Shimizu readily admits that his sole purpose in joining Mahikari was to regain his health. For him, okiyome is a healing technique pure and simple. He turned to it only after he had convinced himself that conventional Western medicine was of no avail. As a former engineer, he was skeptical about the possibility of fixing his car with okiyome. Significant too is his insistence that his illness was brought on by natural causes (overwork), and not by evil spirits, as Yoshida Sensei suggested. In short, okiyome for Mr. Shimizu is a technique for dealing with what cannot be dealt with by science, technology, legislation, hard work, or other human means. As an explanation for misfortune in general, Mahikari holds little interest. His comparatively secular attitude is undoubtedly related to the controlling rationality one associates with men of his wealth and technical education.

Judging from Mrs. Shimizu's resort to okiyome to fix the television set and keep the air conditioner in good running order, she is more inclined toward the miraculous than her husband. For her, okiyome is a way of taking care of things that are apt to "go on the blink." Like other members of the dojo, she is also inclined to call happy coincidences miracles. Nevertheless, her attitudes toward environmental pollution and malfunctioning automobiles reveal a strong no-nonsense streak of self-reliance, responsibility, and social awareness. Only when confronted with mechanical problems involving inconvenience, irritation, and bad luck is she apt to try okiyome, and see.

Kamioka Hiroshi (forty-five) has been plagued by ill health since he was young. For the past eight years, he has suffered from a serious heart ailment:

Sometimes I used to have five or ten heart spells in one day. We even had to call the doctor at night. One doctor told me that my pulse was too fast, and that if he could slow it down I would be okay. The medicine he gave me made my pulse so slow that I became dizzy and couldn't function at all. So I changed doctors. The next doctor told me that my heart was too slow, and that he would have to speed it up. The medicine he gave me made my heart beat so fast that my head began to throb. In this way I went from doctor to doctor, visiting a number of clinics here in Nakayama. I even went to Osaka University Medical Center. Each time I changed doctors they gave my disease a new name.

While seeking medical help, Mr. Kamioka also visited a number of faith healers. Once he saw an advertisement in a newspaper about a "spiritual operation" (*shugenjutsu*) that allegedly had restored the sight of the blind and enabled the lame to walk.* "After I had my operation I did feel better," he said. "But later on I had to go back to the practitioner for more operations. Each one cost me 2,000 yen. Once I went to a healer in Osaka and paid 25,000 yen for a thirty-minute prayer. That seemed to help, too. But three days later I was in agony again. I also visited a Buddhist healer connected with the Mount Minobu branch of the Nichiren sect."

When he was twenty years old, Mr. Kamioka joined Soka Gakkai. After four or five years he became disillusioned, both because his health did not improve and because he was too weak to do the proselytizing (*shakubuku*) demanded of him. He also disliked the fact that in Soka Gakkai (a Buddhist laymen's movement) there were no priests to come to his home at the Obon and Ohigan festivals to recite sutras in front of the butsudan. Later, at the prompting of his boss, he joined another New Religion called Reiyūkai. As a Mahikari member, he now believes that Reiyukai's method of dealing with ancestral spirits is "mistaken," since it was no more efficacious than Soka Gakkai. (Mrs. Kamioka later confessed to me that they had joined Reiyukai out of an obligation [*giri*] to her husband's boss and had never been firm believers.)

Just when he was about to give up on both medicine and religion, Mr. Kamioka saw a newspaper advertisement about Mahikari. Reading the claim that 80 percent of all disease is caused by evil spirits, he immediately thought to himself, "*This* must be my prob-

---

* This operation seems to have been similar to the one Shimizu Masao had on Mount Koya. In both, the practitioner uttered spells and incantations (*kiai o kakeru*) over the body of the patient.

lem." For about a month and a half he visited the dojo to receive okiyome. At first nothing happened, and he wondered whether the people having spirit seizures around him were just pretending to be exorcised in order to get him to join the church. In spite of his doubts, he took the training course in February 1976:

About two weeks later, I had a violent spirit seizure that wouldn't go away even after the benediction was pronounced. I jumped up and down. My left side went completely numb. When I went back to the dojo the next day, the same thing happened. Once when I received okiyome everything became pitch black. I lost consciousness and felt that my body was drifting up into the clouds. I must have been lifted up by about ten spirits that time. I think I got rid of about five of them. At least I haven't had so much trouble with my heart since then.

Because of her husband's lengthy illness, Mrs. Kamioka has become the family's principal breadwinner. Recently, however, Mr. Kamioka has gone back to his job (repairing sliding doors) on a part-time basis. Thanks to Su-god, he can even go for a long ride in the car without feeling pain. And even if his heart does bother him, he does not have to see a doctor: he can just raise his hand.

Mr. Kamioka's attitude toward miracles in general is similar to Mr. Shimizu's. He is sure that okiyome would not be able to repair a broken piston rod; in such a case, he would take his car to a garage to be fixed. If the engine merely sounded bad, he said he *might* try okiyome. As for environmental pollution, Mr. Kamioka maintained that the most efficient way to solve the problem would be to control automobile emissions and begin to use electric cars. The real dilemma, he pointed out, is that the government cannot do anything about pollution without upsetting the national economy. This makes government intervention a moot point. But from this highly realistic analysis he drew an unexpected conclusion: "Since evil spirits probably have a hand in causing pollution, Mahikari members should pray to Su-god in order to solve the problem." Mr. Kamioka also informed me that whenever his Persian cat has diarrhea, he is able to fix her up with just one dose of okiyome.

For Mr. Kamioka, the important thing about Mahikari is that, unlike the other New Religions he had joined, it works miracles you can see with your own eyes. That is, at the dojo you can see people having spirit seizures and getting rid of both evil spirits and diseases. Thus his attitude seems to be deeply colored by the typically unrestrained experiential outlook of Japanese folk religion: try it and see.

There are many reasons why people join religions like Mahikari. Although the influence of the mass media has often been commented upon, my survey of Mahikari members points to the continuing influence of kith and kin, *Blut und Boden*, in the spread of the sect. These, of course, were the dominant influences in the spread and maintenance of religious groups when Japan was still a folk society. We have also seen that before joining Mahikari, many members had been exposed to a wide range of religious and occult beliefs and practices. Although they often describe themselves as having been unbelievers before they joined the dojo, their "secularism" does not seem to have been disciplined by any deep, theological reflection. Nor did it create any absolute distance between them and the traditional religio-magical customs of their families. In most cases, one senses that before meeting Su-god, they simply had not had the need for, or found the occasion to join, a religious group.

In this chapter, as in Chapter 6, we have seen that the practice of folk medicine (whether Chinese herbs, massage, or plain magic) is closely related to both folklore and folk religion. One point universally missed by scholars who have studied the New Religions is that the momentous growth of these organizations corresponded with an impressive revival of popular interest in Chinese herbal medicines (*kanpōyaku*) in Japan after the end of the war. Mr. Shimizu's interest in herbal concoctions is by no means atypical.

There were several reasons for this renaissance of traditional medicine. Compared with Western doctors, herbal specialists seem to take their patients' complaints more seriously. Moreover, Western doctors sometimes resort to the most radical treatment even before the patient is in pain. If traditional medicine's weakness lies in its primitive analysis of the causes and nature of illness, its strength seems to lie in its wide range of cures and its unflagging optimism. Here, Western medicine is just the opposite. Although it can diagnose terminal illnesses with terrifying accuracy, it may offer no hope at all for their cure. What is more, the traditional herbalist does not specialize and is therefore better able to treat his patient as a whole person. Because his herbs are thought to be "natural" substances, the medicines he uses are believed to have far fewer dangerous side effects than Western medicines. Little wonder, then, that so many Japanese have turned to traditional therapies, which they regard as more humane and hopeful, and that some, concluding that "medicine is poison," have turned to Su-god for help.[9]

Most of those who join Mahikari are motivated by serious human needs, such as sickness or difficult personal relations. Ill health, however, seems to be the predominant motive for joining. Many informants said they had joined out of curiosity, but I found no clear-cut cases of members who joined simply to learn about the meaning or composition of the universe. Many cases of curiosity, both in my interviews and in the survey, seemed linked, at some point, to less than intellectual motives. Some of the curious, especially the younger ones, are simply obliged to participate because their parents are members. Others seem to have cited curiosity as a motive because to admit that they had more serious needs or had experienced personal frustration would have meant "losing face." But as we shall see in a later chapter, many of the young people who joined out of interest in miracles, spirits, or religion have actually been possessed by evil spirits more often and more intensely than their elders. Also, they often are able to perform a greater number of miracles than their more seriously motivated parents.

8 The Psychology of Possession and Exorcism

What really happens to people when they become possessed and exorcised? Answers to this question, which seems innocuous and straightforward, differ greatly. Religious responses, for example, run the gamut from an orthodox affirmation of the testimony of believers to an equally orthodox rejection of such "trafficking with the devil" by members of other faiths. Setting aside religious debates, in this chapter I shall take a different tack.

First, based on my interviews and statistical survey, I shall review what Mahikari members have told me about their own possession experiences. We shall find out what it "feels like" to be possessed, to be exorcised, and to exorcise others. Second, we must account for these psychological descriptions. Here we shall move beyond phenomenological description to a comparative, psychosocial analysis. Although this analysis may fall short of genuine explanation —the unhappy fate of many a psychological approach—I shall argue that because it enables us to relate our data creatively to other human experiences, the psychosocial approach essayed in this chapter is a necessary, albeit preliminary, step if we are to move beyond a simple religious understanding of religious facts.

Without denying the reality of the supernatural for believers, the psychological approach taken here rests on a purely secular worldview. Such an approach to the subject of possession is hardly novel. Freud, whose opinions on religion are too well known to rehearse, bluntly denied that evil spirits had any external reality and insisted that their origin was in the "inner life of the patient in whom they manifest themselves." [1] T. K. Oesterreich, in his monumental comparative study of possession, maintained that serious students of the subject today are convinced that "the states of mind apparently belonging to a second ego [that is, the possessing spirit] are really a part of the original individual [the person possessed]." [2] Sheila Walker, in her study of possession in African and Afro-American groups, is still more specific, declaring that possession falls into the category of altered states of consciousness, and that it "can be explained in large part within the framework of hypnosis and hypnotically induced behavior." [3] The analysis put forth in this chapter rests on the perspectives elaborated in the works of these and other like-minded students of possession and related phenomena.

Okiyome as Experience

Because social space helps to mold inner feelings, a few words must be said about the general atmosphere of the dojo before we turn to the experience of okiyome. In spite of the many testimonies that speak of people bounding around the dojo while they are possessed or are being exorcised, the dojo is usually a quiet, one might even say peaceful, sort of place. On the whole, there are violent spirit seizures in the Nakayama dojo only a few times a month. During the day, the building is sometimes empty, except for Nakata Michiko, a middle-aged "Old Miss" who lives on the first floor. (Sensei has allowed her to live there so that someone will always be on hand should a person be unable to find a partner for doing okiyome.) By late afternoon, as many as fifteen or twenty people may gather. Only on festival days and on Thursday evenings, when spirit investigations are given by the staff, is the dojo filled.

When people close their eyes to receive okiyome, they hear around them the sound of hands clapping before the altar, prayers being mumbled, and of course, the Exorcist's Prayer itself being intoned throughout the room. When I asked people what they feel when they receive okiyome, they naturally tended to give very orthodox answers, saying that they had experienced exactly what they were told in the training course they would experience. They affirmed that when they were given spirit investigations, their hands automatically traced Chinese characters on the floor, or their heads automatically nodded in reply to the exorcist's questions. Nearly everyone stated that he had been fully conscious of all that transpired during the ritual. This too was an orthodox reaction, since all are instructed beforehand that they will remember everything after the Treatment is over. Many people claimed that they could feel toxins melting in their bodies and running down their necks, another orthodox response.

Going beyond these predictable replies, some people confessed that they have no special feeling when they receive okiyome. One or two admitted that they simply daydream while it is going on. One woman, still in mourning for her husband, said that she had the feeling of being in a "dreamlike state of non-ego" (*muga muchū*), a response that seemed rather idiosyncratic. Mahikari leaders explain this wide variety of reactions in terms of the relative preponderance of "water spirits" and "fire spirits" in a person's body. People harboring water spirits, they say, are more sensitive and can feel evil spirits working within themselves even when they have no visible spirit movements, whereas those with fire spirits are less susceptible to possession experiences or emotional outbursts.

The church publishes a number of cartoon books filled with vivid pictures of the spirits of foxes, badgers, snakes, *tengu* (long-nosed demons), and ancestors.* One would expect that these pictures might have a direct influence on members' perceptions of evil spirits. It is therefore rather surprising that members seldom, if ever, claim to see the spirits that possess them. On the contrary, they seem to discover the identity of these spirits in the same way, and at the same time, that their exorcist-partner does—through their own automatic writing, manual spirit movements, verbal responses, and head nodding in response to spirit investigations. Gradually, the pieces of their possession-puzzle are put together, and a spirit story begins to emerge.

---

*Pictures of semi-naked women being tortured are used in church cartoons to explain the origin of vengeful ghosts. These illustrations seem to reflect the influence of popular sado-masochistic literature sold throughout Japan.

ke all forms of communication and social interaction, okiyome upposes a certain amount of regularity and patterned behavior. We have already seen that each type of spirit produces unique motions in the body, especially in the hands. This is virtually a code by which spirits can be identified. I had not been long in the dojo before I noticed that people tend to develop their own stereotyped repertoire of spirit movements. Some regularly leap up or fall to the floor in fits of emotion; others invariably let their hands drop to the floor and sit as though in a psychogenic stupor.[4] Every evening, the hands of one woman moved rapidly in small circles as though she were possessed by the spirit of a tiny, burrowing animal. Other people report hot sensations each time they have a spirit seizure. Some women invariably cry, especially when they act as the proxy for a scolded spirit.[5] Others predictably wag their heads back and forth as the spirits inside them try to flee from the Light pouring forth from their partner's hand. Whenever I gave one woman okiyome, even before I had finished the Exorcist's Prayer her nose began to twitch rapidly, suggesting the movements of a rabbit in a luscious patch of clover. Then, as though she had become the proxy of some wretched soul suffering in the other world, her hands would tug at an invisible noose around her neck. Or she would wipe the sweat from her brow, a sign that the spirit possessing her was in one of the "hot hells." In short, many members seem to be habitually possessed by spirits that manifest themselves in routine ways.

The timing of seizures is also highly patterned. Only in a few instances do members talk about being possessed when they are away from the dojo. Usually their spirit movements and seizures are limited to the ten minutes allotted to the purification of the primary soul. Only an exceptionally violent spirit will take longer to be exorcised. Spirit seizures do not generally occur in worship services, lectures, or study groups, or while the rest of the body is receiving the Treatment.

Compared to the seizures associated with the purification of the primary soul, the reactions to the application of okiyome to the rest of the body are anything but dramatic. Usually this is a period of rest or, after a violent seizure, recuperation. Lying on the floor, passively receiving the Treatment from the exorcist's outstretched hand, the subject finds himself in the position (both physically and mentally) of a patient. Lying in this position, or sitting with his back to the exorcist, the person frequently exchanges pleasantries with his partner or with others who have finished the purification of their primary soul. The conversation often turns to the latest word about Mr. Tanaka's kidneys or Mrs. Oyama's asthma, or to miracles people have seen or heard about. Sometimes the talk is about doctors, faith healers, and mediums visited in the past. Generally, the conversation is no loftier than barbershop gossip, mere trifles and homely truths that can be solemnly affirmed without much thought or fear of contradiction. Except for the time when the primary soul is being purified, the attitude of those engaged in okiyome is not particularly pious.*

These are the more typical experiences people have when they receive okiyome. Now let us turn to their feelings when they switch places and assume the role of the exorcist. Because giving the Treatment to others corresponds to the active part played by the ascetic in the traditional ritual of yorigito, the ideal state of mind for the exorcist is one of control. Some members throw themselves completely into this role and intone the Exorcist's Prayer in a loud, stentorian voice that is bound to arouse the most wicked of evil spirits. Whereas some members, even a minister, have confessed that giving okiyome gets boring after awhile, most seem to be quite interested in what they are doing. After all, it *is* interesting to see what kind of spirit movements the Light coming from one's own hands will produce in the body of one's partner. Purifying the primary soul is a serious business, since a violent spirit seizure could take place at any moment. Most people report feelings of heat or electricity in their palms when they raise their hands over others. Some say that their hand becomes hot whenever it passes over a diseased organ in their partner's body. People with water spirits are especially sensitive to these sensations.

The proper attitude for advanced exorcists is clearly explained in the rules for giving spirit investigations. The exorcist must always

---

* In the testimonies that are given during the monthly worship services, there is always room for humor, some of it rather bawdy. As the neophytes raise their hands for the first time, their mood is buoyant and gay, as though they were learning to use some marvelous new technology.

be on guard against lying spirits. An ancestor, for example, sometimes causes a person's hands to move in the pattern associated
with animal spirits. Only later, in the course of another spirit investigation, will the true identity of the possessing spirit be learned.
Also, spirits are said to be lying if their answers do not accord
with Mioshie. For example, if an evil spirit says it is a god, it is
not telling the truth, since according to Mioshie, gods never possess
people. To take another example: ancestral spirits sometimes demand to be worshiped by unrelated victims. Because this also is
contrary to Mioshie, which teaches that a person need worship only
the ancestors of his own family, their demands should be ignored.

A lying spirit can be made to tell the truth if the exorcist con-
ducts his investigation with a "loving heart." Even if he suspects
the spirit is fabricating, he should push on with the investigation,
using the most respectful language. He should be especially polite
when addressing the spirits of warriors, since by nature they tend
to be headstrong and testy. Only if a fox, badger, or other animal
spirit appears is the exorcist to assume a more aggressive and un-
compromising posture. Animal spirits are notoriously stupid and
have to be repeatedly scolded before they will leave a person's body
and depart this world. In all cases, however, exorcists must avoid
railing at the spirits. Rather, they should admonish or scold them
out of a heart filled with love and truth. When they conduct spirit
investigations, exorcists must therefore be constantly on the alert,
polite, and loving—but in deadly earnest. Since they are acting as
the representatives of Su-god himself, they must never investigate
spirits out of idle curiosity.

The religious and practical benefits of this ritual apply to the
exorcist as well as to his partner. According to Mioshie, by giving
the Treatment to others, the exorcist is getting cleaned up himself.
It is even possible to heal one's own relatives indirectly by giving
okiyome to strangers at the dojo.* Many members report feelings

* One young man in Nakayama City joined the dojo hoping to find a cure for
his mother's illness. When, after all his efforts, she refused to let him give her the
Treatment, he took three days of his vacation to give okiyome to others at the dojo.
Su-god, I am told, took note of the young man's selfless devotion and cured his
mother without the direct application of okiyome.

of deep gratification after spending an evening raising their hands at the dojo. When they go home, they know that they have done something for friends, relatives, and strangers at the dojo, for all of their ancestors suffering in the astral world, and also for themselves. By helping to raise the "spirit level" of others, they have automatically raised their own "spirit level" too.[6] This not only heals current maladies but helps ward off future illnesses and dangers. For this reason, nearly all members told me that thanks to okiyome, they felt safe and secure and had found peace of mind.

My statistical survey reinforced what I had learned from the interviews, namely that people respond to okiyome in vastly different ways. Twenty-three percent had to confess that they had had no spirit movements whatsoever, and 40 percent said that they had had only a few. A full 61 percent admitted that the spirit movements they had had were weak. Only 21 percent could say that they had had "quite a few" spirit movements, and only 15 percent, that they had had "a lot." Thirty-nine percent reported that they had had violent spirit movements. Forty-four percent claimed that they had been repeatedly possessed by the same spirit, and 30 percent, that the same evil spirit had possessed more than one member of their family. In short, some members—very devout ones at that—seem to have no observable reaction at all to exorcism, and others, who constitute a minority, respond dramatically to it.

In my interviews I discovered that members had been possessed by a wide variety of evil spirits, including butterflies, water skippers, and a bear that had died in the Nakayama zoo. The statistical survey gives us a good picture of the overall distribution of the spirits among the dojo members: 62 percent of those surveyed had been possessed by ancestral spirits, 53 percent by unrelated human spirits, and 26 percent by the spirits of foxes, cats, badgers, bears, and other animals. Those who had experienced possession by ancestral spirits were asked to identify them more specifically; the responses are shown in Table 3.

Judging from the dojo members' humble place in Japanese society, one would expect more of them to be possessed by ancestors who had been peasants. Significantly, those in the highest and second-highest categories in our Scale of Possession tended to be

Table 3. Types of Ancestral Spirits Possessing
Dojo Members

Type of possessing spirit	Percent of responses
Grandparent	29%
Warrior	27
Father	14
Mother	14
Brother or sister	13
Townsman	6
One's own (deceased) child	5
Farmer	4
Other (not specified)"	33

NOTE: In Japan, ancestors include not only direct lineal ascendants
but nearly all relatives who have predeceased oneself. Hence
siblings and even one's own children can count as ancestors.
   "This option seems to have been selected by members who could
not discern the precise identity of the possessing spirit.

the most susceptible to possession by warrior spirits (40 percent
and 42 percent, respectively).* This seems to indicate that having
warriors for ancestors is not merely a kinship matter. The prestige
(real or imaginary) that warrior spirits confer on their descendants
must also be taken into account. What is more, the violence associated with medieval warriors offers an obvious reason why their
souls should be in hell and why, in order to escape torment, they
would try to return to this world and possess the living. One suspects that the mixed feelings of members toward these alleged
warrior ancestors may even be a reflection of a nebulous status
consciousness. As T. S. Lebra writes, of a related religious sect:
"Ancestors of high status are uniformly sinful, since there is perfect
correlation in the members' eyes between power and moral deficiency. Such ancestors killed people, exploited poor commoners
to enrich their own coffers, engaged in political trickery, indulged
in sexual promiscuity, even seducing a reluctant virgin, and the
like." [7] As we shall see later, samurai spirits of this sort also play
an important role in sexual karma possession in Mahikari.

* For an explanation of the statistical Scales used in this study, see Appendix A.

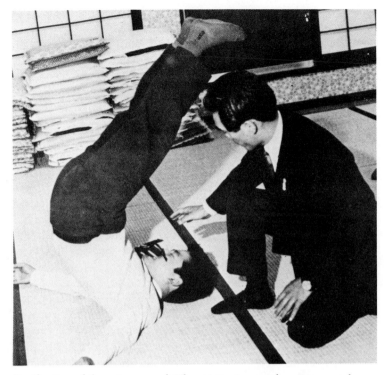

Purification of the primary soul. The spirit seizures of younger members tend to be more numerous and more intense than those of their elders.

Let us turn now to a consideration of the influences of age, income, occupation, and education on the possession experiences of members. The survey shows that younger members tend to have more spirit seizures, and more intense ones, than their elders. In no age group, however, do spirits possess people in a purely random way. That is to say, the religious imagination is not completely spontaneous. On the contrary, spirit seizures and their interpretations are decisively influenced by a person's situation in life. After the age of forty, for example, people tend to be possessed by the spirits of their mothers and fathers, if they are possessed by ancestral spirits at all. Those under forty, however, are often possessed by the spirits of grandparents, unrelated human beings, or animals.

The reason for the spirits' division of labor is simple enough: in order to become an evil spirit, a person obviously must first die! It follows that young people whose parents are still alive cannot be possessed by their mothers and fathers. They will therefore be possessed by the more "available" spirits of their grandparents. Failing this (or in addition to it), the young will be possessed by foxes, badgers, snakes, creatures from outer space, or strangers. Animal spirits therefore tend to possess those who, like the young, have more spirit movements, and more intense ones, than other members. On the other hand, ancestral spirits and spirits of unrelated human beings are more likely to possess members who report fewer and less intense spirit seizures. This seems to account for the reputation that animal spirits have in the dojo for violence. That is, their violence may actually owe more to the youth and nimbleness of their victims than to their own ill will.

As one might expect, higher incomes tend to depress both the number and the intensity of spirit seizures. The most affluent group in the four dojos had the largest percentage of people reporting no spirit movements at all (30 percent, $n = 22$). On the other hand, the poorest group had the smallest percentage reporting no spirit movements (20 percent, $n = 9$) and the largest percentage reporting the maximum number of spirit movements (22 percent, $n = 10$). In the middle-income range, however, there seems to be no correlation between income and spirit movements.

Figure 2 shows the results of my analysis of the susceptibility of the various occupational groups in the dojos to spirit possession (measured in this case both by the number and by the intensity of spirit movements). Although farmers ranked lowest in overall susceptibility to possession, they were the most likely to be possessed by ancestral spirits (78 percent, $n = 7$).* For some reason, low-level white-collar workers (the largest single occupational group in the four dojos) were the most likely to be possessed by the spirits of ancestral warriors (29 percent, $n = 19$).

---

* Only one farmer in the survey was possessed by an animal spirit, and only one by an ancestral warrior's spirit.

When we look at the relationship between education and possession, we find that high-school graduates tend to have more spirit movements, and more intense ones, than those with only a junior-high-school education. Exposure to college education reverses this trend somewhat. But because the levels of change are small, we must conclude that education has only a negligible effect on the members' susceptibility to possession.

High susceptibility

↑

Full-time dojo staff
High-level white-collar workers
Blue-collar workers (skilled and unskilled)
Low-level white-collar workers
Farmers

↓

Low susceptibility

FIG. 2. *Susceptibility to Spirit Possession Among Occupational Groups*

These statistical findings regarding possession, which will be analyzed further later, can be summarized as follows. Although the Spirit, like the wind, "bloweth where it listeth" in Mahikari as in other religions, it is evident from the survey that evil spirits do not go about their nefarious work of possession in a haphazard way. People tend to be possessed by spirits that are both appropriate and available. When members are young, the spirits of grandparents, unrelated human beings, and animals are likely to possess them. As they grow older, they become more susceptible to possession by the spirit of a deceased mother or father. In general, the older the person, the fewer and the weaker his spirit seizures become. Income is related to possession only in the highest and the lowest brackets, high income tending to ward off spirits, low income leaving the person more vulnerable to them. High-level white-collar workers, who because of their generally higher incomes could be expected to be relatively immune to possession, actually are rather susceptible. On the other hand, farmers, perhaps because they have preserved more of the tradition of ancestor worship, tend to be the least susceptible to possession but the most likely to be possessed by ancestors. And finally, we have found that the amount of education has no consistent effect on susceptibility to possession.

The Normalcy of the Possessed

Before we can analyze the experience of exorcism from a psychological perspective, we must establish whether we are dealing with "normal" or "abnormal" people.* Admittedly, the more bizarre kinds of behavior seen at the dojo often prompt outsiders to dismiss the sect as a madhouse and to condemn its members as fools or idiots. I deliberately use this strong language in order to convey the repugnance that many Japanese have for such New Religions and cults. Movements of this sort, after all, violate public decorum and encourage notions and modes of consciousness that differ significantly from those of the workaday world. Possession experiences are offensive not merely to the secular common sense of the Japanese but to the ascetic public spirit and quasi-religious ideology promoted by government and industry alike since the Meiji period.

A cultural bias against the exotic in religion is also deeply rooted in the Western tradition, which has itself been dominated (until recently) by mainline religions characterized by restraint, propriety, and compromise with science, common sense, and property. People growing up in this tradition naturally find possession, divine or demonic, undignified and even repulsive. The usual Western categories of thought simply are not adequate for dealing with possession because, as Walker points out, possession's "behavioral manifestations fall within the traditional Western definitions of pathological behavior."[8] In this study I follow the dominant tendency among anthropologists now working in this field and treat

---

* Although this distinction is notoriously difficult—some would say impossible —to make, I mean by it the practical and legal difference between those who can cope with personal and social life without debilitating trauma to themselves and others, and those who cannot.

the phenomenon of possession as something that, though admittedly unusual to Western eyes, is quite "normal." In any case, we know that, in most cultures, exorcism is not very effective among the clearly "abnormal," which is to say, in cases of extreme mental illness.[9] Because we shall be considering possession as a form of hypnotic behavior, it is also interesting to bear in mind that normal people generally are considered easier to hypnotize than neurotics.[10] Such alterations of consciousness, whether induced by shamans or by psychiatrists, seem more easily achieved by those who are flexible and open than by those whose lives have been scarred by fear or distrust. This, no doubt, is what Freud had in mind when he conceded that religion can help people preserve their mental equilibrium. Although he called religion itself "the universal neurosis of humanity," Freud found that it could protect the believer "against the danger of certain neurotic afflictions; by accepting the universal neurosis he is spared the task of forming a personal neurosis."[11] Freud clearly meant to damn religion by faint praise, but one must not lose sight of the fact that he was giving the believer a relatively clean bill of mental health *as an individual*.

Religion's function of promoting health and normalcy has been acknowledged by many scholars. A case in point is Mircea Eliade's discussion of the mental health of the shaman, which applies equally to members of groups like Mahikari:

It is not correct to say that shamans are, or must *always* be neuropaths: on the contrary, a great many of them are perfectly sound in mind. Moreover, those who had previously been ill have *become shamans just because they succeeded in getting well*. Very often, when the vocation reveals itself in the course of an illness or an attack of epilepsy, the initiation is also a cure. The acquisition of the shamanic gifts indeed presupposes the resolution of the psychic crisis brought on by the first signs of this vocation. The initiation is manifested by—among other things—a new psychic integration.[12]

In the Nakayama dojo, six members out of a total of some 310 have suffered mental illnesses; three of them have been institutionalized at some time. Although my judgment in these matters is not a professional one, I must say that I never encountered any obvious signs of mental disturbance in the members with whom I had contact. One woman who had been committed to a mental hospital on three occasions showed no signs of "abnormality" when I talked with her.

In pre-modern Japan, as in other traditional societies, both the mentally ill and the socially deviant were often stigmatized as victims of spirit possession (*tsukimono*). Spirit possession either channeled and legitimated anti-social behavior or was regarded as a kind of divine or demonic retribution for it.[13] In other instances, entire families were ostracized for generations because they were thought to be possessed by the spirits of cats, dogs, or foxes. In the San'in region of western Honshu, where fox possession is considered a form of sorcery, families said to "keep foxes" are commonly discriminated against, especially in marriage. The same is true of the hereditary "dog-spirit holders" in southwestern Shikoku. Possession of this sort may have had its origin in popular resentment against the nouveaux riches of these areas.[14] Cases of individual (that is, non-familial) possession continue to occur in Japan. Not many years ago, an article appeared in Japanese newspapers about the trial of a man who had accidentally beaten his wife to death while trying to drive a fox spirit out of her.

Of all the traditional types of possession, the practices of Mahikari are most closely related to the possession scenarios of mediums who become possessed on the request of a client. In such cases, the exorcist or ascetic induces a state of possession in his mediumistic partner. The ritual is therefore clearly solicited and controlled. This type of possession stands in sharp contrast to what might be called ingenuous or spontaneous possession, which is often a culturally approved way of expressing and reacting to mental or physical illness or social deviance. The following story is an example of spontaneous possession. It was recorded by E. Bälz, a professor of medicine at Tokyo Imperial University shortly after the turn of the century.

Some weeks after a certain girl had become possessed by a fox spirit, a renowned exorcist of the Nichiren sect was summoned to her side.

Neither excommunication [exorcism?] nor censing nor any other endeavour succeeded, the fox saying ironically that he was too clever to be taken in by such manoeuvres. Nevertheless he consented to come out freely from the starved body of the sick person if a plentiful feast was offered to him. "How was it to be arranged?" On a certain day at four o'clock there were to be placed in a temple sacred to foxes and situated twelve kilometres away two vessels of rice prepared in a particular way, of cheese cooked with beans, together with a great quantity of roast mice and raw vegetables, all favourite dishes of magic foxes: then he would leave the body of the girl exactly at the prescribed time. And so it happened. Punctually at four o'clock when the food was placed in the distant temple the girl sighed profoundly and cried: "He has gone!" The possession was cured.[15]

Although there are many parallels between this case of ingenuous fox possession and the fox possession that takes place in Mahikari, the crucial difference is one of timing and contact. In Bälz's example, an exorcist was summoned only after the girl had been possessed for several weeks. In Mahikari, people are not possessed (in any obvious way) until they step into the dojo.[16] The girl in Bälz's record was obviously a victim of what Oesterreich calls "involuntary" or "spontaneous" possession, whereas members of the dojo seem to experience "voluntary" or "induced" possession.[17]

The spirit experiences, feelings, and socioreligious roles of Mahikari members are all forms of learned behavior that is appropriated and transmitted in set patterns.[18] In effect, members voluntarily seek out and learn to perform both possession and exorcism. This, however, is not evidence for their "abnormality." Quite to the contrary, the strongest evidence that possession in Mahikari is not a pathological phenomenon comes from the simple fact that it is part of a highly structured Salvation Syndrome.

Although Salvation Syndromes can be found in the traditions of ethnic, national, and family religions, they are more obvious, and perhaps more prevalent, in founded religions originating in the revelations of saviors, messiahs, and prophets. Because Salvation Syndromes take shape in the minds of religious virtuosos and are often reworked later on by scribes or scholars, they tend to be internally coherent and schematized (to use Max Weber's word). In their simplest form, Salvation Syndromes are dramatic, all-inclusive oversimplifications consisting of three elements or stages carved like a bas-relief on the souls of the faithful. These I shall call the Problem, the Ideal, and the Way.

Contrary to conventional wisdom, religions do not merely reflect man's existential problems. Quite the reverse: religions create the Problem first and then subsume all of man's specific problems (gout, old age, and the plague) under it. Much as worlds disappear in the maw of a Hindu deity, human problems are swallowed by the Problem of existence. Brought under this awesome, all-encompassing Problem, concrete problems are revaluated and given a new symbolic depth. Life is what it is, not because we have fallen into "the fell clutch of circumstance," but because of the primordial deformity of the world, or the "wound of being," as Nietzsche put it. Religion therefore generates and promotes the very Problem it claims to solve. Saint Paul even assures us that without religion there would be no knowledge of the Judaeo-Christian Problem, sin. Looked at from this angle, religion is not only the devil's prosecutor, but his advocate and co-conspirator as well.

The Fall (or sin) in the Christian religion is a good example of the Problem. It is not merely an inductive generalization about the problems of daily life; it is a dramatic statement that not only describes but creates a picture of man's existence in the world. Obviously, there are as many statements of the Problem as there are religions in the world. The breaking of commandments or taboos, ignorance, craving, disharmony, finitude, and selfishness are only a few of the ways in which the Problem has been stated. Usually, however, the Problem is presented not as a philosophical abstraction, but in the richer garb of symbol, myth, and ritual.

If the Problem is a creative statement of what is wrong with the human condition, the Ideal is a picture of what life could or will be like. Often it is the very opposite of the Problem. In place of the Fall, it holds up before us Ascension and Glory. Instead of endless suffering and transmigration in this samsaric world, it offers the great annihilation of nirvana. The Ideal is often expressed in utopian or eschatological terms.

Finally, each Salvation Syndrome posits the Way to overcome the Problem and attain the Ideal. Again, there is an endless variety of Ways to the Ideal world: faith, sacraments, the observation of decorum or specific taboos, priestly rituals, shamanistic orgies, obedience to divine commands, the gnosis of the wise, the devotion of the simple, and so on. Seldom, if ever, can the Way be reduced to a simple, this-worldly utilitarian or ethical praxis.

Salvation Syndromes can be thought of as sociosemantic processes that sublimate man's problems and aspirations, indeed his very life, by bringing them under the symbols of a sacred world. By creating both a widely shared consciousness of the human condition and sanctioned ritual and moral Ways for dealing with it, Salvation Syndromes enable people to find relief from private dread by bringing it into a therapeutic, social setting. Once a person's own problems become instances of the Problem, they can be dealt with more "objectively"; that is, in a communal or ritual context, be it the Mass, or meditation, or exorcism.

We can now return to the main thread of our argument. The followers of Mahikari, at some psychological level, solicit possession and induce it in others. They do this not because they are deranged or stupid, but because possession and exorcism, taken together, form a systematic Salvation Syndrome in which they see a ray of hope. To review: the Savior, Okada Kotama, saw the Problem as the clouds or dust on the soul caused by sin, bad karma, and evil spirits; this contamination is the source of disease, poverty, war, and other social disorders. The Ideal is a world set free from such impediments; it will be realized in a "non-confrontational" worldwide civilization in which material and spiritual drives will be harmonized. More specifically, the Ideal will be achieved in an eschatological and utopian empire under the rule of the Japanese emperor. In that world, the teachings of the Savior, Okada Kotama, will be supreme, and the Lucky and Healthy Sunshine Children now doing shugyo in the church will rise to places of power and respect. The Way to achieve this Ideal is, of course, okiyome, a ritual that gets rid of man's spiritual and physical impediments and prepares him for his divinized state in the coming Civilization of the Kingdom of God. The dojo is literally the place (*jō*) for practicing this Way (*dō*).

In short, possession and exorcism, even when they result in mental and bodily states of hyperarousal dissociation, or trance, are basically solicited, induced, controlled, and systemic parts of an all-encompassing plan of salvation. In this respect, possession in

Mahikari is identical with possession in many other cultures. To use T. K. Oesterreich's term, it is part of a definite "programme." [19] Programmes or syndromes of this sort are basically self-contained and self-fulfilling, each and every miracle performed in the dojo confirming Su-god's Plan. As Clifford Geertz might put it, the group's ethos and worldview are mutually reinforcing. [20] As unusual as the religious experiences and miracles of Mahikari may be to outsiders, they must therefore be regarded as forms of learned, indeed stereotyped, behavior that by no means presuppose or promote personality disorders of any kind.

Okiyome as Hypnotic Dissociation

I have gone to great lengths to demonstrate the normalcy of Mahikari members and their practices, not just in order to defend them against their secular detractors, but because in the following analysis I use psychological concepts that either derive from abnormal psychology or have been used in the treatment of the mentally ill. Given the provenance of these concepts, some readers might conclude that those to whom they are applied must be abnormal themselves. This is not the case.

Putting our descriptive or phenomenological review of possession and okiyome aside, we can now try to account for these phenomena. But it might be helpful first to examine a more familiar religious phenomenon that, because of its behavioral effects, is similar in many respects to what we have seen in the dojo: I refer to glossolalia, or speaking in tongues. Does research on glossolalia give us any clues for understanding what "really happens" in spirit possession and exorcism?

Glossolalia and the more exotic behavior of Mahikari members have three things in common: both are types of religious behavior that affect gross motor controls; both raise similar methodological problems of interpretation and explanation; and both are an affront to the rational temper of modern scholarship. Apart from field research, students of religion in our universities seldom have occasion for social contact with people involved in either phenomenon. To study them is likely to entail embarrassment, if not a good case of culture shock. It is therefore not especially surprising that the quality of research on both subjects varies enormously.*

In both the Pentecostal churches and Mahikari, adherents report special bodily sensations. We have seen that many dojo members feel a hot sensation in the palms of their hands when giving oki-yome. Likewise, glossolalists may have a warm feeling in their mouths and throats, sometimes described as an electrical sensation, when speaking in tongues. Both possession and glossolalia are regarded by their practitioners as "automatic" behavior. The dojo member is seized by evil spirits; the glossolalist believes he is filled with the Holy Ghost.

I have witnessed spirit movements in the Nakayama dojo that are identical to the kinetic behavior Felicitas Goodman observed in her study of glossolalia: trembling, shaking, twitching (face and thorax), fingers cramping and stretching, head shaking, hand manipulation, the trunk thrown from side to side, jumping, rocking, bowing, and arm lifting. The cliché heard among glossolalists, "He somersaulted all through the church," is regularly heard in the dojos.[21] At the same time, I have also seen relatively sedate exorcisms, which could justly be compared with the less mobile "ecclesiastical glossolalia" of the Neo-Charismatic movement.† Glossolalists also seem to share the dojo members' insatiable appetite for the miraculous. John P. Kildahl, in his study of ecclesiastical glossolalists, found that some think of Jesus as their banker. "He puts money in our pocket. He makes a $5 bill stretch into a $10 bill. He pulls us back from danger and covers us from unknown dangers." One woman claimed that she could recover lost scissors by praying in tongues.[22]

Although glossolalia in the Christian churches and sects covers

---

* Studies of glossolalia conducted by representatives of mainline denominations are sometimes flawed by a deep bias against these heteroprax movements. Another problem complicating this research is the variety of the phenomenon. Glossolalia exists in both Christian and non-Christian cultures and is found today in both the traditional Pentecostal movements and the Neo-Charismatic movement within the mainline churches.

† It is helpful to distinguish between the ecclesiastical glossolalia of the mainline churches (Catholic, Episcopal, Presbyterian, Lutheran, and Methodist) and the sectarian glossolalia of the Pentecostal and Holiness movements. The former tends to be far less kinetic than the latter.

a wide range of activity, it is clearly a kind of learned behavior. Studies of the actual utterances of the glossolalists show that even though "tongues" are not formal languages like French or Japanese, Spirit-filled speech has its own fixed patterns. The various Charismatic groups even have their own recognizable linguistic styles.

These languages are learned both by informal imitation and by formal instruction. In some groups, the elders put their fingers in the mouths of the neophytes and urge them to let themselves go so that the Holy Ghost can fill their mouths. The sights and sounds of fellow believers speaking in tongues beside them also give the Spirit a boost and encourage initiates to receive the Gift themselves. Once learned, the behavior can be initiated by some at will. Others need the spiritual support of the saints before the Spirit fills their mouths. Whereas ecclesiastical glossolalists (Neo-Charismatics) often pray in tongues in the privacy of their own homes, the more ecstatic sectarian glossolalia generally takes place in the emotionally charged atmosphere of the prayer meeting. Sometimes people begin to speak in tongues only after a meeting has gone on for several hours, or when they are on the verge of nervous exhaustion. Various techniques are used to bring the activity to an end. Goodman's glossolalists, for example, rang a "small, clear-toned bell with a very high pitch" to recall members to their everyday selves.[23]

From the more scholarly studies of glossolalia, it is evident that this phenomenon, too, though strange to outsiders, is anything but pathological.[24] Like possession and exorcism in Mahikari, glossolalia seems to be a form of solicited, induced, controlled, and learned behavior. William J. Samarin, in his study of glossolalia, describes it as essentially a "knack" that anyone can learn.[25] This observation, however, overlooks its religious significance, for glossolalia is also part of a systematic and thaumaturgical Salvation Syndrome. But the question remains how to account for this behavior psychologically. Can explanations for glossolalia be applied to possession and exorcism?

After reviewing nearly a century's research on the subject, Samarin concludes that "the attempt to explain glossolalia psychologically is not an impressive one."[26] Without going into the more fanciful or biased interpretations of the subject—of which there are many—I would like to point out only two aspects of the psychological explanation of glossolalia that seem illuminating and potentially relevant to the problem of spirit possession and exorcism. The first of these is the concept of dissociation. Glossolalia is often regarded as a dissociation either of the ego from reality or of "ego material" from the central organization of the ego itself. For Felicitas Goodman it is a form of "hyperarousal dissociation"; for James Lapsley and John H. Simpson, it is a "form of dissociation within the personality, in which a set of voluntary muscles responds to control centers other than those associated with consciousness."[27] The concept of dissociation seems to be stretched too far only when applied to cases of *routine* glossolalia. Samarin, at least, concludes that "the acquisition of charismatic or Pentecostal glossolalia is *sometimes* associated with *some* degree of altered state of consciousness, that this *occasionally* involves motor activity that is involuntary or, *rarely*, a complete loss of consciousness, and that in any case subsequent use of glossolalia (that is, after the initial experience) is *most often independent* of dissociative phenomena."[28] Psychological studies of glossolalia therefore present us with two alternatives: either we can treat the phenomenon as such as a form of dissociation, or we can regard only the more dramatic experiences of the neophyte as a form of dissociation.

Before the concept of dissociation can be used in the context of religious behavior, certain limitations must be set on our use of the term. By Norman Cameron's definition, dissociation reactions are "attempts to escape from excessive tension and anxiety by separating off some parts of personality function from the rest." This process may result in making familiar things strange; or in "an apparent withdrawal from the external world into a world of fantasy (dream-like states)"; or in massive amnesias, fugues, or the formation of multiple personalities.[29] The formation of semi-autonomous ego organizations within the structure of the ego itself is obviously of prime importance for explaining the behavior of people who believe themselves possessed by or filled with spirits, good or evil. When the self divides into a conscious and an unconscious personality, the unconscious personality often communicates with the conscious personality in indirect, symbolic ways. James C. Coleman points out that this "co-conscious personality is usually intimately aware of the thoughts of the conscious personality and of things going on in the world, but indicates its awareness through automatic writing or in some other roundabout way."[30] Behavior of this sort is sometimes referred to as dissociation *in service of the ego*. "Dissociation is an attempt to preserve ego integration by reducing ego span, that is by eliminating some ego functions in order to bring emotional tension within manageable limits"; this is often motivated by "an attempt to gain psychological distance from something traumatic or from something which demands too abrupt an adaptation."[31]

But the view of dissociation as "withdrawing from reality" is riddled with difficulties. It sees reality as a simple state of affairs that anyone can locate, and the imaginary worlds created by dissociating individuals as "unreal." But to define reality in this way is an act of philosophical hubris or naïveté. Today, most psychologists and sociologists prefer to think of life as constituted by many overlapping spheres of reality, each with its own ontological density. From this pluralistic point of view, what is it from which people withdraw when they dissociate?

Dissociation covers a wide range of behaviors. Normal daydreaming and the formation of multiple personalities by mental patients are, alike, forms of dissociation. The imagination itself, whether secular or religious, seems to be predicated on our ability to dissociate ourselves from our present surroundings. Mild dissociative states, therefore, need not be caused by specific traumata. If this is true, dissociation encompasses not only withdrawal from negative or painful situations, but movement toward more positive and pleasant states. It may even be a way of moving toward and attaining what is regarded as a higher reality. To use a simple analogy, we do not always go to the movies just because we are tired, bored, or in need of distraction. Sometimes we go just to see John Wayne or one of Hollywood's other "higher realities." Likewise, dissociation might better be thought of as an unconscious mechanism for transporting the self to different spheres of reality, or for transforming the present world into one that is less threatening, more enjoyable or "real." Broadly conceived, dissociation can therefore be seen as respite from the "world of working" governed by "common sense" (Schutz) and as a transition to a realm filled with different realities and companions, and governed by different rules.[32]

Yet useful as broad psychological definitions of this sort are, they tend to be too generous and inclusive. I shall therefore try to restrict my use of the term dissociation to cases involving (1) dramatic outbursts of motor and psychic energy and (2) the generation of symbols (gods, spirits, supernatural powers) not associated with the workaday world. As a third restriction, I shall limit the term to those cases in which, had we enough information, it would be likely, or possible, to regard the symbolic formations of the person's withdrawal or regression as instances of dissociation in the service of ego maintenance. I am thus not interested in daydreaming as a form of dissociation. Although some of the cases I cite below can justly be described as instances of "mild" dissociative states, Samarin's conclusions regarding glossolalia hold true for most cases of possession and exorcism in Mahikari: these experiences occur too routinely, and with too little emotion, to be considered dissociative phenomena properly speaking.

A subtle dialectic is constantly going on in sects like Mahikari between dissociative behavior and the saintly routine. The neophyte's religious career often begins with a deeply emotional experience of salvation. The Salvation Syndrome itself—because it creates such tension between the Problem (unbearable surplus dread) and the Ideal (unthinkable surplus hope)—often generates altered states of consciousness. At least, many people are incapable of personally appropriating the Way of salvation, thus relieving this (systemic) tension, until they have fallen into a dissociative state of mind. However, from the history of enthusiasm, we know that such a pitch of emotion can seldom be sustained for long. In Mahikari, for example, as the subject gets cleaned up, he is expected to display fewer and less violent spirit seizures, signifying that his spirit level has gone up, and with it, his immunity to possession. Exorcism, like conversion, must therefore lead to a new way of life, a sanctified routine, in short, to the *habitus* of the saints of the Lord. The altered states of consciousness initially induced by the sect are finally transformed, through constant care and nurture, into altered but sustained modes of thought and behavior. Ideally, a distinctive set of "powerful, pervasive and long-lasting moods and motivations" will emerge among the elect.[33] At this point, dissociation must yield to the organization and regimentation of the faithful.

The other clues we find in the literature on glossolalia for a psychological analysis of okiyome are the related concepts of hypnotic suggestion and regression. In religions that institutionalize "hothouses" of emotion and expectation, dissociative experiences are often induced by means of hypnotic suggestion. The social and emotional atmosphere generated by these groups is filled with clues and incentives that help elicit the desired behavior. Mahikari literature and advertisements are filled with pictures and stories describing in great detail the spirit movements people have when they receive okiyome. Photographs on the walls of dojos show people literally somersaulting or standing on their heads as they receive the Treatment. A suggestible person needs to see only a few of these posters before the pre-conscious process of learning the new behavior begins.

The training course is the main conduit of these suggestions. When Yoshida Sensei explained the movements made by the various spirits, I noticed a number of people in the audience moving their hands in semi-conscious imitation of the lecturer's hands. They were, in effect, *rehearsing* the movements of the spirits that would soon be possessing them. When the individual is given okiyome, the autopoetic words of the Exorcist's Prayer and other healing songs create a feeling of deep expectation. The words of the Chorei Hymn, which are directed not to the subject, but to the evil spirits possessing him, naturally create the feeling that a third party is indeed present. Testimonies and the common sight of other people being seized by evil spirits make possession and exorcism seem all the more real.[34] When exorcists probe for the body's "vital points," they are forever telling their partners that they can feel a tightness here or a lump there. This naturally suggests the presence of coagulated toxins (and therefore evil spirits) in the body. (As is well known, suggestion can be used both to induce diseases and to cure them.)

The ministers and other members of the dojo staff constantly drop hints to members about the spirits possessing them. Once, Yoshida Sensei noticed that my hands were shaking slightly when he gave me okiyome. He immediately suggested that an evil spirit had possessed me while I was visiting Shinto shrines in connection with my other research.* Often the suggestions made by the staff are of the vaguest sort. (We have already seen how Yoshida Sensei blamed Shimizu Masao's illness on a "big, bad spirit," even though Shimizu had failed to have any spirit movements at all.) People on the staff are in a good position to provide these suggestions because they regularly ask people about their problems before giving them okiyome. They also try to learn whether the person is worshiping his ancestors. According to one minister, the exorcist will often have a hunch that a certain spirit is possessing his partner. The next time he gives this person okiyome, he might use this hunch to formulate questions for the spirit investigation.

Many people join Mahikari in a state of extreme nervous prostration—for example, after having been told that they have an incurable disease. This frame of mind naturally tends to increase their susceptibility to suggestion, especially if they believe that Mahikari is their last chance in life. Numerous studies of possession in various parts of the world have shown that when people experience a nervous collapse or a deep trance, they often display some degree of hysterical suggestibility. The imagination then becomes quite lively and impressionable, so that what is experienced in this state is apt to seem especially real and significant. "Conceptions of a general order of existence" take shape in the mind of the neophyte, which become clothed with "an aura of factuality." [35]

I observed one of the clearest examples of group suggestion during the national Mahikari festival, which is held in Tokyo at the end of every year. At the climax of the festival Okada Keiju, the Spiritual Leader of the church, stood on a dais before the assembled throng to give them okiyome. Before she raised her hands over them, the assembly was carefully instructed—I should say rehearsed—in the proper way to receive this purification. Since the spirit rays between the Spiritual Leader and Su-god are extremely "thick," their effect is said to be overwhelming. Because a direct purification of the forehead would be too powerful a dose, every-

---

* I found it nearly impossible to press palm against palm and hold my hands perfectly steady for a full ten minutes, especially while being watched by such attentive eyes.

*Okada Keiju, Spiritual Leader of Sukyo Mahikari, giving okiyome to her
followers at a national festival in Tokyo*

one was asked to lower his head so that the spirit rays could enter
through the top of the skull. Dozens of helpers wearing red headbands were stationed in the aisles throughout the hall. The audience was told that if anyone felt faint or if his spirit movements
began to get out of control, he should call one of these wardens
for assistance.

For nearly ten minutes, the audience was repeatedly warned of
the ritual's powerful consequences. As might be expected, no sooner had the Spiritual Leader intoned the Exorcist's Prayer and raised
her hands over the bowed heads of the faithful than the cries of
evil spirits could be heard from all corners of the hall. Wardens
darted here and there offering their help. Nearly a dozen young
women, some wearing the green and white uniform of the Mahi-

kari Youth Corps, collapsed and had to be carried out of the hall. When the exorcism was over, the lady next to me asked whether I had felt anything. I ruefully admitted that I had not. She, however, had felt the toxins in her head melting and running down her neck.

Hypnotic states are known to be related to infantile regression, in which many ego functions are abdicated, including reality-testing and volition. In this state the individual is sometimes capable of creating a new persona for himself. Or, the ego can be split into multiple personalities. When this happens, not the entire ego, but rather a subsystem within the ego structure is relinquished. In cases of spirit possession, we can hypothesize that this subsystem within the ego *becomes* the possessing spirit. As such, it becomes an object of transference (for example, of guilt) and the occasion for outbursts of pent-up emotional energy. (We shall see, however, that not all spiritual apparitions can be accounted for in this way.)

A person in a state of hypersuggestibility also tends "to accept and/or automatically to respond to specific statements (i.e., commands or instructions of a leader, shaman, demagogue, or hypnotist)." Under these conditions, religious healers, preachers, and therapists can become "omnipotent authoritative figures."[36] In prolonged psychoanalysis, for example, it has been said that

a hypnoid state of brain activity may result. Patients may come to feel that in some way they are in the hands of a person of almost divine wisdom; they avidly accept suggestions from the therapist about altering their behaviour, which would have been quite unacceptable to them in their more normal state of mind. Quite bizarre interpretations are accepted and false memories are believed as facts if they fit in with the analyst's own beliefs.[37]

This relationship between hypnotic suggestion and authoritative figures is not surprising, since suggestion itself is a "regressive transference based on a relationship to the hypnotist as in some sense a parent substitute."[38] Applying this notion to religious behavior, Kildahl found that in comparing glossolalists with non-glossolalists, "the glossolalists developed deeply trusting and submissive relationships to the authority figures who introduced them to the practice of glossolalia. Without complete submission to the leader, speaking in tongues was not initiated."[39] Kildahl goes on to suggest that the feelings of euphoria among glossolalists derive not from speaking in tongues per se, but from their submission to authority.*

In Mahikari's training course, the first thing newcomers are told is that they must accept Mioshie "with a humble heart." The teachings and practices of the church are authoritative. The relationship between the subject and his exorcist-partner, though not authoritarian, is based on trust and acceptance. Respect for the exorcist increases in direct proportion to his rank in the church, for those in the highest positions not only can conduct spirit investigations, but can give the most potent benedictions. The therapeutic effects of this personal relationship will be discussed later. For now, it is enough to point out the elements of hypnotic suggestion that seem to underlie it.

Of course, to speak of possession and exorcism as forms of hypnotic suggestion goes directly against the teachings of Mahikari. Both in its lectures and in its literature, the church insists that it does not use hypnosis. Two arguments could be made to support the church's position. First, people who have experienced states of hypnosis or trance are said to be unable to recall later what has happened to them, whereas those who have had spirit seizures in the dojo can recall everything. Therefore the seizure is not a hypnotic experience. In reply to this argument, let me point out that post-hypnotic amnesia is by no means universal. It could even be said that when members are told repeatedly that they *will* recall their experiences after the benediction, hypnotic suggestions are actually being slipped to them that will ensure their post-purification recall. Not remembering one's actions can be a simple defense mechanism for denying one's responsibility for them. Looked at in this way, the guarantee of post-hypnotic amnesia can help ensure the success of the hypnosis by releasing the subject from responsibility. In Mahikari and other possession cults, the subject's responsibility for bizarre or unusual behavior is denied *a priori* on the ground that the possessing spirit is to blame. Thus the ability to recall a possession experience does not necessarily mean that it was not a hypnotic alteration of consciousness.

---

* Some investigators have found that glossolalists were less subject to suggestion than non-glossolalists. See Felicitas D. Goodman, *Speaking in Tongues: A Cross-Cultural Study of Glossolalia* (Chicago, 1972), p. 25.

A second phenomenon that argues against the hypnotic nature of possession and exorcism is spontaneous possession. A number of people I interviewed said that they had read none of the sect's literature and had no idea what would happen to them before their first spirit seizure. Some even reported having spirit seizures while at work or at home in bed. Likewise, several of Goodman's glossolalists stressed that they never had an inkling of what they were about to do, that they "just did it"; from this she concludes that "some people may achieve dissociation spontaneously."[40] Now, it is quite possible that many of these people were not aware that they had been subjected to suggestion because of its subliminal nature. Or, they might simply have forgotten the details of their experience. On the other hand, assuming that some possession experiences are genuinely spontaneous, we can account for them psychologically as instances of hyperarousal dissociation. Cases of spontaneous self-hypnosis, for that matter, are well documented.[41] That possession sometimes occurs spontaneously, therefore, does not seem to count against our understanding of the phenomenon as hypnotic behavior.

To sum up our argument thus far, although the interview and survey questions did not deal directly with psychological issues, the more dramatic possession experiences I observed in the dojo seem best accounted for by the psychological concepts of dissociation and hypnotic suggestion. Since I was not equipped to test the relationship (if any) between the hypnotizability of Mahikari members and their susceptibility to possession, much of what I have written above must remain in the realm of speculation. Although my approach must therefore be tentative, there are clear advantages in looking at possession and exorcism as a kind of "hypnodrama," or more accurately, "hypno-sociodrama," to use Sheila Walker's apt expressions.[42] This approach helps us account for things that would otherwise remain a mystery. If we regard possession as a form of hypnotic behavior, we can see why during the quiet of okiyome (deprivation of external stimuli) the subject will sometimes erupt with outbursts of repressed emotional energy. We can recognize the dojo members' feelings of floating and their weeping as responses widely shared by those in hypnotic states.[43] We can understand why repressed guilt, taking the symbolic form of evil spirits, often comes to the surface.[44] Because some people are more easily hypnotized than others, we might expect the dojo members to vary widely in their susceptibility to spirit possession. This has been borne out by the statistical survey. Studies of hypnosis also help us understand the respective psychological postures of the exorcist and his subject, that is, the people- and world-controlling stance of the exorcist (hypnotist) and the passive dependency of his subject (the hypnotized individual).[45] From this perspective, receiving okiyome can be regarded as "institutionalized regression in the service of the ego."[46] Finally, the theory of hypnotic suggestion offers a well-documented explanation for the healing power of religious rituals like okiyome. This phenomenon has been known and debated in medical circles since the time of Franz Anton Mesmer (d. 1815), who was himself something of a thaumaturge.

Psychological Forms and Functions of Okiyome

Dissociation and hypnotic suggestion, though they provide a foundation for explaining the religious experiences and miracles observed in sects like Mahikari, apply directly only to the most dramatic cases. Even in these cases, more must be said about the specific symbolic forms possession experiences take and the functions they serve in the subject's conscious and unconscious life. Even though spirit seizures may be hypnotically induced states of consciousness, what the subject experiences is clearly not determined by his exorcist in any mechanical way. Even hypnotized subjects, far from being putty in the hypnotist's hands, make substantial additions to the suggestions he makes.[47] Likewise, in okiyome there seems to be plenty of room for the experience to take form through the symbolic projection of psychic material from the subject's unconscious.

Okiyome can be thought of as an algebra of dissociation, projection, and catharsis. The ritual relies on no iron law of association but on the (partially conditioned) spontaneity of the religious imagination itself. When okiyome results in spirit seizures, specific spirits, having their own motives and personalities, are instantiated for the x, y, and z of the Salvation Syndrome. In some cases, the substitution is clearly reflexive, such as when a spirit represents real feelings of guilt or shame. In other cases, it is chanced upon randomly, but it still enables the "formula" to work. Okiyome is therefore a compound of the fixed and the loose, the traditional and the novel, the essential and the existential. Mircea Eliade aptly expressed this dialectical aspect of religious behavior when he wrote: "Religious man is not given; he creates himself by drawing close to divine models." [48] Mahikari shows us that even *demonic* models can have a role to play in this self-creation.

Figure 3 summarizes and categorizes by form and function the various types of spirit seizures that I observed in the Nakayama dojo or learned about in published testimonies. I cannot claim that the chart is exhaustive. Furthermore, the typical spirit seizure falls into more than one category. For example, it might take the form of a homeopathic projection, while serving the functions of expressing repressed emotion, symbolizing retribution for past sins (guilt), and creating a new persona.

In Figure 3 I use the word projection not to denote the deflection of guilt from the ego to others, but to denote the psychological process of objectification or reification. To take a non-religious example, when the blues singer Leadbelly sang "Good mornin' blues and how are you?" he was reifying, or personifying, the blues within him as a blues "out there." Through his music, he projected his blues and—who knows?—perhaps even exorcised himself from their grip. Aside from the obvious differences of expression, the main distinction between artistic and religious projections lies in the degree of freedom the artist and the believer have to structure their experiences. In the arts, it is primarily the form (that is, style)

TYPE OF PROJECTION	FUNCTION					
	Theodicy					
	Retribution (blame-guilt-shame)	Exoneration	Etiology (cause)	Legitimation	Creation of new persona	Expression of repressed emotion
Homeopathic						
Non-homeopathic						

FIG. 3. *The Functions and Symbolic Projections of Okiyome*

that becomes fixed; but in religion, both the form and the content of rituals, myths, and dogmas, even while being embellished and enriched, tend to become stereotyped. The believer's creativity therefore consists in the way he instantiates the Salvation Syndrome in his own life.

Religious projections may conveniently be divided into two sorts: homeopathic and non-homeopathic. The notion of homeopathy is, of course, taken from Sir James George Frazer's classic study of magic. In its simplest terms, homeopathy (or the Law of Similarity) means that similar causes produce similar effects: "Like produces like." [49] Not limited to magic, homeopathy is a mode of thought that runs through a wide range of religious symbolizations, one of the most important being karma. The biblical phrase so often used to explain karma—"Whatsoever a man sows, that shall he also reap"—is a perfect example of homeopathy. Many of the possession scenarios I encountered in Mahikari fall under the category of homeopathic projections of karma. For example, the husband of one zealous member of the Nakayama dojo died from facial cancer. After his death, his widow learned through spirit investigations that his illness had been caused by the spirit of a snake whose head he had cut off when he was a boy. This is a simple case of homeopathic revenge: a head for a head.

Non-homeopathic projections, by contrast, posit no apparent similarity between the person's past or present experience and the projected symbol. Cause and effect are therefore asserted without recourse to the magical Law of Similarity. For example, a woman suffering from asthma comes to the dojo and discovers she is possessed by a fox spirit. Since nothing besides the simple identity of the fox is known, any possible similarity between the possessing spirit and its victim (or her affliction) is either unknown or unimportant. One important kind of non-homeopathic projection is what we might call catalytic dissociation. In this kind of projection, a seemingly random symbol acts to release a tremendous flood of energy, so that the exorcism itself becomes exceptionally violent and cathartic. The best example of catalytic dissociation is the story of the cat possession I related in Chapter 3. [50] In this case, the person had done nothing wrong to the cat that might have set into motion the wheels of karmic retribution. There was no obvious symbolic correspondence between his own condition and the cat's unlucky death. The cat, in short, was a random catalytic agent through which pent-up motor and psychic energy found release.*

We can treat the various functions of okiyome categorized in Figure 3 as different ways in which individuals respond to a wide variety of needs, such as the quest for moral integrity; the integration of personal experience; the expression of frustration and hurt, approval and love; or the maintenance of order, security, and hope in the face of life's losing odds. Since these needs are too numerous to categorize, I shall simply assume that any of them might be found at work, singly or in combination, in the six functions of okiyome that I am about to elaborate.

The first three functions of okiyome (retribution, exoneration, and etiology) I have grouped together as forms of theodicy. Theodicy is a word that sociology has borrowed from theology to denote the symbolic resources mobilized by a group or a whole society to deal with the ultimate frustrations of life: misfortune, sickness, and death. These adversities include not only the sad inevitabilities of the human condition, but avoidable misery as well. Retribution and exoneration are symbolic responses to the question of responsibility. As forms of theodicy they deal with shame, guilt, or blame. Chapter 9, for example, examines several cases in which women became Mahikari followers because of a serious "role deprivation": the failure to attract or keep a husband. The theodicy Mahikari offers these women is called "sexual karma" (*shikijō innen*). Through spirit investigations, some women discover that their present difficulties closely resemble the scandals of their past lives. Women who stole lovers from other women in past incarnations find that the spirits of those offended women now are taking revenge by causing their husbands or fiances to leave them. Sexual karma may also function to exonerate the possessed. For example, quite commonly

---

* Experiences of this sort seem closely related to the treatment of "shell-shocked" patients in World War II, who were *not* made to recall and relive their traumata. It was found that, after a trance-like state had been chemically induced, "the release of great anger or fear could be more effectively produced around incidents which were entirely imaginary and had never happened to the patient at all, and such abreactions of imaginary events could have remarkably beneficial effects." William Sargant, *The Mind Possessed: A Physiology of Possession, Mysticism, and Faith Healing* (Philadelphia, 1974), p. 5.

a woman discovers that she is possessed by a male spirit who has fallen in love with her. To keep her for himself, the spirit tries to prevent her from finding a husband. Thus women suffering from the consequences of retributive sexual karma seem to be saying, "I am to blame for what is now happening to me," whereas those whose spirit stories represent exoneration seem to say, "I am not, and never have been, responsible for my present plight."

Lonely women are not the only ones to have spirit seizures representing retribution and exoneration, for complicated feelings of guilt or shame within the family are often manifested in seizures of this sort. For example, Nakamura Mariko joined Mahikari in 1975, hoping to find a cure for her rheumatism. She is only forty-one, but because of her illness she has become emaciated and weak, and now looks twice her age. In spite of her exposure to Mioshie, Mrs. Nakamura continues to believe that her illness was originally caused by a fever and not by evil spirits. Her husband's participation in the sect and response to okiyome have been significantly different. As his wife's illness grew progressively more serious, Mr. Nakamura spent all of his free time drinking and gambling. After joining the dojo "in order to cure my wife," he had a spirit seizure in which he discovered that in a previous life he had offended someone. He believes that the spirit of this offended person has taken possession of his wife, making her ill in order to take its revenge. I was surprised to learn that he has never told his wife about this revelation. Perhaps this omission reflects his feelings of guilt for neglecting her during the ten years of her illness. He assured me that since joining Mahikari, he has given up his vices.*

The third kind of theodicy is concerned simply with the cause of misfortune, not with a person's feelings of guilt or blame. Although the etiology of misfortune in Mahikari is almost always personalized—the blame being cast on evil spirits—the emphasis as far as the living are concerned is on cause and not on responsibility. An

---

* Mr. Nakamura is a good example of a dojo member whose family is steeped in folk religion. His grandmother and aunt were both mediums. His grandmother lived in the country, where she exorcised people possessed by foxes and badgers. His aunt lived in Shikoku, where she worked as a diviner and healer. Although she was not connected with any particular sect, she performed purifications using Shinto prayers (*norito*) and recited the Prajñāpāramitā sūtra. Mr. Nakamura himself had several encounters with spirits when he was a child.

etiological spirit seizure therefore deals with issues like *why* Mr. Tanaka burned his hand, *why* he lost his job, or *why* his daughter has bone cancer. Generally, however, because blame, guilt, shame, and causation are often expressed in the same spirit story, it is impossible to distinguish clearly among the three types of theodicy. A purely disinterested quest for the ultimate causes of one's misfortunes is relatively rare in popular Japanese religions.

If theodicy is a sociosemantic device for making misfortune more bearable, legitimation is just the opposite. It justifies an excess of good fortune, power, or wealth in the face of the bad luck, impotence, poverty—*and resentment*—of others. In other words, legitimation is a set of ideas, ideals, and emotions that supports or rationalizes the claims of one person or group against all others. We have already seen one good example of the legitimating function of okiyome in the spirit history of the Yoshida family. The spirit of Sensei's father appeared to the family after their neighbors had begun to snub them. To encourage the family, the spirit told them how much he appreciated all they had done for him, especially by building the dojo, and how their work had improved his position in the astral world. The spirit thereby legitimated the Yoshidas' intrusion into their neighbors' private affairs and their own dedication to the church. As Takie Sugiyama Lebra points out, aggressive attitudes (such as meddling in the domestic affairs of one's neighbors), if assumed under purely secular conditions, "would be embarrassing or would provoke negative sanctions because the norms of Japanese culture emphasize humility, empathetic forgiveness, patience, self-blame, and subtle communication. Possession by a spirit legitimizes taking the roles suppressed or prohibited by the cultural norms." [51]

The relatively large percentage of people who claim to have been possessed by the spirit of a warrior ancestor can also be explained by the legitimating function of possession. Because the warrior class was the mainstay of the medieval elite, to claim a warrior as an ancestor—or rather, to have the warrior ancestor claim you as a descendant!—is both a compliment to you and a point of pride for the entire family.

The legitimating function of okiyome is also seen in the spirit experiences of young members whose parents are opposed to their involvement in Mahikari. In many cases, the staff suggests to them that their parents are opposed to the church because they are possessed by evil spirits themselves. Sometimes a grandparent or other long-dead ancestor will appear to these young people and ask them to rearrange the family's butsudan; since the butsudan is the Holy of Holies of the Japanese family cult, few parents are willing to allow their children to tamper with it. Parents often deny their children's request to become full-time Mahikari ministers, setting off blistering family feuds. The appearance of a grandparent's spirit during okiyome therefore serves to legitimate the position of these young people in their struggles with their parents. As in everyday life, the grandparents and grandchildren have a common enemy, the generation in between.

Although no stigma is placed on members who have not had spirit seizures, having seizures may legitimate neophytes as bona fide members in the eyes of the stalwart. Later, the disappearance of spirit seizures, an indication that the member's spirit level has risen, often precedes or accompanies his nomination to a position of responsibility in the dojo. Depending on the circumstances, then, either the appearance or the disappearance of possessing spirits can have a legitimating function.

The function of some spirit seizures seems to be the creation of a new self-understanding or public image—a new persona. Some people seem to be quite gratified by the recognition they receive when they "somersault through the dojo" or when they present their spirit stories before the assembled group. To me, the lively spirit seizures of some of the young members look like juvenile antics consciously or unconsciously designed to get attention. But my impression could be wrong. Perhaps they really express the need for "existential refreshment" that young people feel when they are beginning to face the pressures of adult obligations for the first time.

The last function of okiyome that I shall mention is the expression of repressed emotions and frustrated drives. Freud may have been over-generalizing when he identified evil spirits with "base and evil wishes, the derivatives of impulses which have been rejected and repressed," but certainly many of the denizens of the astral world fit this description.[52] It may seem strange to think of people expressing pent-up emotions through ritual actions that are so highly stereotyped. Perhaps our difficulty in imagining this process derives from our Western—and romantic—views about the emotions and their expression. Just as the rationalist in us recoils from the murky waters of the unconscious, the romantic in us eagerly expects them to gush forth in uncontrolled torrents of emotion. But this rarely happens. On careful examination, we see that nearly all religious expressions of emotion are channeled and controlled. Even the worldwide myths and rituals symbolizing the return to chaos have their invariant pattern, usually based on a simple rule of role reversal. Likewise, as Goodman points out, in the dissociative behavior of glossolalists, as one moves beyond the threshold of consciousness "there is not disorder but structure."[53] Thus even the most ecstatic kinds of religious behavior have their forms and their limits. Religious symbols and experiences inevitably become fixed and typical. This is especially true in Japan, where emotion is most highly valued when it is expressed with moral or artistic restraint.

How Okiyome Heals

Having laid out the types of projection involved in okiyome and some of its pre-conscious functions, we can now turn to the question of how okiyome heals. Stalwart dojo members have no difficulty giving the answer. Okiyome heals, they say, because of the power of Light (or spirit rays) transmitted from Su-god via the amulets prepared at Mahikari Headquarters.

This study, not being an essay in theology, comes at the question from a different perspective. Unlike believers, we must deal with more mundane considerations such as the psychosocial mechanisms used by the Lord God to work his wonders. Incidentally, although zeal and hope may ingenuously inflate some testimonial claims, I see no reason to doubt that in Mahikari and related religions, healing miracles do take place.

Since there is no uniform psychological response to okiyome, we can be assured that healing, when it does take place, does not occur in the same way or for the same reasons. Here I shall discuss only four ways in which okiyome heals: by ritualizing social interaction, by catharsis, by the quiet restoration of confidence, and by creating a new persona.

In Japan, a common personality disorder is a feeling of total immobilization. A housewife, for example, may become so neurotic about pollution, food additives, and how to avoid carcinogens that she can no longer cook the family's meals. Individuals in this state can go neither forward nor backward. Wherever they turn, everything seems to lead to an impasse (*ikizumari* or *toraware*), so that life itself becomes stagnant and futile. Traditional Sino-Japanese medical lore may clarify the conceptual world underlying these symptoms. Broadly speaking, it attributes disease to obstructions of the "energy flows" within the body. Therapy therefore consists of unclogging the system and restoring its proper balance, rhythm, and movement. These concepts are reflected in Japanese *shiatsu*, in the various thaumaturgical manual therapies discussed above, and in Mahikari's ideas about the coagulation of toxins, spirit obstructions, the "melting" of tumors, and so on.[54]

Okiyome not only melts tumors and spirit obstructions in the body; it also restores the flow of the social interactions that are necessary for leading a normal life. The most important of these are interdependency and reciprocity.[55] One of the most thoroughly studied types of social interaction in Japanese society is called *amae*, from the verb *amaeru*, meaning "to depend and presume upon another's benevolence." A reciprocal type of relationship, amae presupposes an Ego who avails himself of the Alter's kindness, nurturance, and protection. At the same time, it requires an Alter who desires to indulge or coddle the Ego (*amayakasu*). This intimate dependency relationship is typical of human relations throughout Japanese society, but is especially notable in the relationships between mother and child, wife and husband, and even bar hostess and male client.*

In okiyome, the subject receiving purification is ritually placed in

---

* The amae relationship is probably not as important in many Japanese industries as the promoters of paternalism would like us, and their Japanese workers, to believe. Amae is sometimes closer to the ideal form (*tatemae*) of social and economic relationships than to the real feelings (*honne*) of the people involved. One must therefore distinguish between amae in ideology and amae in actual conduct.

the position of one who is "doing amaeru." His role is not only passive (as we saw when we compared it with the medium's role in yorigito), but also dependent. He must "depend and presume" on the benevolence of his exorcist. Without his exorcist there obviously would be no okiyome, and no one would get "cleaned up." The subject must trust his partner properly to "entrance" him; to interrogate, reprimand, and dispatch the spirits possessing him; and finally, to pronounce the benediction over him and bring him back to the everyday world.

When we relate this ritual amae to our discussion of suggestion, we can see that the subject of okiyome is in a position conducive to the hypnotic processes of regression, transference, and the abdication of adult ego functions. The ritualization of amae frees the subject to gratify his infantile urge to relinquish ego controls and indulge in what otherwise would be regarded as childish behavior. As in hypnosis, the subjects of okiyome revert "nostalgically to a phase of life in which passive-receptive mastery was the major means of coping with the outside world, when their security was achieved by participation in a greater unit, the all-powerful parent." [56] Because this regressive stage of okiyome is in effect a victory for the magical "omnipotence of thought," it is not surprising that possession scenarios tend to fall into the classic categories of magic itself: homeopathy, sympathy, and contagion. Regression makes it possible to withdraw temporarily from the threatening events of adulthood, but the real magic of possession-regression lies in the fact that some people emerge from the experience in greater control of their lives, and with their health restored.

This is only half of the story. Since okiyome is a reciprocal ritual, once the subject has been purified, he switches places and becomes the exorcist. Ego becomes Alter. The one who "depended and presumed" on his partner now has the chance to indulge and nurture him. Taking his partner's side, the exorcist will scold the spirits for him and try to ensure their departure. The exorcist can therefore be thought of as the partner in control. This role may have more psychological significance than meets the eye, for the wish to be an exorcist, like the desire to hypnotize others, may be related to an infantile need for magical omnipotence. [57] After all, when dojo members raise their hands and assume the exorcist's posture, they are in a position not only to heal the sick, but to repair automobiles, to change the weather, and so on. The exorcist, in short, is the thaumaturge par excellence.

Although okiyome is a spiritual duet, to revert to an earlier metaphor, the two parts are not only different but unequal. The exorcist and subject routinely exchange places, but one could argue that when a person comes into the dojo for the first time, his spirit level is so low that he is *essentially* a subject for okiyome. The mutuality of the ritual may even make it easier to assume the subject's passive role. While being purified, the subject is actually giving the exorcist an opportunity to do shugyo and raise his own spirit level. The subject therefore knows that, far from being a burden to others, he is playing a useful, if passive, role.

But the subjects of okiyome have their own aspirations. Above all, they desire to get cleaned up and progress from their lowly roles (and low spirit levels) to the exalted level of master exorcist and thaumaturge. Shugyo can therefore be regarded as a ritual of social interaction that allows people gradually to exchange their passivity, frustration, and vulnerability for the active body-, people-, and world-controlling stance of the magician. As they practice and act out following and leading, obeying and commanding, amaeru and amayakasu, they are also reaffirming the natural interactive roles that Japanese are expected to play in daily life. For those in a state of psychological deadlock, this proleptic ritual "unplugging" of spiritual and social obstructions can have the most therapeutic effect.

There is yet one more bilateral relationship in the ritual of purification that must be mentioned: the relationship between the subject and his ancestors. Even though the ancestors are dead, the interplay between subject and ancestors in okiyome can be considered a ritual of social interaction.[58] In essence, Japanese ancestor worship extends the relationship between parents and their children in this life by means of a ritual relationship that takes over when the parents die. As Meyer Fortes, writing of ancestor worship in a different part of the world, once remarked, "The ancestor cult is the transposition to the religious plane of the relationships of parents and children; and that is what I mean by describing it as

the ritualization of filial piety." [59] In the exchange relationship between the living, the parent provides the child with nourishment,
protection, and care, while the child responds with love, obedience,
and labor. After the parent dies, the child nourishes the spirit of the
parent with offerings made in the butsudan, while the parental spirit
continues to reward or punish the child from the other world. Thus
the exchange, though modified, continues.

In Mahikari, ancestral spirits and their descendants can assume
either a positive or a negative attitude toward one another. If the
descendant neglects his butsudan, ignoring the order of the memorial tablets in it, his ancestors will starve in the astral world or bear
grudges against him. But if he tends his butsudan faithfully and
cleans up his ancestors through okiyome or by making contributions to the church, their spirit levels will rise in the other world.
He can even give okiyome to the corpses of his deceased parents
and spare them from suffering the same fatal afflictions when they
are reborn in the next life. Filial piety of this sort will naturally
win the ancestors' approval. The ancestors, for their part, can take
revenge for ritual omissions by possessing their descendants. In
some cases, they may randomly take revenge on their descendants
for offenses committed by strangers in their own generation. Because the descendant in such a case had nothing to do with the
offense, possession serves an exonerating or etiological function.
Sometimes the ancestors simply declare that they are attracted to
their descendants' amulets and want to get cleaned up. On the positive side, the ancestral spirits can act as guardians, ensuring the
happiness and well-being of their descendants.

This system of ritual exchanges in effect distributes guilt and responsibility in a way that is quite foreign to Western notions. One's
misfortunes and failures need not be borne alone, since those in the
spirit world share the responsibility. In other words, responsibility
is partially shifted to an external cause, reducing individual guilt.
On the other hand, *surplus* guilt and responsibility (the Problem)
is placed on the living because they must provide for the well-being
of ancestors in the astral world. The boundaries of the ego are
therefore conceived differently from the way Westerners or secular
Japanese might see them. Because the traditional concept of karma

literally "con-fuses" the sins of the individual and his family in past incarnations and in the present, it extends the ego both through time (through successive incarnations) and through a more intimate identification with the family. The creation of surplus guilt and responsibility that results is alleviated by ritual mechanisms that improve a person's karma (the Way). In Mahikari, these mechanisms are okiyome, rearranging the family's butsudan according to proper rules, and apologizing for any errors in ritual practices.

When mistakes are found in their butsudan, people are expected to apologize to their ancestors. Apology for ritual omissions, it should be added, is apology par excellence. Rarely do people apologize for moral sins or shortcomings. Apology therefore tends to be restricted to infringements of ritual norms and should not be confused with confession as we use the word in the West.

Indeed, the public confession of specific moral sins is avoided in Mahikari. Ritual apologies, moreover, entail no real loss of face, since they are not tied to individual responsibility in a social or moral context.

Ancestors also apologize. After being scolded by an exorcist, they often shed copious tears (through the eyes of the subject receiving okiyome), and promise to stop bothering the living and return immediately to the Fourth Dimension. Both kinds of apology—the descendants' apology for neglecting their butsudan and the ancestors' apology through the "sympathetic weeping" (*morainaki*) of their descendants—have potential cathartic value. Apologizing for ritual mistakes frees people both from guilt and from the checkmate of karma, restoring the flow of normative exchange relations between ancestors and their descendants. As a result, the family's karma improves, diseases are cured, good fortune returns, and so on. Okiyome can therefore be thought of as a ministry of reconciliation between the living and the dead. Given the historical religious traditions of Japan, the restoration of proper filial piety can have very gratifying therapeutic effects. No wonder ancestor worship is such an important ingredient in so many of the country's New Religions.

The word catharsis, meaning a purging or cleansing, is simply the Western (actually Greek) equivalent of the Japanese word okiyome.

The therapeutic value of catharsis—whether induced by psychiatric abreaction, electro- or insulin-convulsive therapy, sodium amytal, sodium pentothal, sexual orgasm, or religious ritual, to name a few well-traveled routes—requires no documentation here. In Mahikari, the nervous collapse following a violent spirit seizure appears to be a cathartic experience, probably similar to the climactic stage of possession-trance in various religions around the world. In this state of emotional prostration, people are said to be hyper-suggestible, meaning that the words of surrounding authority figures seem especially vivid and important to them. Spirit investigations conducted under these conditions are likely to have strong therapeutic effects. Catharsis may also take place when an exorcist scolds a person's ancestors and takes his side against fate, and during sexual karma exorcisms, when women can indirectly express and, ideally, cleanse themselves of their resentment and fear of male domination. Since only 39 percent of the dojo members report having strong spirit movements, how many actually achieve a catharsis in the classic sense of the word is open to some doubt. It may be that catharsis sometimes works in quieter ways.

Okiyome also heals by restoring confidence. From the statistical survey we can conclude that for the majority of members, significantly altered states of consciousness and dissociation properly speaking are not the driving forces behind their conversion and spirit experience. After all, 23 percent have had no spirit movements whatsoever, and 61 percent report that their spirit movements have been weak. Since many of these "dry" (and older) members are leaders of the dojos, we must account for their commitment to Mahikari in other ways. What dissociation and catharsis do not achieve, a gradual socialization into the world of spirits and miracles does: thus these members display the same alteration of life and fortune and the same zealous commitment to the church. Their sense of confidence may be no more ecstatic than the feeling a jogger has after his daily run, but it does reassure them that they have found the key to long life, health, and happiness. Thus the typical dojo member is confident that okiyome not only cleans up the toxins he has already accumulated, but also prevents future disease and misfortune. The Treatment is thus both purge and prophylactic. Most members attribute their peace of mind to the mere possession of an amulet, which—as long as they do not forget it at home—keeps good luck coming their way.

Finally, okiyome helps create a new persona. When people become members of the dojo, they literally open the door to personal recognition. Everyone who enters the dojo is ritually greeted by those in the room. Likewise when each person leaves, he is saluted with the words *gokurōsama deshita*, "thanks for all of your help." However much he may need help himself, each person is made to feel that he has helped someone else. Now that he too can perform miracles, he can be a "little Buddha" or a "little Christ," roles that naturally heighten his self-esteem. Members who have dramatic, entertaining, or emotionally moving miracles to report at the monthly festival naturally attract much attention. Likewise, the discovery of a spirit story helps create a new public image for the person within the religious community. At receptions held for new members, the older members are introduced along with their spirits: "Wakimoto Kanako, possessed by a samurai who died four hundred years ago," or "Watanabe Mariko, a girl who was possessed by two hundred fox spirits from a shrine in Kyoto." The possessing spirit thus enriches the new persona. Over 45 percent of the members are eventually given some position of responsibility in the dojo, further enhancing their feeling of importance.

Okiyome itself plays a vital role in the discovery of a person's new identity. Before the person can get cleaned up, he must recognize that his spirit level is very low. As he gets cleaned up, his spirit level goes up, his luck improves, and miracles abound. The new Mahikari persona is therefore based not just on a ghost story, but on a success story as well. Okiyome is a ritual process whereby a person's dignity and worth are rediscovered and affirmed. The ritual's effectiveness is greatly increased by the subject's feeling that someone cares enough to reprimand the evil spirits plaguing him. At last, someone is on his side.

The new persona often extends to a new spiritual identity for the whole family. Since the social status of a Japanese family traditionally rests on the mythological status of its ancestors, a ritual that cleans up ancestors and raises their spirit level in the Fourth Dimension obviously promotes the upward mobility of their descendants in the Third. The discovery of this new individual and collective persona may have healing effects for many members of the dojo.

What really happens in okiyome? Something different each time it is given. Yoshida Sensei would explain this by saying that every evil spirit has its own will and bag of tricks. An outsider, however, might attribute this variety of religious experience to the predispositions, personal histories, and imagination people bring to the ritual. However we explain it, the reactions people have to okiyome clearly range from hypoaroused, semi-meditative states of tranquilization (externally similar to hypnotic lethargy or psychogenic stupor) on the one hand, to hyperaroused states of excitement and dissociation, and altered states of consciousness on the other. One might surmise, however, that what most people feel when they receive okiyome is not much different from what most Christians experience when they pray: very little. Of course, some Christians —for example, the Charismatics mentioned above—feel quite a lot when they pray. In this chapter I have suggested that they may even provide us with important psychological hints for understanding okiyome.

From the comparative point of view, we have seen that, like glossolalia, possession is part of a self-contained Salvation Syndrome. Although it is rooted in such unconscious psychological processes as dissociation, hypnotic suggestion, regression, and catharsis, it is also a solicited, controlled, systematic, induced, and learned form of behavior. Although it is statistically unusual in modern Japan, I have found no reason to regard this behavior as pathological.

Members of Sukyo Mahikari will not agree with much that I have said in this chapter. Even non-members who are wary of psychology might object that the psychological jargon I have used is as spooky as the testimonies it aims to explain. Admittedly, the concepts found in psychiatric textbooks (Id, Ego, and Superego, for example) are no more palpable than evil spirits. By turning to the arcane concepts of psychology, are we not violating Aristotle's venerable rule that the less known should be explained in terms of the better known?

In response, I can only say that what is less known or better known naturally depends on one's own range of experience and knowledge. The most helpful aspect of the psychological study of possession is its capacity to lead beyond itself into a comparative study that includes clinical and anthropological data alike. From the impressive literature that already exists, it is clear that the religious experiences of dojo members are related, mutatis mutandis, not only to glossolalia but to trance, ecstatic and meditative states of mind, shamanistic visions, hallucinatory revelations, personality transformation dreams, and other altered states of consciousness.

I am aware that the technical psychological terms I have used function primarily as labels to tag similar psychological and religious phenomena, and that to label something is not the same as to explain it. The advantage psychological language offers, compared with the theological descriptions given by church members, is not that it tells us what really happens in okiyome. It is no better equipped than Mioshie to distinguish between reality and illusion. I would argue, however, that because of its comparative thrust, a psychological approach gives us more powerful tools for dealing with possession and exorcism both as general phenomena and as phenomena with specific psychosocial environments generally ignored by theological discourse.

Taking my clues from Mesmer, Freud, and their followers, I have treated possession and exorcism in this chapter as psychosocial phenomena. I have tried to give the theory of projection more specific content than it usually receives in religious studies by relating it to the clinical concepts of dissociation and hypnosis. Where possible, I have also tried to show how these psychological categories mesh with experiences that one thinks of as typically Japanese, for example, by relating hypnotic regression to a ritualization of amae-type relations. I part company with Freud only when he naïvely assumes that an absolute distinction can be made between reality and the "collective illusions" of religion; for reality is no simple thing. Although the concepts generated by Freud and other psychologists may fall short of genuine scientific explanation, they enable us to comprehend the basic similarities in the transitions we make when we move from the workaday world of common sense into the realms of art, religion, and mental darkness.

9 Women and Their Sexual Karma

One of the salient features of the New Religions is the large percentage of women in their rank and file. Since my survey questionnaires were distributed on a Sunday, when most of the male members could be present, we can assume that the percentage of women who replied to the survey (62 percent) is a good indication of their representation in Mahikari as a whole. Women have always played a major part in Japanese religion. Even in the Shinto tradition, though women are generally excluded from the public celebration of rituals, they play crucial roles in the organizations charged with festival preparations. Since prehistoric times, women have functioned as mediums and shamanistic healers. Many of the New Religions were founded by charismatic women and only later were organized by male leaders and ecclesiocrats. Even today, most of the people who visit mediums and healers because of spirit possession are said to be women.[1]

There are several reasons for this significant involvement of women in religious affairs. Excluded from public rituals as they have been from public life in general, women have specialized in, and relied heavily on, the private functions of religion, such as divining, consoling, and curing. Today, because of the flexibility in her schedule, the Japanese wife, who is often unemployed, may be freer than her husband to attend religious services. Women in general continue to have a reputation for having deeper religious emotions and a keener sensitivity to the supernatural than men.[2]

In Mahikari, for example, when members were asked which sex they thought was more likely to have more spirit seizures, 54 percent said women, and 15 percent men; 31 percent said that both sexes are equally possessible. Both male and female members regard women as more possessible, but as might be expected, a higher percentage of men than women hold this opinion (men, 62 percent; women, 49 percent).* The survey confirmed the accuracy of members' expectations: women *do* have more spirit seizures ($r = .22$; $p = .001$), and more intense spirit seizures ($r = .20$; $p = .001$), than men. A greater percentage of women than men suffer from multiple possession and from possession by ancestral spirits, unrelated human spirits, and animal spirits. Also, more women than men are possessed by their spouse's ancestors (35 percent to 14 percent).†

This chapter examines the religious experiences of some of the women in the Nakayama dojo. I must stress from the outset that my purpose is not to psychoanalyze these women. For that I have neither the necessary credentials nor sufficient data. Rather, by placing the stories of their spirit seizures in the context of their concrete life situations—and by making what Clifford Geertz calls "clinical inferences"—I shall try to explain and interpret the significance of their experiences.[3] When possible, I shall also relate their experiences to the analytical framework established in Chapter 8. Since most of the women I interviewed had joined Mahikari because of illness, a subject dealt with in detail in Chapter 7, this chapter concentrates on the specific problems of being a woman in Japanese society and the ways in which Mahikari deals with these problems.

My specific interest is in the years a Japanese woman spends between graduation from high school and the birth of her first child —years that can be among the most trying in her life. Following the anthropologist Arnold Van Gennep, we can consider these years

---

*It is curious that those who expect men to be more possessible than women tend to have more possession experiences themselves. The sex of these respondents was not sufficient to account for this difference. We can therefore postulate that these people associate possession with masculinity (or perhaps seriousness) in order to gain social approval for themselves. Trafficking with evil spirits is not something for sissies!

†On the other hand, men are more likely than women to be possessed by their own ancestors (86 percent to 65 percent).

an extended transition period that is divisible, like rites of passage, into three stages: (1) *separation* from the person's previous station in life; (2) a period of *liminality*, when the person, now between statuses, has an anomalous position on the periphery of society; and (3) *reincorporation* into new roles rewarded with enduring prestige and social status.[4]

Until high-school graduation, the social role and identity of the typical Japanese girl is relatively secure. Generally, she is part of a close and supportive network of structured relationships at home, at school, and among her friends. At about the time of graduation, however, she is separated from many of these personal ties and embarks on a short career characterized by temporary social roles and positions. During this liminal period, whether she goes to college, works in a factory or office, or simply stays at home, her status is somewhat nebulous. Because she is regarded as a social and economic transient, expected to leave her job or position as soon as she can marry, even a career-minded woman is not taken very seriously. Only after she has become someone's *okusan* (wife), has adjusted to her new family, and has had a child, is she fully reincorporated into society. Although marriage may not signal everlasting bliss or the end of her personal development, generally it is only after she is married that a woman feels secure in her status and identity.

Since in Japan a woman's social standing is largely determined by her domestic status, the greatest threat a young Japanese woman faces is the possibility of ending up an old maid. Young women often enjoy the first few years of their new lives as students, store clerks, or factory workers, despite their marginal position in society. But if a woman reaches twenty-five and still has no marriage prospects, she begins to worry. Hints and less subtle pressures from family and friends may turn worry into sheer panic. Although romantic love is accepted in post-war Japan, chances to mingle freely with members of the opposite sex outside one's place of work are limited. Young people therefore must often depend on formal and informal intermediaries to help them become acquainted. Under these circumstances, dating is often stiff, awkward, and embarrassing.

Few women pass through these liminal years without heartaches, but on the other hand, few experience really serious traumata. As during other times of transition, society mercifully provides the individual with approved ritual activities that make the passage endurable, and even pleasant. In Japan, women at this stage of life generally participate in what might be called "rituals of refinement." As though to symbolize both good breeding and availability, some take lessons in one or more of the traditional arts, such as the tea ceremony, flower arranging, the samisen or koto; others try their hand at Western arts, such as painting or playing the piano. Overnight, the most blushing and plodding "Hanako san" becomes a whirlwind of culture. Even girls who do not go to college practice these rituals of refinement. Work in an office or factory is often legitimated as a good experience that will make a girl a better wife and mother. In this way, work of marginal significance is beautified as a ritual activity that will prepare her for marriage.

The following quotation is from an interview with a young woman from a blue-collar family who was working as an OL (Office Lady) in a large company. It is an excellent example of the aspirations of a "neo-traditional" woman at this stage of life.

As for me, I have no special person in mind, but I have a dream of marriage. It is stronger now than when I was graduating from high school. My dream is to create a warm atmosphere in a home even if it turns out to be a humble home. To find someone, first I must polish myself. That is what I am doing now. I am improving myself so that I can find an ideal husband.[5]

Today, about 21 percent of Japanese women enter regular four-year colleges. More often they go to junior colleges, where women make up 86 percent of enrollments.[6] The laxity and formalism of most higher education in Japan make college an excellent place to practice the rituals of refinement. Like office work, education often becomes a ritual in itself. What more pleasant Bridge of Dreams could the young, middle-class Hanako san take to cross the emotional abyss of her nubile years?

This chapter deals chiefly with less fortunate women who, for lack of time, money, talent, or good looks, are not successful in practicing the rituals of refinement, or who, because of the alleged influence of malignant spirits, otherwise fail to find happiness in marriage. For such women these marginal years are filled with broken engagements and estrangement from parents and lovers, not to mention unhappiness with their jobs or college life. In extreme cases, the psychological pressures of the new situation may result in hysterical illnesses and neurotic or even psychotic behavior patterns.

More often, the maladjusted display less dramatic physical symptoms. For example, a survey conducted by a Japanese firm in 1976 concerning the health of its unmarried office girls in Osaka and Tokyo found that two out of every three of these women claimed to be ill: 67 percent of those twenty to twenty-four years old, and 69 percent of those twenty-five to twenty-nine. The principal maladies cited were stiff neck, menstrual pain, and constipation. Also mentioned were low blood pressure, allergy, headache, gastritis, and gastroptosis.[7] Many of these tension-related symptoms are identical with the complaints that bring women of this age to the dojo. The survey I conducted shows that around the age of twenty-two, there is a precipitous jump in the percentage of women who say they joined the church for reasons of health. Many women who do not join a New Religion turn to more traditional healers and exorcists. Carmen Blacker found that a large proportion of those who visit Buddhist temples for exorcism are "young housewives between the ages of twenty-five and thirty-five."[8]

My statistical survey clearly shows that in general, single members tend to have more, and more intense, possession experiences than married members. They are also more likely to experience repeated possession by the same spirit (see Table 4). But which is

Table 4. Types of Possession Experience by Marital Status

Category	Single		Married	
	Number	Percent	Number	Percent
Number of spirit movements				
Low	130	59%	238	66%
High	91	41	122	34
Intensity of spirit movements				
Weak	100	58%	137	64%
Strong	72	42	78	36
Experienced multiple possession	60	44%	86	40%

Table 5. Sexual Karma Possession by
Age Group and Marital Status

Age group	Members having sexual karma possession		Percent single
	Number	Percent	
0–17	14	44%	100%
18–22	30	47	98
23–29	33	43	55
30–39	27	28	13
40–56	23	17	7
57–65	4	11	7
66–	0	0	18 [a]

[a] Largely widows and widowers.

the more important influence on possession behavior, age or marital status? To answer this, we must look more closely at a kind of spirit possession of great importance to young people. We have already seen that the church explains the breakdown of romances, engagements, and marriage as the work of vengeful or lustful spirits, or as a result of bad sexual karma (shikijo innen). The statistical survey confirms what is generally recognized in the dojo, that sexual karma is significantly related to the victim's age and marital status. As Table 5 shows, this type of possession seems to be especially common among single people under thirty. At thirty, there is a sudden drop, both in the percentage of members who are still single and in the percentage troubled by sexual karma.

All told, 44 percent of the single members surveyed have been beset by bad sexual karma, compared with only 21 percent of the married members.* When we control for age and marital status, we find that being single definitely increases the incidence of sexual

---

* When we control for sex, we find that single members, male or female, tend to be more susceptible to sexual karma possession than married members. (See Appendix B, Table B.1.) Single members are also more likely to believe that their families have been possessed by an evil spirit than married members (32 percent to 21 percent). This finding probably reflects the suggestions made to single members by leaders, who try to explain away parental opposition to the church by intimating to the young person that his entire family is possessed by an evil spirit.

karma possession, and that being young increases it still more. This means that younger members tend to blame a broken engagement or a bad marriage on bad sexual karma. Older single members, however, are less likely to blame sexual karma—in spite of their failure to marry.

Judging from the comparatively passive role that tradition assigns to women in courtship *and* the social pressure put on them to find a mate, one would expect them to be more susceptible to sexual karma possession than men. This, in fact, is the case. Thirty-four percent of the women members, but only 20 percent of the men, have suffered from sexual karma possession.[9] Thus women are more susceptible than men, whether they are single or married.[10]

Before we turn to the spirit stories of young women victimized by bad sexual karma, let us look at the story of what the Japanese call an "Old Miss" or "High Miss," that is, a woman who has never married. Hers, after all, is the fate that every young Japanese woman fears most.

An "Old Miss"

Nakata Michiko is a diminutive, rather plump lady of fifty-four who lives by herself in a small room on the first floor of the dojo. Every day she can be seen bustling about the dojo in strange floor-length dresses of indeterminate shape. Miss Nakata was born and raised in Seoul, Korea, where she was graduated from a Japanese high school. According to her mother (who also became a member of Mahikari), Michiko never did very well in school and used to fall asleep under her teacher's nose. After the family returned to Japan, Michiko (then twenty-three) tried to maintain herself in various ways. Unlike her elder sisters—one of whom became a physician in Tokyo, and the other, the owner of a button shop—she never was able to hold her own. When she joined Mahikari she was working in a camera shop and living on the edge of poverty. Hearing this, Yoshida Sensei decided to give her about $30.00 a month to give okiyome to people who dropped into the dojo during the day. On Wednesdays, when the building is closed, she goes about the city selling cosmetics.

Before one of her sisters introduced her to Mahikari, Miss Nakata used to go to a Protestant church. Although she thinks that the Savior, Okada, was greater than Jesus Christ, she continues to regard herself as a Christian. She likes to point out that when Jesus cast out evil spirits in the country of the Gerasenes (Luke 8:26–33), the spirits entered a herd of swine that went berserk and drowned themselves. Okada, on the other hand, was able to save not only demoniacs, but the demons themselves. She had always been impressed by Jesus's saying, "There is nothing outside a man which by going into him can defile him; but the things which come out of a man are what defile him" (Mark 7:15). It was only after she entered Mahikari that she began to understand what these internal defilements really are: evil spirits.

The day after she completed the intermediate training course, Miss Nakata had a spirit seizure that recurred each time she received okiyome during the next two weeks. The evil spirit possessing her was that of an older sister in a previous life. Bedridden with tuberculosis from the age of eighteen, this woman had died when she was only twenty-eight. Just before she passed away, she married a man who was willing to take her family name and thereby preserve her family's identity. Because of her unfortunate death, she became a malevolent ghost, possessing and killing off her own family, so that finally she had no one left to care for her own memorial tablet. As a result of her murderous career, she was demoted by Su-god and transformed into various animal spirits. Originally these animal spirits, which also possessed Miss Nakata, were "as big as elephants." Gradually, as she got cleaned up, they became smaller and smaller, until finally they seemed "no bigger than dragonflies." After two weeks of okiyome, her sister's spirit once again took on human shape, confessed all of her evil doings, and wept bitterly.

Before Miss Nakata joined Mahikari, she had always been sickly. "Once my abdomen became filled with water so that I looked pregnant," she said, stretching out her hands in front of her stomach. Finally, she had to go to her sister's clinic in Tokyo for an operation. She also had been afflicted with a serious cough. For years, wherever she was, whether on a streetcar or in the bathtub, once she started coughing she was unable to stop. After her elder sister's spirit apologized to Su-god, the cough disappeared. "It was this evil spirit who, because she could not be healthy and happily married herself, became jealous and caused me to be sick." The spirit also had caused her to remain single. "When I was younger I had some suitors. But either they grew tired of me or I of them. Sometimes a third party came into the picture. If only I had met Su-god two years earlier, I could have found a husband," she sighs to her friends.

Miss Nakata has had several other interesting spirit experiences. The spirit of a young man who broke his neck in a motorcycle accident has appeared to her several times. She has also been possessed by the spirits of aborted infants. Sometimes she has been possessed by as many as twenty animals at the same time, miserable creatures that perished in fires and earthquakes.

One year, on the day after the Obon (All Souls) Festival in midsummer, the ghost of Miss Nakata's grandmother appeared to her to complain that she was hungry. This surprised Miss Nakata, since Obon is a festival for worshiping and feeding the souls of all the departed. "Grandmother should be full," she thought to herself. Nevertheless, she sent a postcard to her mother to suggest that special offerings be placed before her grandmother's memorial tablet. "In spite of this, her ghost continued to appear every day. Finally, I decided to go home to see what was wrong. There I discovered that a member of our family who had converted to Soka Gakkai had wrapped grandmother's tablet in white cloth and put it away for storage. In its place stood a new tablet. Grandmother's spirit obviously had not moved into the new tablet. No wonder she was hungry!" Miss Nakata put the two tablets side by side to induce her grandmother to move from one to the other. At last the spirit received her offerings and "went away rejoicing."

In the summer of 1975, the seizures finally stopped. "The evil spirits were cleaned up the same way I was, through okiyome," she explained. In December of that year, she was made a member of the dojo's auxiliary cabinet (*junkanbu*) and vice-chairperson of the Helpers' Society.

Miss Nakata's spirit experiences at the dojo seem to be reflections of the traumata of the single woman. Although one can only guess the unconscious origins of these spirits, it would seem that possession by the spirits of aborted children—and a disease that made her look pregnant—might be symptomatic of her own frustrated desire to marry and bear children. It is not impossible that the spirit of the young man killed on a motorcycle was a would-be intended. But this is mere speculation. What is certain is that the appearance of an "elder sister" from a previous existence was a case of homeopathic possession. Possession by this spirit also explained why Miss Nakata was sick and never married (etiology), and removed all personal responsibility or guilt for her failure to find a husband (exoneration). It is curious that this "elder sister" married an "adopted husband." Miss Nakata's real elder sister actually did take an "adopted husband" in order to continue their family line.

Happily, the dojo has become both a home and an ersatz family for Miss Nakata. By giving okiyome to hundreds of people who visit the dojo every month, she feels that she is raising her own spirit level, so that in future lives she will avoid the same diseases and frustrations. Although she has come to terms with her fate through her religious experiences, her life is obviously no model the single young Japanese woman would want to emulate.

Young Single Women

The following case deals with a girl still too young to worry a great deal about marriage. Nevertheless, since a girl begins to think about her prospects early in adolescence, thoughts of marriage may loom behind this case too. I cite it here at length, both because of its dramatic interest and because it is an excellent example of the folkloric quality of the spiritual autobiographies popular in Mahikari. This version of the story is my reconstruction of details provided by Yoshida Sensei and Miss Watanabe herself on several occasions.

Sometimes a physical irregularity, however slight, can cast a shadow over a young woman's entire self-image. Although I could never muster the courage to ask her, I had the suspicion that this was true of Watanabe Mariko. Miss Watanabe, a young lady of nineteen, is remarkably plump. She also has a large gap between her two front teeth that causes her to speak with an occasional whistle. Whatever the reason, as soon as she entered Nakayama Commercial High School, Mariko began to hate herself, feeling that she was a weakling with no real purpose in life, but with a great fear of death. For some time there were also (unspecified) problems in her family. To escape from all of this, Mariko threw herself into the activities of several high school clubs. But even there, though she had a wide circle of friends, she had no one to whom she could freely unburden herself.

Mariko was introduced to Mahikari by a friend and took the training course in November 1974. Although she claims to have entered the sect "out of curiosity," she experienced a healing miracle soon after she joined. This occurred when a doctor informed her that she had kidney stones. After taking X rays, he declared that she needed an operation. To make sure, he wanted to take more X rays the next day. Her parents, who from the beginning had adamantly opposed her religious activities, urged Mariko to have the operation. When she argued that Su-god would heal her, her mother finally agreed to let her postpone the operation, thinking that, after all, a religious cure would be cheaper than a medical one. The next day, after going to the dojo for okiyome, she went back to the hospital for more X rays. This time not a trace could be found of the stones. After this "miracle," Mariko's mother reluctantly allowed her to continue going to the dojo, but warned her that she should not let her father know about it. To this day, she tells me, her greatest sorrow is that she cannot go home and tell her parents about the "marvelous" spirit seizures she has at the dojo. Were it not for her parents, she would become a minister of Mahikari. Yoshida Sensei believes that her parents must be under the influence of a malicious ghost, and points out that because they will not allow Mariko to rearrange their butsudan, the Watanabes' ancestors are still in agony in the astral world. Gradually, however, they are being saved by her discipline at the dojo.

So loyal has Mariko become that whenever she goes out to enjoy herself, she begins to feel guilty for not being at the dojo. Yoshida Sensei believes that absenting herself from the dojo causes her spirit level to go down, and that this, and not some adolescent identity crisis, is what causes her to hate herself. Although Sensei gives her credit for persevering in spite of her parents' hostility, both he and Mariko believe that her spirit is still at a low level. Sometimes, when the Youth Corps goes out to put on a testimonial meeting, she becomes possessed by "loitering ghosts." When she was still in high school, she once became possessed in the classroom, and all of her friends thought she had lost her mind. "People who don't know Mahikari just don't understand these things," she complains.

Sometimes, Mariko does things that she can only attribute to the influence of evil spirits. Once, for example, she refused to carry out orders from a superior at the bank where she now works. Another time, she did not feel like going to work and stayed at home without bothering to call the bank. Her employer phoned her at home and threatened to fire her if this behavior continued. When her mother heard about it, she went straight to the dojo to complain. "You must help me," she said to Mrs. Yoshida. "Mariko is just too big for me to handle."

Because of her low spirit level, Mariko is constantly surrounded by evil spirits waiting to attack. No sooner is one spirit cleaned up and sent back to the astral world than another jumps into her body to take its place. Fortunately, none of them seem to make her ill or cause any serious problems.

Mariko's spirit seizures are dependably dramatic. Once, when one of the ministers was giving her okiyome, she crawled with slow, sluglike motions to the side of the room and started to go up the wall. As she began her ascension, she beat her head against the wall. To keep her from injuring herself, the minister—all the while giving her okiyome with his right hand—held a pillow behind her head with his left. When she began to pull out the cord to the electric ceiling fan, he gently took it from her hand. Another member quickly removed a stack of towels when he saw that she was about to mount it. On at least one occasion, she fell to the floor of the dojo with a crash that shook the whole room, and lay there several minutes as though reduced by the spirits to a heap of defeated humanity. When this happened, the ministers had to pronounce the benediction over her several times before the spirits would leave her in peace.

After one violent seizure that left Mariko looking especially haggard, I asked her what had happened. She replied:

Oh, a badger spirit has been possessing me. Actually, in its previous life this animal was a human being who belonged to another New Religion and tried to sabotage Mahikari. Because he had put himself in the service of a secondary deity, Su-god changed him into an animal spirit. Whenever I am possessed by spirits who sincerely want to be saved, I feel relaxed when I leave the dojo at night. I only get worn out after I have been possessed by a spirit bearing a grudge or by one who wants to do some harm. My own spirit level is higher nowadays, so that when I go home I am no longer as wiped out by spirit experiences as I used to be.

In fact, after her spirit seizure is over, Mariko usually bustles around the dojo, helping on various projects, chatting with people, and acting genuinely pleasant and happy. Formerly, she used to ponder the spirit seizures she had had at the dojo when she went to work the next day. But now she seldom thinks about them after she leaves the dojo. In general, her seizures are becoming less severe. Whereas she used to try to run away from her problems, she feels that during the past year she has learned to face them directly. She is still insecure about her status at the bank and even at the dojo. Although she is still young and unengaged, Mariko believes that were she to marry now, the heavy clouds still overshadowing her soul would cause the marriage to break up. Nevertheless, she does hope to marry one day—preferably someone who has already been cleaned up.

Mariko's most dramatic spirit adventures were caused by a pack of fox spirits from a Shinto shrine. Some time ago, she went with a group from the dojo to a suburb of Nakayama to put on a testimonial meeting. When she received okiyome at the dojo the next day, an evil spirit caused her to cross her arms and legs and sit like a man, haughty and proud. It even made her criticize Su-god. When the benediction was pronounced, the evil spirit refused to settle down. Yoshida Sensei changed places with her exorcist and gave her the benediction himself. Still no results. And so he began to interrogate the spirit. A fox spirit from the Fushimi-Inari Shrine on the south side of Kyoto made its appearance. No ordinary vulpine, the evil spirit boasted that he had 200 retainers of his own.

"If you're so great, why bother to come down to our dojo?,"

Sensei asked the fox. The fox finally admitted that he was hungry. In the old days, he used to be worshiped and fed fried bean curd by merchant families in Kyoto. Now neglected, he had been attracted to Mariko's amulet.

"I thought that if I came here, someone would give me something to eat," the fox confessed. "What is more, if you don't give me a drink, I'm going to beat Mariko up."

"I'm not going to give you a drink just because you tell me to," Sensei objected. Then he thought again, and proposed this to the fox: "If you want a drink, you must begin to serve Su-god and start to behave yourself."

The fox thought for a while. "Very well, I'll be good," he promised.

"This is quite a turnabout," Yoshida Sensei thought to himself. After all, the fox was a messenger of one of the secondary deities.

As it happened, at that time Yoshida was giving lectures for a training course in one of the suburbs of the city. On this, the second day of the course, one member of the class, a certain Mr. Suzuki, had not shown up. Here was a way to test the real intentions of the fox. Sensei explained to the fox what the three-day course was all about and told him how Suzuki had failed to come to the second lecture. "Make him come back tomorrow, and I'll give you some sake," he challenged the fox. The fox agreed, and Yoshida Sensei pronounced the benediction over Mariko.

An hour later a telephone call came for Sensei. It was Suzuki calling to say that something unforeseen had come up that day, making him miss the lecture. He apologized and promised to come the next day. Yoshida Sensei was amazed. "Here is clear proof of the strength of animal spirits," he thought.

The next day, Suzuki appeared as promised. So did Watanabe Mariko, who had agreed to help out with the refreshments served on the final day of the course. When she met Sensei at the door, she had a weird grin on her face. "Today I get my drink," she laughed.

Sensei thought that she was acting a little spooky, but he said, "Very well, I'll give you okiyome after the lecture is finished, and then you can have a little drink."

After the session was over, small cups of sake were distributed to all of the new members. When the toast was made, Mariko snatched up two cups. "One for me and one for the fox," she chortled. Yoshida thought that this was strange, since Mariko seldom drinks. After she had finished her two cups, she went about the room with her tray, collecting used cups from the other members. Whenever she found some sake left in a cup, she lifted it to her lips and quickly drained it. When Yoshida saw this disgraceful behavior and tried to stop her, Mariko's eyes flashed with rage. She began to run about the room in a tantrum and finally had to be tackled and held down. Sensei immediately gave her okiyome, and the fox appeared once again.

"You promised, you promised," whined the fox. "Give me some more!"

"Oh no," Yoshida replied, "you're now in Miss Watanabe's body, and the sake will harm her."

I should pause here to explain that during the training sessions, the Light of Su becomes exceedingly intense, causing evil spirits to become quite thirsty. This is why the fox, parched as he was, became so enraged.

"More, more!," he shouted.

"Very well," Yoshida conceded at last. "I'll give you one more cup, but that's all." He filled another cup and gave it to Mariko, who downed it in a gulp. "You certainly have an odd way of drinking," Yoshida chided the fox. "You can't even taste the sake when you swig it down so fast." As though to spite him, Mariko—or rather the fox—slowly and sensuously licked the outside of the cup. Finally, when the fox said he had had enough, Yoshida pronounced the benediction.

The office of the dojo is merely a small corner in the back of the hall marked off by movable room dividers. One evening, some members looked over these partitions and noticed someone in the office drinking a large bottle of sake. When they rushed in to see what was going on, they found Mariko guzzling from the bottle. Because of the girl's size and strength, they were unable to get the bottle away from her. Finally, Yoshida himself came into the office and grabbed it from her. He reprimanded the fox for thinking he could drink the dojo's sake at will: "If you keep doing bad things like this, Miss Watanabe will get sick, and you yourself will be punished by God." Even though animal spirits are not too bright, the fox finally seemed to understand. He even agreed to desert the god Inari and start working for Su. The fox was very happy with this arrangement and returned to the shrine in Kyoto, together with his 200 underlings, to turn in his resignation.

A week passed, and again Mariko was at the dojo to receive oki-yome. This time she had an especially violent seizure and began to blaspheme Su-god. Her exorcist became so upset that Yoshida Sensei was asked to take over. It was the fox again, in spite of his promise to reform. It turned out that when he had returned to the shrine at Fushimi-Inari, his boss—an even more powerful fox in Inari's employ—was extremely put out by his conversion to Su-god. The boss scolded the fox for agreeing to work for Su, and with the help of other foxes at the shrine, pummeled the wretch until he agreed to come back to work for his old master, Inari. Thus it seemed that this time he had returned to Nakayama bearing a grudge against the dojo for getting him into such a mess. Because the other foxes had beaten him up, the fox had come back to hurt Miss Watanabe and do battle with Su himself. The purification went on for some thirty minutes. No matter that Yoshida said, the fox would not listen. All the while, Mariko was having violent stomach cramps and crying out for help. Yet, every few minutes she would begin to roar with laughter, in spite of her pain.

"Now I bet you know how strong I am!," the wicked fox shouted with glee.

By this time, Mariko was causing such a rumpus that everyone in the dojo dropped what he was doing to watch. Many thought the fox would kill her. Later, even Yoshida admitted that he too had been worried. He prayed to Su-god to deliver her from the fox. Suddenly the spirit began to complain about being too hot and started to blow on Mariko's arms and legs as though he were burning up. Mariko picked up a floor cushion and pressed it against her body as thought she were trying to put out invisible flames. Suddenly she let out a cry so loud that everyone in the room turned pale. At last the fox became quiet and stopped moving. Su-god had destroyed the evil creature with fire!

The following week, when Mariko was receiving okiyome, other foxes appeared. Again she developed violent stomach cramps and ran around the dojo as though she had lost her mind. A spirit investigation revealed that these foxes were the retainers of the original fox, who had now come, true samurai that they were, to take revenge on behalf of their martyred lord. "Attack, attack!," they shouted. As soon as Su-god's fire became too hot for them, they ran away. Those who lingered were summarily destroyed by the fire.

Both in high school and after joining Mahikari, Miss Watanabe evidently dealt with her low self-esteem by plunging into various group activities. For her, the dojo seems to be a community where she can gain the approval (and perhaps the attention) that she does not get at home. By raising the spirit level of her ancestors through her religious discipline, she actually may be seeking their approval in her fight with her parents over Mahikari. This legitimation is extremely important, since ancestors symbolize the superego of the family and the individual alike. Their supernatural approval has been reinforced by Yoshida Sensei's suggestion (and Mariko's own belief) that her parents are under the influence of bad karma and evil spirits. Thus, in part, her spirit seizures may be a ritualization of the rebellion of late adolescence.

What is striking about her testimony is its entertaining, folkloric quality. Miss Watanabe's literally enchanted life has virtually become a folktale. The foxes that possessed her are essentially the same tricksters found in Japanese folklore. Because foxes play such an important role in Japanese folk religion, and in Mahikari in particular, I will digress for a moment to say something more about them.

Anyone who has seen a statue of the white fox that acts as the messenger of the god Inari cannot fail to have noticed its phallic character. According to Sino-Japanese legends, the fox is a creature of yin. In order to become a complete "celestial fox" and fly off to heaven, it needs to acquire a yang element. It is this thirst for yang that lies behind the central mythologem of the folktales about the fox: the story of the fox that transforms itself into a beautiful young woman in order to seduce a young man. The fox-maiden typically meets her prey in some obscure place, perhaps on a country road at dusk, and takes him off to some wonderful, faraway place where they marry, have children, and live together in great rapture. Later, the fox-maiden assumes her true vulpine shape and disappears. The young gentleman, left in the lurch, awakens from the fox's spell, only to find himself eating rotten leaves or going about on all fours like an animal. Sometimes he awakens in an open grave, or finds himself sitting in a cemetery, his wife, children, wealth, and palaces all a mirage. Exposed to the laughter and ridicule of his neighbors, he finally dies from shame and disgrace—and from the loss of semen (that is, yang), which is all the fox-maiden wanted from him.

Thus the popular theme of bewitchment by foxes seems to derive from the notion that "the person who experiences the orgasm first loses a unit of life essence and if the partner can restrain orgasm this unit is absorbed."[11] A deficiency in such energy can be made up only by receiving a complementary dose from another person. For this reason the fox, desiring to become immortal, seduces young men in order to absorb their vital sexual energy. When the fox disappears, it takes with it the life force of its victim, who accordingly must soon die.

The symbolism of the fox, though complicated, is undeniably sexual in nature. The fox symbolizes fertility and abundance. On the other hand, it also symbolizes the mirage of love: love without an object, the waste of sexual substance, impotence and humiliation. The famous cartoon by the twelfth-century Tendai abbot Toba Sōjō shows a fox stroking a "tail" drawn up between its legs.[12] It does not take a psychiatrist to suggest that the "fox-fire" (*kitsune-bi*) emitted from the end of its "tail" is semen. Now, in medieval China and Japan, masturbation (for this *is* what we are talking about) was considered as debilitating as it was in nineteenth-century Europe and America. Ilza Veith points out that

in men it was believed that the semen carried the essential life force and that, at birth, each male was endowed with a specific quantity. Each ejaculation expended a portion of this vital essence which could never be fully replenished. . . . Because of this intense concern with the preservation of semen, an irresistible urge towards masturbation and nocturnal emissions was usually interpreted as the work of vengeful spirits who took the shape of seductive young women and even pursued their victims in dreams. The consequent psychic disturbances were doubtless often due to fear of the dire effects which followed the irreplaceable loss of vital substance.[13]

Although I would hesitate to say how much, if any, of the erotic side of this fox lore entered into the unconscious generation of Miss Watanabe's spirit seizures, it is clear that because of the richness of traditional lore about the fox, the evil creatures that possessed her had the symbolic *potential* for expressing a wide range of desires and fears: abundance, fulfillment, fertility, and childbirth, on the one hand; humiliation, impotence, poverty, sickness, and death on the other. The analysis of these themes is complicated by the fact that though women are commonly possessed by foxes, most of these tales are told from a man's point of view. Tales about foxes, therefore, often reflect fears of losing one's wife, prestige, wealth, and above all, semen (as in wet dreams or masturbation, where the beloved is an illusion). Common in the bewitching of both sexes, however, are the themes of impotence and deception.

I suspect that the innumerable spirits that have possessed Miss Watanabe and are still waiting to possess her may satisfy her need for new experience. I tend to believe that in her case, these foxes are not so much projections of unconscious dilemmas or desires as they are non-homeopathic catalysts for the cleansing of her own spirit. Thus they function as dramatic occasions, excuses, or moments of (somewhat stereotyped) cathartic experiences in which emotional and physical energy is released. Whatever the case—and these remarks are merely speculation—it does seem that by means of spirit possession experiences patterned after the drama and denouement of a folktale, her own lackluster existence has acquired a "plot." She has found a new persona, as well as the reason (or etiology) for her unhappiness. She therefore has hope for a better life through Mahikari. In spite of the foxes' mischief, there is still time for her to get cleaned up and find herself a nice young man.

The next case is that of a young woman who suffered from mental illness. When Najita Kayako was twenty-two, she was engaged and about to be married. One month before her wedding day, she suffered a mental breakdown, was hospitalized, and was pronounced schizophrenic. This was to happen four times. Every time there was talk of marriage, she suffered a relapse. When she was released from the hospital, she visited mediums to inquire about her prospects for marriage and the cause of her illness. After all, there were no other cases of mental illness in her family. Perhaps it was a curse. One of the mediums told her that a certain ancestor of hers had died some time ago without marrying. If she wanted to get married, she would have to become reconciled with this spirit. "Don't have just one chat with him," the medium advised. "Talk things over with him in a leisurely way and get his approval for your marriage. Then he will stop bothering you."

When she heard this, Kayako began to study her family register and discovered that, in fact, her great-great-uncle Denmatsu had gone to America and died there at the age of twenty-seven, before he could marry. "Since he died without leaving any heirs," she thought to herself, "his spirit must still be attached to this world."

After Kayako was released from the hospital for the third time, she and her mother joined Tenrikyō, one of the largest of Japan's New Religions. Kayako even took a lengthy training course at the sect's headquarters in Tenri City near Nara. In 1976, when she was released from the hospital for the last time, she read a magazine article about Mahikari and took the elementary and intermediate training courses. Her mother later joined too, but continued to believe in Tenrikyo as well. Kayako admits that the two religions are similar, but feels that Mahikari's teachings about spirits are clearer. After she began to receive okiyome, the spirit of her great-great-uncle began to appear, just as the medium had predicted. Now, at the age of twenty-nine, she has made her peace with this spirit and once again is engaged to be married. This time, because she can talk freely with her fiance, she is not afraid of a relapse.

While Kayako is recuperating, Yoshida Sensei has allowed her to live on the first floor of the dojo with Miss Nakata. She has decided not to work until she is married, so that she can avoid upsetting situations. She is now quite happy, especially since she has the opportunity to talk with so many different people as she raises her hands at the dojo.

Miss Najita's story shows again how close dojo members are to the folk religion of their country. Although the spirit of her great-great-uncle appeared to her at the dojo, it was a medium having no connection with the dojo who first suggested its existence. (Later on, a Mahikari minister warned Kayako never to visit the medium again.) Her homeopathic spirit possession helped her understand the reason for her illness and failure to marry. The experience also seems to have been an exoneration: she herself was not to blame for her misfortune. Now she knows that there is something she can do to break the hold of bad karma: through okiyome she can get cleaned up, get married, and find happiness.

One of the most dramatic stories of sexual karma possession was told to me by Katada Toyoko. Born twenty-nine years ago in a remote mountain village in the middle of the prefecture, Toyoko attended school only as far as the ninth grade. When she was in her early twenties, she quarreled with her mother and left home to live by herself in the city. Although she has had several jobs, she has yet to find a permanent position.

The greatest miracle she has experienced since joining Mahikari has been a divine deliverance from boyfriends whom she describes, without reserve, as "double-faced cheats and liars." All of them seemed "nice" at first, but in the end they turned out to be "real oddballs." Two even had criminal records and were being kept under surveillance by the police. Unsavory as they were, once she had become emotionally involved with one of these men, it was almost impossible for her to break off the relationship.

Her most recent lover was the worst of the lot. Each time she saw him coming to her apartment, she would try to run out the back door, since he always caused a commotion. One night he even tied her up and beat her. She was afraid that these scenes were making her a nuisance to the whole neighborhood. She began to wonder whether she was not under a curse of some sort. Finally, when things were getting completely out of hand, her elder sister (who has no special interest in spirits) took her to a Mahikari Purification Center on the north side of Nakayama City. There she talked with a minister who listened carefully to her story and told her that she was probably possessed by *many* evil spirits. If she wanted to "get saved" she should take the training course as quickly as possible. Toyoko took his advice and enrolled in the next course given at the dojo.

About two days after she had received her amulet, Toyoko's boyfriend waylaid her on the street and forced her into his car. She used to be mealy-mouthed around him, but with her new amulet, she felt more confident and put up some resistance. Enraged, he started to pull her hair and pummel her. Since they were still in the middle of the city, he decided to drive out to the coast where they could not be seen. By the time they reached the waterfront, it was dark, and not a soul could be seen for miles around. Once again he started to beat her up. Finally, he pulled out a knife and threatened to murder her on the spot. Just when she thought she was about to be killed, five policemen materialized out of nowhere and arrested her boyfriend on charges of assault with a deadly weapon.

Since this miracle occurred, Toyoko has had many spirit seizures at the dojo. Even before she took the training course, an older sister (who had died ten days after birth) appeared to her when she was receiving okiyome. At other times, foxes and other animal spirits have made their appearance. Through spirit interrogations, she has been able to piece together the story of her previous existence. It seems that during the Warring Countries period (1467–1568), Toyoko was born into an upper-class family and was known as Princess Saiyuri. The princess once stole the lover of one of her chambermaids. The miserable chambermaid then killed herself and became a malicious ghost. When Toyoko was reborn in the twentieth century, this spirit attacked her left leg and made it shorter than the other, causing her to walk with a slight limp. Later on, Princess Saiyuri became engaged to the younger of two brothers. But she was unfaithful to her fiance and married the elder brother. The younger brother hanged himself in despair, and like the chambermaid, returned from the astral world to possess Toyoko in her present life. During the spirit interrogations, the spirit of the younger brother spoke in classical Japanese, using words peculiar to the warrior class that Toyoko herself could not understand. It was after she was possessed by her ancient fiance that she began to argue with her mother and be fooled and manipulated by boyfriends.

Thanks to Su-god (and the police), Toyoko was finally able to get rid of her unwanted lovers. When I last talked with her, she was still living by herself. She now knows that her lovers have been inflicted on her because of the evil things she did in her previous existence. Before she gets married, she believes, she must get cleaned up, or she will get into trouble again.

The thaumaturgical powers of her amulet clearly gave Miss Katada the courage to get out of a destructive relationship. She does not seem interested in why she repeatedly got involved with men of this sort as a psychological question. For her it is enough to say that they were "double-faced cheats and liars." Only in the once-removed context of spirit experience did she seem to be able to wrestle with the question of personal guilt and responsibility. The fact that her spirit story makes her guilty in a past life for the misfortunes of the present may reflect the guilt she feels for having left home to set up her own apartment in the city—an action that most Japanese would not regard as proper behavior for young single women. It may even be a symbolic way of dealing with her own responsibility for getting involved with hoodlums in the first place. Finally, one wonders whether her possession story explaining why she was born with one leg shorter than the other was a reflection of her feelings of guilt, and fear of (need for?) punishment. About these things we can never be certain.

The last single woman I shall describe is Suzuki Tanio, a young woman of twenty-one. Tanio has been afraid of men since she was a child. To this day, she tries to avoid dates. If she must go out, she prefers the kind of group dates that are popular among young Japanese. Whenever she finds herself alone with a man, she feels paralyzed by fear. This paralysis, however, does not prevent her from pushing away a date who tries to touch her. Whenever she finds a boyfriend, they inevitably start to fight and finally break off the relationship. The very thought of marriage is irksome to her. Although there has been some talk about setting up an arranged marriage for her, she thinks that, feeling as she does, such a proposal at this point would be insulting to a man. If she must marry, she hopes she can find someone who will understand her, since as she acknowledges herself, she is a "little different" from most other women.

Tanio first came into contact with Mahikari when she injured her left hand. A distant relative of her mother was visiting the family at the time. When she heard about Tanio's injury, she said, "Here, let me try a little charm on you," and gave her okiyome. The woman described Mahikari's teachings about evil spirits to them, but Tanio and her mother felt that Mahikari was too frightening to get involved with. The next day, however, Tanio felt a strange desire to learn more about the religion. She contacted the relative and went with her to the dojo.

There, from the very beginning, Tanio experienced violent spirit seizures, falling down unconscious on the floor and saying things that she herself did not understand. When Yoshida Sensei saw how violent her seizures were, he told her, "Since you are under the influence of sexual karma, evil spirits will continue to interfere with your life until you get cleaned up." Thinking that her seizures were "strange" and "scary," she decided to take the training course at once. The following year (1976), she went on to take the intermediate course as well. When she receives okiyome, she has various reactions. Sometimes she has a "good feeling," but other times she suffers sheer agony. Once, while she was at work in a department store, she had a seizure that caused her to feel depressed and raise her hand "automatically" in the air. Fortunately, she was able to get control of this spirit herself without calling the dojo for help.

Spirit investigations have revealed that Tanio is being possessed by the spirit of a woman whose husband she stole in a previous existence. Whenever this spirit appears, her seizure is so violent that three people cannot hold her down. She has also been possessed by a rather vague spirit whose lover she stole in an earlier life. Once she was possessed by the spirit of a young man who returned from the astral world and fell in love with her. Aside from these major possession experiences, there have been a number of less serious ones, such as the appearance of the spirit of a cockroach she had accidentally stepped on and killed.

Before she joined Mahikari, Tanio was convinced that she was suffering from "neurotic androphobia" (*dansei kyōfusho*), as she put it. Now she realizes that her fear of men is the work of evil spirits, and ultimately, her own wicked deeds in a previous existence. She has often discussed her problem with one of the ministers, who has advised her to find a boyfriend who is a dojo member. He pointed out that evil spirits were causing her to get involved with men who were not members in order to drive her away from the dojo.

Even now, Tanio does not like herself. "When I was a child, I was honest, but after I grew up I became deceitful," she said. She is convinced that when she talks to people (she is, incidentally, a stutterer), she gives them a "bad feeling" because of her selfish and aggressive attitude. When she worked at the department store, she used to have fairly good relationships with her fellow clerks. But since she took her present position as an OL (Office Lady) at the electric company, she has become less patient and often has "explosions of stubbornness," sometimes clashing with her superintendent. In the training courses she learned that if she comes to the dojo every day, she can "absorb the Light" and raise her spirit level. Nevertheless, evil spirits sometimes make her feel that going to the dojo is unpleasant, and so her attendance is erratic at best. Shortly before our interviews, she was having a lot of trouble with a boyfriend and stayed away for two months.

Mrs. Suzuki opposes her daughter's involvement in Mahikari, especially when she returns from the dojo late at night. Because of her opposition, Tanio has not yet been allowed to rearrange the family's butsudan. Moreover, Mrs. Suzuki belongs to a sect that places more emphasis on the scroll hanging in the butsudan than on the memorial tablets themselves. When Tanio first started to go to the dojo, she used to return at night and tell her mother about her violent seizures. She also told her that she had been warned at the dojo that she might even be killed by evil spirits. Her mother found these tales appalling and suggested that the people at the dojo were trying to frighten her. Then Tanio started lying to her mother. When she went to the dojo, she would tell her mother that she had gone somewhere else. When she went to Mahikari festivals in Tokyo, she would tell her mother that she was visiting friends. Unfortunately, the evil spirit that Tanio assumes is possessing her mother saw through all of this. Nowadays, when she goes to the dojo, she no longer bothers to lie about it.

When I asked Tanio whether she had had any traumatic experiences as a child that might account for her abnormal fear of men, she told me the story of her family. For years, Su-god had brought financial difficulties on the family in order to make them atone for their sins. (The other members of the family, who are not Mahikari members, do not realize this.) Her parents were always quarreling, and when Tanio was in middle school they were legally separated, though they apparently had already been living apart. Tanio, a brother, and a sister were raised by their mother. Because her father was often drunk and violent, Tanio's mother kept her from seeing him, even when she wanted to. Since childhood, Tanio says, she hated him and hoped he would die. In 1973, while Tanio was on a trip, her father did die. After his death, he appeared to her twice while she was receiving okiyome. Because her older sister was married in 1976, Tanio's mother wants her to put off marriage and live with her for another three years.

The important role the dojo leaders play in suggesting various spirit solutions to people's problems is obvious throughout this case. It was Yoshida Sensei who told Tanio that she was suffering from bad sexual karma. It was at the dojo that she learned that her mother's opposition to the sect is the work of an evil spirit possessing her. Likewise, she accepted the suggestion that when she does not feel like going to the dojo, she is being misled by evil spirits. Nor did she reject a minister's suggestion that her problems with boyfriends are caused by spirits trying to take her away from the dojo. Whatever benefit these suggestions may have for individual members, they clearly help uphold the importance of the dojo as an institution in their lives.

For a woman suffering from a (self-diagnosed) case of androphobia, I was surprised at how freely Miss Suzuki discussed her problems with me and with a male minister. Her possession by the spirit of a young man who had fallen in love with her suggests that in spite of her fears, she hopes men will find her attractive. Her other spirit stories seem to be cases of retributive possession, whereby present misfortunes are explained in terms of her own misdoings in previous existences. When I suggested that her father's violence and her mother's possessiveness might have influenced the development of her androphobia, Tanio was skeptical. It was the anamnesis of her previous lives, not her childhood, that she found significant, and healing.

Having seen some of the ways in which evil spirits affect the lives of single women, we turn now to what happens when a woman marries.

A Young Married Woman

Araki Eiko is a short woman of twenty-nine, with coarse hair, tinted reddish-brown, that wants to stand up in any and all directions. As we spoke, her eyes moved restlessly, perhaps insecurely, about her.

After her graduation from high school, Eiko worked as an office girl, and later studied dressmaking for a year. When her father became ill, she gave this up and returned home to live with her parents. Worried about her prospects for marriage, she once telephoned a well-known clairvoyant in Yokohama. Without even seeing her face, the man seemed to know all about her and assured her that she would find a young man. She followed up her telephone call with a letter to which he responded, instructing her to visit the local headquarters of the "Sunshine Civilization Fellowship" on such-and-such a street in Nakayama City.

When she went to the address, she was confused, because the sign in front of the building said Sukyo Mahikari, the new name of the sect. Nevertheless, she thought it quite miraculous that the clairvoyant would know about this place, especially since he was not a Mahikari member himself. But when she went in to talk with the minister, she was quite disappointed. She had gone there hoping to find a husband, and all he wanted to talk about was how to worship her ancestors. In spite of this, she decided to take the training course held the following week (November 1974). Gradually her fixation on marriage began to disappear, and she became more relaxed. She gave more thought to her family's butsudan and how to help her ancestors in hell. She even gave some thought to becoming a minister herself, so that she could "save people." Her family was unhappy about this turn of events. "Instead of worrying about the butsudan, why doesn't she think about getting married?," they grumbled.

The family began to put more and more pressure on Eiko. Finally, she recalled—by this time sobbing so that she could hardly talk—they began to berate her openly. "No," she answered them, "marriage is not the same thing as happiness. With my new amulet I can make the whole world happy." In December of that year, she went to the Great Purification Festival held in Tokyo. During this festival, all participants are given envelopes for making contributions and prayers, which, they are assured, will be presented before Su-god by the Spiritual Leader herself. Prayers of this sort are guaranteed to be heard. Because her father was ill at the time, Eiko decided to pray for his recovery, and not for a husband. Su seemed to appreciate her selflessness, for the next month she met her husband-to-be.

Araki Yoshimitsu, a quiet and serious young man, is six years younger than his wife. Born and raised in the countryside near Kumamoto in Kyushu, he attended technical high school and then went to Osaka, where he worked for three years as a house painter. After that he moved to Nakayama City, where he continues to ply the same trade. Under his wife's influence, he took the Mahikari training course and has become extremely devout.

It was also under Eiko's influence that her parents and older sister finally took the training course. To receive their amulets, the whole family went to the Osaka dojo. After the ceremony, somebody gave okiyome to Eiko's little niece, who had come along to see her mother receive her amulet. Unfortunately, the girl suffered a violent spirit seizure and began to run around the floor of the dojo. Yoshida himself interrogated the spirit. The child's great-grandfather appeared and said that he wanted to be saved. "When I was alive, I was hated by the whole family," the spirit complained. "They were happy when I died. Now I've fallen into the deepest part of hell." Finally, after an hour of turbulence and interrogation, the benediction was pronounced. Although the child seemed to recover somewhat on the way home in the train, her mother and grandparents were appalled at what had happened to her. Yoshida Sensei tried to explain to them that without this kind of seizure, the child would still be possessed by the evil spirit without their even knowing it. Eiko also tried to allay their fears, and took advantage of the situation to warn them that if they did not change their butsudan right away, something dreadful would happen to the family.

By the time the train had arrived in Nakayama, the family seemed to be more or less pacified. But when they told the little girl's father what had happened, he became furious and forbade his wife ever to go to the dojo again. Shortly after this, Eiko's parents also stopped coming. They never have rearranged their butsudan. Eiko, of course, was deeply upset that her attempt to win her family for Mahikari ended so traumatically. Yoshida too was perplexed by this outcome. "Since they had taken the training course, they *should* have understood," he grumbled. He is still convinced that the family's opposition to Mahikari is the work of a vengeful spirit that is possessing all of them.

Shortly after Eiko met her future husband, she began to be possessed by a variety of spirits, most of them her own ancestors. Although she admits she cannot tell when a spirit is approaching her, she is aware of its presence the very moment it enters her body. Sometimes this happens when she is walking along the street. The first sign is a feeling of enormous pressure on her chest and right shoulder. When she is receiving okiyome, she sometimes gets a numb feeling or a tingling sensation that runs from her right shoulder down to her hand. At other times she is "paralyzed" by an evil spirit when she gets into bed. Her husband was once possessed by a fox spirit as he lay in bed. He quickly recited the Exorcist's Prayer, and the fox disappeared.

The most significant seizures Eiko has experienced have been caused by ancestral spirits. In August 1976, she and her husband went back to Kumamoto to look up the posthumous name of her husband's grandfather, who had died about thirty years before. While they were on the trip, Eiko cut her hand, which soon became badly infected. After they returned to Nakayama, she went to the dojo to receive okiyome. There, through a spirit investigation, she learned that her injury was the work of her ancestors, who were jealous when they saw that she was worshiping her husband's ancestors before her own. The ghost reminded her that, after all, when she had entered the dojo it was in order to save *them*. Yoshida Sensei, who was doing the cross-examining, defended her by explaining to the spirit that she had not yet been allowed to change her family's butsudan and therefore was not to blame. When the seizure was over, her ancestor's spirit had scolded her, and Yoshida Sensei had scolded the spirit. One of the purposes of okiyome, Eiko pointed out to me, is to scold (*satosu*).

Since she was a child, Eiko has had trouble with her ears. Her parents took her to various doctors and made her take pills and tonics. Now, of course, she believes that medicine is poison, and that her problem is caused by evil spirits. Sometimes her ears begin to hurt when she is worshiping before the butsudan. One day Eiko and her husband had some *sushi* for supper. Although she had hardly had anything to eat all day, she felt full as soon as she finished her first piece. Thinking that this was strange, she went to the dojo for okiyome. The spirit that appeared to her that night was her husband's grandfather, who was suffering in hell for the violent life he had led. It was he who had caused a recent earache. While he was alive, he had suggested to Eiko's mother-in-law that she abandon Yoshimitsu, who was her sixth child. Ironically, it was now Yoshimitsu and Eiko who, by faithfully tending their butsudan, were saving him and their other ancestors. At first, the spirit said, he had been in a dark place. Now, thanks to the Arakis, his position had improved so that he could see things, and even overhear conversations between neighboring ghosts. The spirit cried with joy, as did Eiko when she related this story to me. Before he returned to the astral world, the spirit predicted that an earthquake was about to hit Japan, but he could not say when it would happen or how many people would perish.

Eiko's ears began to hurt one night when she was helping put on a fireworks exhibition. When she returned home, she was unable to fall asleep because of the pain. When it became unendurable, she begged her husband to take her to the hospital. As a pious follower of Mahikari, he refused. Instead, early the next morning they went to the home of their squadron leader, Mr. Murakami, to receive okiyome.* The spirit that appeared to them was a human being in the shape of a badger. He had taken possession of her when she went to the fireworks display, hoping to "get saved" himself.

When her ancestors are hungry, Mrs. Araki feels a pain in her stomach. Once when this happened, her husband gave her okiyome, and on her closed eyelids she could see ten people with Tokugawa-period hair styles rising up to heaven. Then the pain subsided.

The dojo plays a large role in the Arakis' lives. Even though they live on the brink of poverty in one of the tiniest apartments I have

---

* The membership of each dojo is divided into territorial units called squadrons, each with its own leader (*hanchō*).

ever seen in Japan, they manage to donate about $60.00 every month to the dojo. They pay no rent, since their apartment is owned by a bakery where Eiko works. When I visited their home, they showed me the miniature butsudan they had bought at the dojo. The small offering trays were filled with tidbits from their own supper: beans, eggs, rice, and some Coca-Cola. There was some milk in a baby bottle on one of the trays, even though the Arakis have no children. When I asked why the bottle was there, they replied that it was for ancestral spirits who may have died in infancy or in the womb. After they installed this butsudan, some ancestral spirits that had been bothering Yoshimitsu vanished. Eiko believes that she has been possessed by evil spirits because her parents will not allow her to correct the mistakes in their butsudan. She believes that their stubbornness may be the work of ancestors in hell who have not yet apologized to Su-god. Nevertheless, if her parents really wanted to worship their ancestors properly, Su-god would let them, she reasons.

She contrasts her family's intransigence with the attitude of her husband's family. Because his ancestors have apologized, his family allowed him to set up a butsudan with replicas of the family's memorial tablets. Rather humbly, she wonders whether his family's attitude might not also be the result of her husband's superior discipline. In fact, he is exceptionally devout for a young man his age (twenty-three). Through okiyome, he has fixed the door of their car and repaired their television set. One day, he ran out of paint and had to go back to his supplier for some more cans. On the way he began to feel through his shirt for his amulet. This appears to be a nervous habit, but his wife regards it as a sign of his great faith in the amulet. He suddenly discovered that it was not resting against his chest, but had fallen over his shoulder and was hanging behind his neck. At just that moment he noticed in the rear-view mirror that his truck had barely escaped a rear-end collision with another vehicle. He believes that his amulet, sensing the danger, had moved to his back in order to protect him.

As we have seen, religion not only reflects human problems; it also creates a major problem (the Problem) that can in turn be "keyed," as Erving Goffman would say, to the more concrete problems a person has.[14] The problems of everyday life, therefore, are solved not *just* by a Divine Solution (the Ideal and the Way), but by the generation of this Greater Problem. One major Problem created by the Japanese folk tradition and reinforced by Mahikari is the responsibility laid on a person for his ancestors' well-being in the afterlife. The Problem-consciousness associated with ancestor veneration is both ethical and magical in nature. It fosters a deep, moral sense of family identity, a potentially volatile surplus of guilt (for moral or ritual misdeeds), and the hope that if a family cares properly for its butsudan, it will reap an abundance of good fortune.

Because of her heightened consciousness of both family and butsudan, Araki Eiko seemed to be caught between the rival claims of two sets of ancestors. Since by custom the Japanese wife worships her husband's ancestors, it is far more likely that a woman who joins Mahikari will be possessed by her husband's ancestral spirits than that her husband will be possessed by hers. Mrs. Araki has been possessed by spirits from both her own and her husband's side of the family. When the Arakis went to Kyushu to help save Yoshimitsu's ancestor, Eiko's ancestor grew jealous and attacked her. Yet, when she worshiped Yoshimitsu's ancestors in their tiny butsudan at home, she got earaches and stomach cramps. Thus, though her problems (finding a husband, earaches, and stomach cramps) may have been solved in the Mahikari Way, the solution itself depends on the creation of an extraordinary Problem for the Japanese woman: how to marry, and change family identities and ritual obligations, without offending ancestors on either side of the family. Both the etiology and the cure for her specific problems depend on *the artificial creation of a Problem*—contentious ancestors.

Because it offers a whole battery of reasons for the evils of life— some of them consistent, others not—a religious theodicy tends to become laminated or coralloid in its form and complexity. Although Mrs. Araki believes that many of her problems have been caused by jealous ancestors, she also believes that the reason why she has had so many spirit seizures in the first place is that her parents have not properly rearranged their butsudan. At the same time, she seems to shift the blame for her spirit possessions and personal trials from her parents to ancestors in the astral world who have not yet "apologized to Su-god." She also wonders whether her parents would have let her fix up the butsudan if she had been more zealous in her own shugyo. I strongly suspect, however, that this self-deprecation is merely an instance of the Japanese wife's typical reflex response to almost any problem that comes up in the family: "I alone am guilty." [15] At no point in Eiko's reasoning did the scandal of her niece's traumatic spirit seizure come up as an explanation for why her family had become antagonized. I first learned about this episode from Yoshida Sensei.

So far, we have seen how sexual karma and evil spirits have plagued the lives of an Old Miss, single girls, and a married woman. We turn now to the story of a woman whose two marriages have broken up, as she believes, because of interventions from the Fourth Dimension.

A Divorcee

When she was in her early teens, Matsumoto Chioe determined not to go to high school. Instead, much against her parents' wishes, she enrolled in a school for dressmakers. After her graduation from this school at the age of nineteen, she went to work in a dress-maker's shop. It was there that she had her first convulsive fits. Whenever one of these spells came on, several people had to hold her down and put something in her mouth so that she would not swallow her tongue. After it was over, she would fall into a deep sleep. When she awoke, she always had a headache, and was unable to remember anything that had happened. Her parents took her to several hospitals in the area, including two mental institutions. Although her symptoms seemed similar to epilepsy, her doctors did not want to use this word for the disease. If it was epilepsy, they said, there would be a way to treat it. Because her doctors could not tell her the nature of her illness, what had caused it, or what it might lead to later, she became all the more anxious.

Chioe was married for the first time in May 1974. By the end of that year, the marriage had broken up because of her convulsions. Although she vowed not to remarry, by January of the next year she had found a new husband. On their engagement trip, she had one of her spells. In order to test her fiance, she exaggerated the serious-ness and frequency of her seizures. He assured her that they did not matter to him, and for some time they got along quite well. She became deeply attached to a child her husband had had by his former wife. Then the trouble began once again. Before long it seemed to her that her husband could talk of nothing but her seizures, and she herself developed an "inferiority complex" because of them. She blamed herself for being lazy and for being unable to get pregnant. At night her body was racked with pains, which mysteriously disappeared only after she went back to work the next day. Finally, her husband was able to put up with her no longer, and he ordered her to go back to her parents' home. "While he is pleasant to other people, he is terribly cold to me. You could hardly call him a husband," she complained. By the end of the year (1976), they seemed headed for a divorce.

When her second marriage fell apart, Chioe began to look for a religious solution to her problems. One night, at 2:00 A.M., she heard the voice of Saint Kobo Daishi calling her to perform austerities. Obeying the voice, she went to a river in the forest, where the voice commanded her to remove her skirt. Then she waded out into the water and stood reciting Buddhist sutras for two hours. As she stood in the freezing river, she could feel an evil spirit pounding her over the back with a bamboo rod. She got out of the water, took a pencil and piece of paper, and wrote down the words of a sutra. She was amazed to see her fingers automatically writing the unfamiliar characters of a sutra that she had never seen or heard before. When her relatives came to the forest to fetch her, she refused to go back with them, preferring to stay there and continue her austerities. During the following months, she went on several other pilgrimages and even visited a medium.

Her first contact with the New Religions was through Reiyukai. Although this sect is not known for spirit seizures, she claims that during one of its mass rallies, she and some other people became possessed by spirits and had to be put into a separate room. In March 1976, after participating in the sect's activities for three or four months, she quit. "All they do, day in and day out, is pray, recite sutras, and take your money," she muttered. Looking back, she believes that all of these religious experiences merely paved her way to Su-god.

After Chioe took the Mahikari introductory training course in June 1976, she stopped thinking about her other religious experi-

ences. The first time she received okiyome, someone's face appeared
to her. Then she felt a heavy weight pressing down on her shoulders
and began to have difficulty breathing. Just as when she had performed austerities in the river, she felt an evil spirit pounding her
over the back, making her cry and sway back and forth. Because
the spirit beat her, the minister giving her okiyome concluded that
it must have been an ancestor who was a bailiff or executioner in
his own lifetime. Her grandmother, however, thought that it was
probably the spirit of the girl's uncle.

Chioe has also been possessed by the spirit of her cousin, a girl
who was once very close to her. At the age of twenty-four, this
cousin was engaged to be married, but on the day the furniture
arrived for her new home, she committed suicide. This took place
three years before Chioe's convulsions began, when she was only
sixteen. Because the cousin was not able to marry and be happy, her
spirit in the astral world became jealous when she saw Chioe about
to be married. The spirit therefore inflicted an illness on Chioe that
made both of her marriages break up.

Since this illness had never appeared before in her family, Chioe
was at a loss to explain it until she entered Mahikari. When I
asked whether she had had any traumatic experiences as a child
that might have caused it, she replied that once, when she was in
the eighth grade, she had hit her head in a school bus accident.
Other than that, there was only the death of her cousin. She asserts
with confidence that she has such a good relationship with her
parents that they are the envy of other people.

Thanks to okiyome, Chioe has had no fits in recent months, not
even on the eleventh day of the month, when for some reason, she
always used to have one.

Here we have yet another young woman who came to Mahikari
from a tradition in which celestial voices, religious austerities, and
demon possession were commonplace.

Since Chioe's doctors were unable to name or explain her illness,
I cannot pretend—with less skill and information—to be able to
diagnose it. As in the other cases, all that I can hope for is to put
forward some clinical inferences. Were a psychiatrist to study her
disorder (assuming that it has psychosomatic origins), he would
probably be interested in her break with her parents over leaving

home. As we have seen, her convulsive fits began as soon as she started work. A psychiatrist would also be interested in her cousin's suicide, which took place three years before Chioe first became ill. Here, at least, his diagnosis and the revelations of her spirit interrogations might coincide, since she believes that it was this cousin who possessed her and caused her illness and marital difficulties.

One point Chioe stressed several times during our interview was that the failure of her doctors to explain her disease doubled her anxiety. As we saw in Chapter 7, the way to the dojo for many members has been paved by the failures of Western medicine. Mahikari's ability to provide an explanation (etiology) for Chioe's illness and divorces has been one of the most important aspects of the religion for her.

Childlessness

The women whose spirit stories we have been considering have all had trouble finding or keeping a husband. They are all victims of what sociologists call role deprivation. Those not deprived of okusan-hood have suffered from being deprived of motherhood. Childlessness has long been regarded as a curse in Japan. Among the most sought-after charms sold at shrines and temples across the country are those that promote fertility and safe childbirth. The Tenrikyo sect, the fifth largest of the New Religions, got its start when its foundress, Nakayama Miki (1798–1887), became known for her ability to ensure safe childbirth. In Mahikari, many women are looking for the same kind of divine assistance. One woman tells the following story, which I have summarized from her testimony in *Mahikari* magazine.

Five years ago I became a member of Mahikari. The following year I was married. When I found that I couldn't get pregnant, I took the advice of my mother-in-law and went to see a doctor. As I feared, the doctor told me I had a tipped uterus. This must be an omen from Su-god, I thought to myself. He must be warning me that I haven't taken enough time to go to the dojo to give and receive okiyome. When I saw other woman playing with their children, the tears would come to my eyes, and I would think, won't I ever have a child of my own?

To make up for lost time, my husband and I decided to spend our vacation at the dojo doing odd jobs. I brought fresh flowers and arranged them before the altar every day. One day, a spirit investigation showed that I was being possessed by the spirit of a woman bearing a grudge against me. It was this spirit that was preventing me from having a child. As I continued to do shugyo, my fixation (*shūjaku*) on getting pregnant began to go away, and before long I stopped praying for a baby. Soon I felt better than I had since we got married.

One day I woke up feeling very tired. I began to sweat and vomited up a lot of impurities, so that in just one day I lost five kilograms. Once again I went to the doctor. At last I was pregnant! But our joy did not last long, for soon I learned that I had developed an ovarian cyst the size of a baseball. The doctor said that it would have to be removed surgically because it was endangering the life of the baby. There must be some mistake, I thought. And so I went to three more doctors. Every time the diagnosis was the same.

When I look back on this experience, I realize how shallow I was. Through okiyome I discovered that a spirit had caused my cyst, too. I continued to do evangelistic work for Mahikari, bringing in two friends who were also childless and encouraging lax members to "raise their hands." Finally the cyst disappeared without a trace. Even the doctor was amazed.

Although this testimony was presented before the actual birth of her child, the woman credits Mahikari with the double miracle of conception and the disappearance of the ovarian cyst. Here, again, we have a "laminated theodicy" that explains suffering in terms of multiple causation. The woman attributes her previous inability to become pregnant to a tipped uterus, and at a deeper level, both to possession by a grudging spirit and to her own lack of religious zeal. The notion of getting rid of fixations or attachments to things (shujaku) is, of course, an ancient Buddhist idea that often has therapeutic effects.

In some societies the possession of women by evil spirits seems to be a symbolic excrescence of the battle of the sexes. For example, in the male-dominated society of the pastoral Somali in northeast Africa, women are regarded as weak and submissive. As though seeking to redress the wrongs committed against them by unfaithful lovers and stingy husbands, Somali women often become possessed by jinn-like spirits called *sar*. Because the sar spirits are thought to be "consumed by envy and greed, and to hunger especially after dainty foods, luxurious clothing, jewelry, perfume, and other finery," women who have been "entered" by them are free to make all sorts of extravagant demands on their menfolk.[16] For these women, I. M. Lewis points out, spirit possession is actually an oblique strategy of retribution.

Does spirit possession serve the same function for Japanese women? After all, Japanese men have the reputation for being among the most "sexist" in the world, and despite constitutional guarantees to the contrary, Japanese women are said to be treated as second-class citizens in many regards. In nearly every aspect of public life, they play secondary or subordinate roles. A woman is expected to use polite forms of speech when talking with men, to leave major decisions to her husband, and to show herself humble in all ways. She is even expected not to take her bath until all the other members of the household have taken theirs. Although women do have considerable power over and responsibility for their children, the kitchen, and the family purse, the image of the ideal woman promoted and approved by nearly all institutions, secular and religious, is that of the self-sacrificing and submissive wife and mother. Even today, older Japanese women can recall the days when "the three obediences and the seven grounds of divorce" were the rule.* Only in the roles of okusan-hood and motherhood does the typical Japanese woman seem truly secure. And though change is in the air, the Japanese feminist responds to improvements with the charge *plus ça change, plus c'est la même chose*—or the Japanese equivalent.

Although romantic love was once the norm among Japanese peasants, after the Meiji restoration (1868) the samurai ideal of arranged marriages was promoted as part of the government's drive to spread the ideals of the warrior (*bushidō*) among the common people. The marriage customs of the traditional warrior class were completely different from those of the peasants. Because the bride and groom often came from distant parts of the country, marriages

* Traditionally, a Japanese woman owed three obediences: to her father as an unmarried girl, to her husband after marriage, and to her children after her husband's death. The seven grounds of divorce were disobedience to parents-in-law, failure to conceive, diverting household money for her own personal use, sexual indulgence, jealousy, serious disease, and talkativeness. Iwao Sumiko, "A Full Life for Modern Japanese Women," in *Text of Seminar on "Changing Values in Modern Japan,"* Stanford University (Nihonjin Kenkyūkai in association with the Asia Foundation, 1977), pp. 95–96.

had to be arranged by the family heads and by go-betweens. Marriages of this sort were obviously predicated on considerable self-denial.

Suppression of individual desires in the choice of mates and after marriage in one's general conduct for the sake of the well-being of the corporate family was demanded of both husband and wife. In this context, any mutual affective gratification, including sexual satisfaction, which tended to undermine the corporate interest of the family, was understandably suppressed. The male dominance of the society, however, enabled men to find sexual satisfaction in the entertainment world, whereas women were not allowed to seek such gratification outside the marriage.[17]

Having so little choice in marriage, the Japanese have often taken a fatalistic attitude toward it. Marriage is part of a person's karma. In fact, the Japanese word for karma (*en*) can be used to refer to marriage itself. Karma ties the knot of marriage (*en-musubi* or *en-gumi*) and thereby creates relatives (*en-pen*, *en-biki*, or *en-kosha*) that a person might not have chosen had he or she had any say in the matter.

Mahikari's notion of sexual karma is closely related both to this fatalistic attitude toward marriage and to the ideological subordination of women in the samurai code. Although women ultimately are equal to men in the eyes of Su-god, Mioshie assigns them a subordinate place in society. The Mahikari cosmogony itself legitimates this discrimination. Mioshie tells us that the "spiritual pattern" (*hinagata*) of the male was created 20,000 years before that of the female and is naturally associated with the general superiority of the yang principle. One of the proofs of the superiority of Japanese culture over Western culture is its masculine (or yang) nature. In his lectures, Yoshida Sensei insisted that if women's liberation succeeds in Japan, the country will be doomed. Furthermore, if women do not properly respect their husbands, they will be unable to worship their ancestors correctly. For women to be happy, they must therefore realize that their marital and other problems are simply instances of the Problem of bad karma, and that the Way out of these difficulties lies in the Mahikari Treatment.

In the spirit stories I have presented in this chapter, we have seen the resentment and fear some Japanese women feel toward men. Najita Kayako, for example, has suffered a mental collapse each

time she was about to be married. Katada Toyoko describes her
lovers as "double-faced cheats and liars." Suzuki Tanio speaks of
herself as an androphobiac, and we have suggested that her fear of
men may have arisen from her traumatic relationship with a violent, alcoholic father. In the main, however, these women seem to
regard their frustrations with the opposite sex as something to be
overcome, not avenged. Unlike the Somali women, who seem to be
interested primarily in compensation, these Japanese women are
seeking fulfillment. Like the traditional laborer, who seeks to better
himself without changing the "relations of production," Mahikari
women who have been troubled by sexual karma are not trying to
revolutionize sexual roles, but trying to fulfill the roles they are expected to play as women in Japanese society. Sexual karma possession and exorcism—taken together as a syndrome—can be regarded
as a symbolic process for effecting a woman's upward domestic
mobility. It transforms singleness into okusan-hood, barrenness
into motherhood. In Chapter 12 we shall see that this ambition
directly parallels the members' quest for a higher religious status,
and that, like upward domestic mobility, the upgrading of religious
status is accomplished within the established ideals, customs, and
institutions of society.

10 *The Magician's Will*

Sukyo Mahikari is, above all else, a religion of miracles. In my survey, only twelve people out of 688 admitted that they had experienced no miracles at all since joining the church. Up to this point, I have used Bryan R. Wilson's word thaumaturgy, or the adjective thaumaturgical to refer to this kind of practice and orientation.[1] Perhaps the word magic would be even more appropriate. In this chapter, we shall review Mahikari's practical "response to the world" in order to see whether the use of this stronger and perhaps more specific term is justified.

According to my survey, at least 39 percent of the members of the four dojos in the Osaka area have experienced healing miracles.* Members reported, for example: my brain tumor went away; my asthma was cured after I began to receive okiyome; my warts and corns disappeared; I began to spit up impurities and vomit (that is, bodily "toxins" were expelled); I no longer stutter; my menstrual cramps went away after I worshiped my ancestors; I

---

* In Japanese, the words *kiseki o itadaku* mean to receive humbly, or be blessed with, a miracle. Although the expression puts the individual in a passive role vis à vis Su-god, the source of all miracles, linguistic form alone should not determine our interpretation of miraculous experiences. This is particularly true of a language in which deference and humility are de rigueur. In spite of the passivity suggested by verbal habit, the actual use and conceptualization of okiyome seem to imply that when the individual raises his hand he takes an active, controlling role in the production of miracles. I have therefore used the English verbs "to receive," "to experience," and "to perform" miracles more or less synonymously throughout this book.

Giving okiyome to a movie projector

overcame mental illness or alcoholism. Many of the miracles reported went far beyond the limits of psychosomatic therapy. For
example, I heard about, but did not meet, a woman who was born
with six breasts, four of which allegedly disappeared when she received okiyome. Relatives who did not want to receive okiyome
have been purified and healed while they were sleeping. Members
regularly give okiyome to infants and children, so that they will be
healthy and tractable when they grow up. None of these miracles
seems to fall under the category of psychosomatic healing.

Likewise, miracles performed on animals or inanimate objects
fall into what we might call a more objective class of wonders.
When movies or slides are being shown in the dojo, members gather
around the projector to give it okiyome before the meeting begins.
Before members leave for festivals in Tokyo, the stairwell of each
charter bus is purified to ward off traffic accidents. Similarly, forty-
two respondents to the survey said that they had fixed their televi-

sion sets just by raising their hands over them. Twenty-nine had repaired their wristwatches in this way. Sick animals are believed to
be easier to purify and heal than human beings, since in the first
place, they are not unbelievers, and in the second, they have not
taken a lot of medicine. One woman told me that she had cured
a growth in her cat's mouth by raising her hand over it. After the
miracle, the cat took a nap on her prayer book every time it wanted
to receive okiyome, as though to give its mistress a hint. Another
cat had kittens, two of which died at birth. Before the owner buried
them, he held his hand over them for fifteen minutes and noticed
that the back of their necks became "soft." He regarded this as a
special miracle, since the neck is where rigor mortis sets in first, or
so he told me. The kittens did not revive, however. Similarly, when
the same member's father died, ten dojo members gathered around
the body to give it okiyome. They noticed that the complexion of
the corpse began to change from the dusky pallor of death to the
color of living flesh. The face also lost its look of pain.

Climatic miracles also fall into this objective classification. In
1976 a dojo in southern Kyushu that was threatened by Typhoon
Number 17 telephoned the Spiritual Leader of the church in Tokyo
requesting a Divine Notification.* She accordingly informed Su-
god, "If the typhoon hits the Kyushu dojo, it will not be able to
have its monthly festival." Miraculously, the storm remained
stalled off the coast of the island for thirty hours and lost most of
its fury. In Gifu Prefecture the same typhoon, which did much
damage to the rest of the area, left the local dojo standing high and
dry. When I pointed out that this storm had also miraculously
spared the Nakayama dojo, while flooding neighboring buildings,
Yoshida Sensei objected. This was no miracle, he said, since he had
purposely selected high ground when he bought the land for the
dojo. It was good to be reminded that not everything is a miracle!

Aside from healing miracles, the survey revealed that members
have experienced a wide variety of other miracles, many of which

---

* Divine Notifications (*onenji*) are one of the Spiritual Leader's special preroga-
tives. On request from a local dojo, she simply presents a case of need or emergency
before Su-god as a statement of fact. Divine Notifications are therefore not prayers
or petitions. One might think of them as broad hints.

could be called objective. Somewhat arbitrarily, I have classified them into seven categories as follows:

(1) *Physical miracles* (36 percent): Such miracles include those performed on inanimate objects, animals, or infants. For example: I cured my cat's (dog's, bird's) disease; I fixed the electric fan (or the bathtub or the chain saw) by giving it okiyome; I stopped the crying of a baby in a neighboring apartment by giving it okiyome through the wall; I revived my withered morning-glories; I made our car run without gasoline by raising my hand; I improved the taste of noodles (rice, wine) by giving them okiyome; I changed the weather.*

(2) *Coincidental miracles* (13 percent): I accidentally met a relative at the festival in Tokyo; I found my way when I was lost; I caught a bus when I was late; I got my own way; I found some money on the street; I was able to get a fishbone out of my throat; nothing bad happened to me.

(3) *Evangelistic miracles* (5 percent): I got a relative (or friend) to join the dojo; my parents allowed me to attend a festival in Tokyo, even though they are opposed to Mahikari; my husband stopped criticizing the church.

(4) *Financial miracles* (5 percent): I found a job; I made some money, so that I could go to the festival in Tokyo.

(5) *Spiritual miracles* (5 percent): I am allowed to live each day; my ancestors are being saved in the astral world; my spirit (*seishin*) became bright; I got cleaned up; I was hurried and pressed, but I prayed and things became smooth; I stopped playing around; a fox spirit disappeared; some "gold dust" (a good omen) appeared in my teacup.

(6) *Human and family relations miracles* (2 percent): I became engaged; I was reconciled with my parents (or children); relations with fellow workers improved; I was saved from a maniac; Su-god brought back my runaway child (husband).

---

* Since members were asked about physical miracles in a separate question (see Appendix A, Question 24), the number of physical miracles reported is probably higher (compared with the other categories) than might otherwise be expected.

(7) *Academic miracles* (2 percent): My grades improved; I passed my college entrance exams.

Of the 359 people who answered Question 26A, concerning the number of miracles experienced, 60 percent claimed that they had been blessed with up to fifteen, and 37 percent claimed even more than fifteen. Many in the latter group wrote on their questionnaires that they had experienced "innumerable" miracles. As a shorthand device, I shall refer to those who reported a moderate number of miracles (one to fifteen) as the Mercy Drops Group, and to those who reported fifteen or more as the Showers Group.*

One of my purposes in conducting the survey was to investigate the influences of age, sex, marital status, income, occupation, and education on the occurrence of miracles.

Although the survey turned up no overall correlation between age and the number of miracles experienced, when we divide the sample into the Mercy Drops and Showers groups, we find that older members are more likely to fall into the Mercy Drops Group —those reporting a moderate number of miraculous experiences. Older members also are less likely than younger members to experience objective, physical miracles, such as fixing a wristwatch by okiyome. The highest-ranking age cohort in a cross-tabulation of physical miracles and total number of miracles experienced is the group eighteen to twenty-two (37 percent, $n = 16$). The same cohort scored highest in a cross-tabulation of the number of miracles experienced and the occurrence of healing miracles (25 percent, $n = 11$). Thus, in sheer number of miracles experienced, the younger members of the dojo are either the most skilled wonder-workers or the most easily convinced of their own powers and blessings.

A paradoxical reversal of this finding occurs, however, when we look at the responses to Question 25, which confronts the respondent with a problem designed to tease apart practical common sense from a "thaumaturgical response to the world." The question reads: "If your car broke down, in what order would you do the

---

* The names of these groups are taken from the old Protestant hymn "There Shall Be Showers of Blessings," the refrain of which is: "Showers of blessings, / showers of blessings we need. / *Mercy drops* 'round us are falling, / but for the *showers* we plead."

following: (a) look for the cause and fix it yourself, (b) give it oki-yome, (c) call a garage?" Of those who answered it, 47 percent said that they would first look for the cause and fix it themselves; 51 percent would give the car okiyome; and a mere 1 percent would call a garage.

When we cross-tabulate responses to this question with the age of the respondents, we find a discernible relationship between "thau-maturgical auto repair" and advancing age ($r = .19$, $p = .001$). That is, the older a person is, the more likely he or she is to try to fix a malfunctioning auto by using okiyome before trying to repair it in a "secular" way. Figure 4 shows the overlap between this correlation and the fact that, as members become older, they be-come more likely to experience only a moderate number of mira-cles. The relatively high percentage of older members in the ranks of those who said they would use okiyome first to fix an automobile may indicate that those with the least exposure to the actual work-ing and breakdown of autos are the most likely to rely on a thau-maturgical response to a mechanical failure.

Turning to the influence of sex and marital status on the occur-rence of miracles, we find that both sexes have been about equally blessed with healing miracles (women, 39 percent; men, 38 per-cent). Likewise, nearly the same percentages of both sexes have per-formed physical miracles (women, 36 percent; men, 38 percent). When we look at the total number of miracles the individual claims to have performed, women dominate the Showers Group (women, 40 percent; men, 33 percent), but the situation in the Mercy Drops Group is just the opposite (men, 63 percent; women, 58 percent). Perhaps because women, like the elderly, have been relatively less exposed to the harsh realities of auto mechanics, in answering Question 25 they tended more often than men to say that they would first try okiyome to fix a car (women, 57 percent; men, 46 percent). Men, on the other hand, are more likely to try to fix the car themselves first (57 percent to 48 percent). On the whole, there-fore, women have an only slightly more thaumaturgical attitude to-ward automobiles than men. As for marital status, 44 percent of the single members fall into the Showers Group, compared with only 32 percent of the married members. This finding apparently reflects the relative youthfulness of the single members.

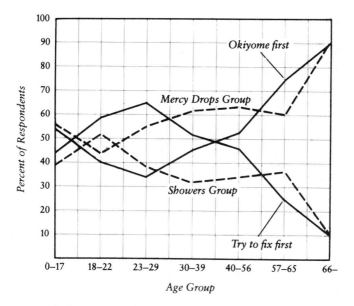

FIG. 4. *Miracle Record and Preference for Thaumaturgical Auto Repair by Age Group*

Whereas the survey shows no real correlation between a member's income and the number of miracles he has performed, income does seem to be somewhat negatively related to the use of okiyome in auto repair. That is, the higher a person's income, the less likely he will be to try to repair his car by simply raising his hand over it.[2]

When we compare the general susceptibility of different occupation groups to spirit possession with the percentage of each group that would use okiyome first to fix an auto (see Table 6), we find that the full-time dojo staff and the high-level white-collar workers remain in about the same relative positions. The blue-collar workers become more clearly divided into skilled and unskilled, and farmers move up in rank.

As for educational level, the Mercy Drops Group shrinks with rising education, but the Showers Group actually increases.[3] This trend can be explained, in part, as the result of the work of the Mahikari Youth Corps among high-school and college students.

Table 6. Spirit Possession and Preference for Thaumaturgical Auto Repair Among Occupational Groups

Rank order of susceptibility to spirit possession	Rank order of preference for giving okiyome to auto first	Percent of group preferring okiyome first
Full-time dojo staff	Full-time dojo staff	67%
High-level white-collar workers	High-level white-collar workers	58
Blue-collar workers	Farmers	52
Low-level white-collar workers	Unskilled blue-collar workers	47
Farmers	Low-level white-collar workers	40
	Skilled blue-collar workers	35

The same explanation accounts for the high percentage of members aged eighteen to twenty-two who fall into the Showers Group (see Fig. 4, above). We must also remember that the older members, who are largely in the Mercy Drops Group, have had fewer years of schooling on the whole.

We can now summarize our review of the miraculous experiences of dojo members. As we have seen, Mahikari's World of Miracles, far surpassing faith healing, takes in a wide variety of wonders, including even inexplicable transformations in both animate and inanimate objects at a distance. Only a dozen members out of the entire sample reported that they had yet to experience a miracle. About the same percentages of both sexes have performed healing miracles and objective physical miracles. Being female and single, however, somewhat increases a person's chances of having Showers of miracles. Women also are somewhat more likely than men to try to fix a car by raising their hands over it. Of the ranked occupational groups, the full-time dojo staff and the high-level white-collar workers are the most likely to try to fix a car by using okiyome. The same two groups, as noted earlier, are also the most susceptible to spirit possession. On the other hand, low-level white-collar workers, who represent the largest employment group in the four dojos, rank next to the bottom in both lists.

Our most interesting finding is the correlation between age and the occurrence of miracles. The older a member is, the more likely he or she is to experience only a moderate number of miracles.

Likewise, older members are less likely than younger members to perform objective physical miracles. The members most likely to be blessed with Showers of miracles are generally under thirty years of age. Since younger members have usually had more years of schooling than older members, education itself is positively correlated with the performance of miracles. This astonishing thaumaturgical talent among the youth of the dojo probably has more to do with the zealous evangelism of the Mahikari Youth Corps than with the state of public education in Japan. Only in response to the question about fixing a car did the older members display a more thaumaturgical outlook, perhaps because they, like female members, have had less personal experience with automobiles and the usual ways of repairing them.

Now that we have reviewed the general contours of members' miraculous experiences, we must ask the question "Is what they are doing magic?" Mahikari members, of course, do not regard their miracles (*kiseki*) as magic. The Japanese words for magic—*majutsu*, *mahō*—have all the negative connotations of the English word. When I asked members to compare miracles with magic, they usually pointed out that magic is the work of people (such as mediums) controlled by a fox or some other evil spirit, and that it is only concerned with curses and spells.

Scholarly opinion on the nature and definition of magic has in general been as divided as scholarly opinion on religion. The Australian rites treated by Frazer as magic were regarded by Durkheim as religion par excellence. Some scholars make a clear distinction between magic and religion; others see none. For some, magic naturally falls under the broader category of the sacred. For others, it is as profane as technology and science. Some, like Freud, would emphasize the compulsive or wishful nature of magical acts (for example, spells), whereas others, like Malinowski, would emphasize their pragmatic function in ritualizing the optimism needed to face dangerous situations. Much, of course, depends on the research orientation of the investigator. Those interested in the sociology of knowledge follow Frazer, and try to locate magic and religion on cognitive maps showing the way from superstition and falsehood to science and truth. Others, in search of the psychosocial dimensions of culture pay homage to Malinowski, treating magic and religion as expressive gestures closer to man's emotions and instincts than to his rational faculties. Unfortunately, most of the early discussions of the problem, such as the works of Frazer himself, Edward Burnett Tylor, John Ferguson McLennan, and Herbert Spencer, were caught in the quagmire of evolutionary theory or in the slough of speculation concerning the historical origins of social and cultural institutions. It was Andrew Lang, in his book *Magic and Religion* (1901), who first showed that magic and religion often coexist. But it was left to Malinowski to demonstrate that the topic could be discussed more fruitfully by putting evolutionary and historical questions aside. In general, later twentieth-century anthropologists have followed suit, approaching magic either from the angle of its social and psychological functions or as a problem in the sociology of consciousness. Only sociologists entranced by such evolutionary notions as Weber's "disenchantment of the world" have resisted this retreat from historical speculation. Today, most anthropologists regard religion and magic as interrelated phenomena representing a continuum of beliefs and practices. Hence the popularity of such clumsy adjectives as magico-religious and religio-magical, words that commit their users to much and little at the same time.

The English language has contributed to this Babel of theory and speculation. In the first place, unlike the word religion, the word magic has no natural plural in English. Although "magics" differ from each other as much as religions do, want of a proper plural has fostered the mistaken assumption that there is an "essential magic" behind all the rich variety of magical experience. A still more vexing problem is the negative connotations that the word magic has acquired. Here, we must bear in mind the religious influences on our language. English and other Western languages are, in effect, Christian. The distinction between prayer and spells, religion and magic, was originally made not by anthropologists in their nineteenth-century armchairs, but by Protestant theologians and Puritan saints in their sixteenth- and seventeenth-century pulpits.[4] Protestantism both destroyed the ritual and magical praxis of historical Christianity and sponsored a narrower conception of religion based on faith alone. In the countries and languages singed by the Reformers' zeal, magical customs became synonymous with base superstition. All that was left to the Enlightenment was to deliver the coup de grâce.

In spite of the bewildering uses of the term and its polemical thrust in Western religious literature, the concept of magic is so central to the comparative study of religion that one abandons it at peril. I therefore intend neither to give up the concept nor to propose still another definition for it. In place of a definition, I shall follow William P. Alston's treatment of the definition of religion and apply it to magic by merely presenting a set of "magic-making characteristics." Based on Wittgenstein's notion of "family resemblances," Alston's approach attempts to avoid the conundrums of essentialist definitions and put the definition of religion on a more practical footing.[5] Since there is no universal essence of religion or magic behind the actual religions and magics we find in human experience, no single predicate can sufficiently define the phenomena. Drawing up lists of predicates that generally characterize them, we find that some religions or magics correspond with nearly everything in the set, whereas others correspond with a much shorter list. This, after all, is what family resemblances are all about: not every member of the family has the same nose. When we review the characteristics generally imputed to magical phenomena in anthropology and the history of religions, we arrive at a list that includes, among others, the following adjectives: impersonal, mechanical, automatic, compulsive, coercive, practical, and efficient.[6] To these I would add palpable and quick. Out of this family of adjectives, we can best describe Mahikari's magic as (1) quick; (2) palpable (being both this-worldly, or practical, and human-oriented); and (3) automatic (coercive and mechanical).

Mahikari's magic is quick. So intertwined is Mahikari's magic with religious faith that one is tempted to say that its magic is quick religion, its religion slow magic. Although speed is not often mentioned in definitions of magic, it does seem to be one of magic's more important characteristics, perhaps because of magic's wish-fulfilling function. As Marcel Mauss puts it, "Between a wish and its fulfillment there is, in magic, no gap."[7] The magician, therefore, is an efficiency expert. His "presto!" is to "abracadabra" what "amen" is to prayer. In China, for example, the tempo of Taoist

charms used in exorcism is sometimes indicated by their final
words: "Quick, quick!" or "Quick as fire!"[8] The magician, like the
medium, gets a "moment-to-moment reaction" from his manipulation of gods, spirits, and ritual media. This is a strong contrast to
the priest in established churches, who observes little or no immediate "feedback" from his gods.[9]

Magic nourished in the "hothouse" of sectarian emotions is especially impatient for results. In Mahikari, traditional methods of
meditation and spiritual discipline are regularly criticized for taking
too long and for being too difficult for the average person. Mahikari members claim to acquire magical skills in only three days that
an ascetic would need years to master. As one woman in the Nakayama dojo explained to me, "Okiyome is especially useful in emer-
gencies, since you can use it immediately" (*tossa no baai*). Another
put it this way: "Prayer is no good [*dame*]. It takes too long. But
with okiyome, if someone has a heart attack, all you have to do is
raise your hand." A member of a dojo in Tokyo also groused about
prayer. When her son became "neurotic," she asked a Catholic nun
for help. The nun could do no more than say, "I'll pray for you."
Okiyome, on the other hand, *did* something for the boy. Again and
again, members stressed that because okiyome was quick-acting
and could be performed anywhere and at any time, they had found
peace of mind.

Mahikari's magic is palpable, active, pragmatic, and this-worldly.
If we imagine religious and magical symbols taking their position
between us and ultimate reality, religious symbols by and large
point to the ultimate "beyond" themselves, whereas magical ones
refer to and act on the human world "in front." Magic therefore
tries to modify a given state of affairs within a tangible, human
Diesseitigkeit. Thus it is, as Mauss says, "a practical idea"; consequently, "there is no such thing as an inactive, honorary magician."[10] Hence the emphasis on shugyo in Mahikari. "Just try it
and see!" is a phrase constantly on the lips of the zealous. Not
once did I hear anyone say, "Believe it!" or "Have faith in it!"
Reversing the adage, believing, literally, has become seeing. Members constantly emphasize that in the dojo you can see for yourself
that spirits exist. Likewise, you can see miracles taking place. This

emphasis on concrete, visible experience—which members confuse with empiricism or an experimental orientation—is often pointed to as a mark of the superiority of Mahikari over other religions. With the advent of the Savior and the founding of his church, Mioshie proclaims, "the era of religious pragmatism has arrived!"

Because magic can work only in the palpable world of human experience, its symbols are inevitably expressed in concrete terms and situations. One of the best examples of this is the spirit rays or cords (reihasen) emitted from the exorcist's palm. Mauss, no doubt, would quickly classify these together with "the idea of effluvia which leave the body, magical images which travel about, lines linking the magician and his field of action, ropes, chains." [11] All are examples of *mana*, the spiritual power that he believed creates magical objects.*

The objective quality of Mahikari's magic is obvious when we consider the beliefs and practices concerning the amulets that transmit spirit rays. Amulets, as Mauss points out, are "concrete impersonal representations of magic." [12] When the neophyte receives his amulet at the end of the elementary training course, he is told to prize it more highly than life itself.

Yoshida Sensei explained the care of the amulet as follows:

Wash your hands before putting on the amulet and then dry them with a clean towel. (It would be especially disgraceful to use the same towel you dry your feet with!) Take off your amulet only when you take a bath or sleep in the nude. If you sleep in pajamas, fix the amulet to them with a safety pin, so that it will not touch the floor. When you aren't wearing it, hang it up on a nail on the wall where people do not pass by. But never hang more than one amulet on the same nail, lest their wave lengths become confused. Never hold your amulet lower than your knees. If you drop it, immediately notify the head office in Tokyo. If you step on it or drop it in a dirty place, it is a prediction of an impending disaster, or a sign that you have committed a sin against Su-god or your ancestors. Dropping the amulet or getting it wet can cause it to become disconnected. To plug it in again, you must bring it back to the dojo and pay 10,000 yen as apology money. If you drop it but do not step on it, you may ask

---

* Mauss's theory, which stands or falls on his identification of magic with mana, has been accepted by some (e.g., Lévi-Strauss) and rejected by others (e.g., Malinowski). Seeing no reason to reject his position out of hand, I prefer to relativize it by subsuming it under a broader set of magic-making characteristics.

Su-god to forgive you and then repair it yourself by giving it three minutes of okiyome on each side. An amulet should be cleaned periodically. Clean it twice a year if you sweat a lot. Be sure to keep up your monthly dues. We offer this money to Su-god in order to keep the line connected for the next month.

In fact, those who have failed to maintain their amulet in good shape have suffered the consequences. Someone once checked the amulet of a member who had recently died and noticed that the paper scroll inside was missing. Yoshida Sensei speculated that this was why the person died. Another member told me that she once forgot to put her amulet back on after taking a bath and consequently developed a bad case of hiccups. As soon as she put it on again, her hiccups went away.

As a rule, magical objects such as amulets tend to be surrounded by taboos that underscore the reality of their power. In the end, the object loses its symbolic, inanimate character and becomes an active agent, or a subject in its own right. The rules for this transformation can be better seen as we turn to the third characteristic of the church's magical practices.

Mahikari's magic is automatic, sometimes coercive, and somewhat mechanical. This characteristic is illustrated by the accounts of physical miracles given in the classification near the beginning of this chapter. According to Mahikari members, okiyome does not depend on faith, though when applied to humans it works more effectively if the subject believes. Accordingly, no fuss is made if people fall asleep during lectures: since the dojo is thought to be filled with True Light, they are being helped even while dozing. Another example of the automatic character of Mahikari magic is the special training course held occasionally in Tokyo and offered by invitation only. According to Yoshida Sensei, "After a person takes this course, his innermost thoughts become so strong that he can get whatever he wants just by wishing for it. For example, if you want a woman, you just have to think about one. Since this can get you into trouble, the church has to limit the enrollment in this course. Not everybody wishes for things that are good for him!"

Contrary to popular opinion, the secular worldview is not necessarily dominated by the laws of science and technology. People with a secular outlook—with their greater capacity for suspended or detached judgment—are content, or at least are prepared, to give Fortune her just due. Thus they regard the events in their lives as the outcome of an untidy compromise between natural causation and plain luck. The magician finds this intolerable. He is ill at ease in the world until by a wave of his hand—or simply by raising it—he has made cold necessity and contingency disappear. The rule of his art is: where Fortune was, there let human control be.

The roots of this "magical response to the world" have been traced back to infantile delusions of grandeur and to the unconscious wish to control uncontrollable parents. However this may be, to build an alternative world, the magician must first revolutionize his own prehension of existence. The most critical of his initial feats is the bold transformation of language, which in turn will make possible all of his later accomplishments. This linguistic legerdemain has been skillfully exposed by Edmund Leach in his book *Culture and Communication*. Although Leach's analysis itself is straightforward enough, it presupposes certain definitions that I will present in summary form for the purposes of our discussion:

(1) *Signal*: When A is a signal for B, the relationship between them is mechanical and automatic. A triggers B. The message and the message-bearing entity are simply two aspects of the same thing.

(2) *Index*: When A indicates B, A can be said to be an index. A and B are no longer two aspects of the same thing. Whereas signals are causal, indices are descriptive. For example, in Pavlov's experiments with dogs, "the bell was an index for the presence of food, but was treated as a signal." Within this general class, Leach includes *Natural Indices*, in which the association between A and B is natural; for example, "smoke is an index of fire."

(3) *Symbol*: When A stands for B by arbitrary association, A is a symbol.

(4) *Sign*: When A stands for B as a part standing for a whole (metonymy), A is a sign. Thus, "a crown is a sign for royalty." But where a crown is used as a trademark for a brand of beer, it is a symbol and not a sign. *Sign* relationships are contiguous and thus mainly *metonymic*, whereas *symbol* relationships are arbitrary assertions of similarity and thus mainly *metaphoric*.[13]

Leach's key observation about magic is that like Pavlov's dog, the magician has learned to treat indices as though they were signals. Thus he is able to persuade himself and his clientele that his metaphoric nonsense makes metonymic sense. Actually, the magician (or sorcerer, as Leach calls him) must play three tricks before his stunt comes off. First, he must treat the metaphoric symbol as a metonymic sign. Second, he must treat the imputed sign as though it were a natural index. And third, "he interprets the supposed natural index as a signal capable of triggering off automatic consequences at a distance." In this way, the magician's words become the active agents of his own benevolence or wrath.[14]

From the secular point of view, words "have no effect but on those that understand them," as Hobbes once observed. For most of us this rule is quite obvious, but for people like Okada Kotama, words are independent actors directly related to events in the physical world. In fact, they are events themselves. According to Mioshie, our innermost thoughts (*sōnen*), when vocalized, set up vibrations and thought waves that are directly related to autopoetic words (*kotodama*), which in turn act directly on people and things. Thus the various sounds of the Japanese syllabary are linked to specific functions in both the Third and the Fourth Dimension. The sound SU, for example, sets up decisive, unifying spirit movements (*reidō*) or functions (*hataraki*) that can "stop anything." Thus we are told that even the English word stop (pronounced SU-toppu in Japanese) has been influenced by the primordial "SU-function." Thanks to the logopneumatology of the syllable SU, we also know that the ancestors of the Japanese emperor (SUmera Mikoto) were incarnations of SU-god. Personal names with this sound are said to have the power to bring about peace. Thus SUmera means "a person who unifies."

The Mahikari prayer book and scriptures are filled with autopoetic words of this sort and are therefore no ordinary tomes. The prayer book must never be put on the floor, unless it is protected by a special cover sold at the dojo. Spirit seizures have been induced in people simply by touching the prayer book to their foreheads. The Exorcist's Prayer works by the same kind of word magic. Newcomers are told not to worry about how they will respond to the Prayer and the Treatment. Spirit movements and spirit writing alike are said to be automatic. Leach's analysis of the language of magic also helps explain the importance of the Savior's eisegetical wordplay. In all of these cases, the literal incarnation of symbols and metaphors makes it possible for index words to function like signals. The magician can therefore change the world by words alone: *ex opere operato*.

Thanks to this marriage of signals and indices, a bilateral relationship is established between words and events. Words not only cause events; the occurrence of events is, itself, an indication that words have been spoken. Thus, behind all events there is an intention, be it in this world or in worlds beyond. This is the logic of omens. In Mahikari, omens play an important role in the guidance of everyday life. Often the omen is a warning from an ancestor. By heeding it, a person can cure maladies that are presently afflicting members of his family and ward off future misfortune. Spirit investigation itself might be thought of as a way of changing opaque misery into a transparent omen. Through it, the possessed become oracles of their own destiny.

There are also good omens. Once, during an evening service I attended at the Nakayama dojo, a girl noticed a speck of "gold dust" on the foot of the young man sitting in front of her. A group of people quickly gathered around him to see the omen for themselves. Yoshida Sensei explained that gold dust is a "materialization of Light" and a sign of Su-god's favor.*

The most dramatic omen that I witnessed during my stay in Japan occurred in Osaka's Grand Dojo. In early December I took the train from Nakayama to Osaka to distribute my questionnaires at a festival being held there. The Grand Dojo is on the second floor of a large two-story building. The 500 people who attended the festival that afternoon nearly filled the room. At precisely one o'clock, the ceremony started. Shinto liturgical music was piped into the hall. As I listened to the uncanny whine of the archaic reed instruments, I wondered whether this music created in the hearts of those present feelings at all similar to the *mysterium tremendum* that Rudolf Otto identified as the religious response to

---

* The skeptic will point out that the interior walls of Japanese homes are often sprinkled with a similar "gold dust" for decorative effect. One can easily pick up a good omen simply by brushing against them.

Mahikari altar, offerings, and acolytes

the Holy. Or did it merely inspire the "dreadful," "scary," and "weird" feelings that members so often mentioned when they related their own spirit experiences? [15] The music *was* perfectly suited to thinking about spirits and ghosts.

Two girls appeared, dressed in the red and white robes of Shinto shrine maidens, and started to make their offerings before the altar. The first girl, moving with a quiet ceremonial dignity, brought offerings on lacquered trays from a back room into the main hall. Lifting the trays slightly above her head, she passed them to the second girl, who then walked to the altar, knelt, and deftly placed them before the altar scroll. Tray after tray was brought in, heaped with gifts of fruit, rice, bean-paste soup, canned foods, beer, and sake. In the very center, before the altar scroll itself, they finally placed a large, pink sea bream. A string tied from the fish's mouth to its tail caused its still quivering body to arch gracefully upward on the tray. The performance of these essentially awkward ceremonial movements with agility—especially with 500 people watching so intently—was a spectacle in its own right.

After making their offerings, the girls took their places at the side of the altar and sat down. The music was turned off. Then, before the master of ceremonies could reach the microphone, the offering placed before the god Ōkunitama-Ōkuninushi (Daikoku) suddenly slipped from the step of the altar and crashed to the floor. Instantly the mats in front of the altar were covered with the most unholy mess—broken dishes, scattered chopsticks, spilled soup, rice, and vegetables.

The reaction of the congregation was one of shock and disbelief. The same impression seemed to cross the mind of everyone in the hall: an angry god had reached out with an invisible hand to push away the offerings from the altar. Was this an omen, or a warning to someone? While five or six people scrambled for towels and began to clean up, the leader closest to the microphone called for silent prayer. Most of the congregation quickly complied and bowed their heads. Others turned to their neighbors and began to whisper about what had happened and to speculate about what it might portend. One old man in front of me (said to be a former gangster) bent over in prayer, shaking his head from side to side as though repenting some heinous sin. Throughout the room, women were sniffling and drying their tears. The two young ladies who had presented the offerings sat quietly weeping at the side of the altar.

Finally, another leader took the microphone, and in a voice shaking with emotion said, "I am very sorry about what has just happened. Perhaps we have made some mistake that caused this to occur. We don't know what it was. The festival will now be postponed until two o'clock." Because the president of the dojo was absent, the vice-president mounted the small platform in front of the altar, bowed down before Su-god, Ōkunitama-Ōkuninushi, and the portrait of the Savior, and apologized profusely. Then he turned to the congregation, bowed, and again apologized, taking on himself all of the blame for this great sacrilege.

The atmosphere in the room was perceptibly tense and gloomy. Some routine announcements were made in order to kill time. Then someone showed three lengthy reels of eight-millimeter film taken at the annual summer outing of the dojos in the Osaka area. As the congregation watched the movies of potato-sack races and other picnic frolics, the mood in the hall finally became more cheerful.

At two o'clock, the festival began once again. The same tape of Shinto music was played. I had wondered whether the two altar girls would be replaced. They were not. Needless to say, every eye was fixed on them and the offering trays to see whether disaster would strike a second time. People in the back of the room craned their necks to get a better view. The mood of the congregation seemed to become especially strained when the girls replaced the tray before the statue of Okunitama-Okuninushi. Judging from the tension in the air, I am sure that had the offerings fallen again, pandemonium would have broken out. Fortunately, all of the trays stayed in place. Finally, the vice-president mounted the dais to thank the deities that this time the festival had gotten off to a "safe start."

Three hours later, when the festival came to an end, many people stayed behind to receive okiyome and chat. Naturally, there was a good deal of talk about the fallen offerings. Some people thought that the tray had fallen because one of the women in charge of preparing the offerings was menstruating.* Others, especially the women, disagreed with this explanation. Perhaps someone had had "wrong thoughts" (*machigatta sōnen*), they said.

That evening, when I returned to Nakayama, I dropped by the local dojo. The members of the staff were having a party and invited me to join them. Naturally, I told them about the spilled offerings. The story created an instant, electrifying sensation. Immediately everyone had his or her own opinion on the subject. One man, a bank teller, repeated over and over, "This is something that science simply cannot explain!" All agreed that it was "strange," "odd," and even "scary." One young man, a leader of the Youth Corps, jumped up to telephone a friend who had attended the festival in Osaka that day. According to his friend, some of the Osaka members felt that the fallen offerings were definitely a sign of Su-

---

* In Japan, women are often excluded from Shinto rituals because of their periodic "red pollution." But this was the only time that I heard of this taboo in Mahikari.

god's displeasure. They recalled that a month earlier, when the regional festival of the Osaka-area dojos was held, everything had gone wrong. Preparations were hastily made and nothing was properly coordinated. This time, all of the top leaders of the dojo were in Tokyo attending a conference at the sect headquarters instead of paying attention to their festival obligations in Osaka. Perhaps Su-god was trying to tell them that they should take greater care in putting on his festivals.

Everyone I talked with, both in Osaka and in Nakayama, was ready to see the incident as an omen and to speculate on its significance. I thought it rather curious that no one who had witnessed the event seemed to pay any attention to the fact that the steps of the altar were narrower than the ill-fated offering tray, and that the oversized tray had been set precariously on a piece of thick cardboard placed over the step to widen it.

Omens are events or things that express the will of agents in the astral world. Like magic, they are quick, palpable, practical, and effective. Their logic simply reverses the rules for making magic. In magic, as we have seen, it is the magician who, by making index words perform like signals, establishes a mechanical relationship between his own words or will and physical events. Omens, on the other hand, *are* events—ones expressing the will of the unseen.

In his magisterial study of the Azande, E. E. Evans-Pritchard emphasized the systemic network linking witchcraft, oracles, and magic.[16] In the next two chapters we shall see that in Mahikari too a similar triangulation of possession-exorcism, omens, and miracles lays a foundation for a worldview with its own coherence and resilience. What holds Mahikari's triangular praxis together is, first of all, its members' own will to get cleaned up and raise their spirit level. We have seen in Chapters 7 and 8 that this will is conditioned by human, all too human, needs. Furthermore, this will and its specific needs can be satisfied only when people are ready to subscribe to the Greater Need posed by religion itself. Thus, beneath the religious will and the intricate symbolic structures and reticulations of religious thought there goes on an endless seesaw between everyday needs and spiritual Need, or between life's problems and the Problem of life itself.

Mahikari's cosmos is also held together by a different kind of will, namely, that manifested in the grudges, lusts, appetites, and concerns of the beings that inhabit the Fourth and higher Dimensions. It is the will of these spirits that accounts for the otherwise dumb and senseless tragedies of the Third Dimension. Likewise, it is their will, revealed through omens and spirit investigations, that enables people to know their fate—and do something about it. Since the spirits that control us have thoughts, feelings, and intentions of their own, we can, in effect, manipulate them by coaxing them, apologizing to them, teaching them Mioshie, and honoring them with flowers and other treats. If all else fails, we can warn them of the punishment that awaits them if they do not return to the astral world.

Since will, and not blind chance, lies behind misfortune, we have a key for unlocking and even improving our fate. Indeed, fate, destiny, and luck, not to mention the grace by which some would live, are pulverized by the magician's will. All are reduced to spiritual cajolery and a battle of wills. Hence the ritual combat between the exorcist and the evil spirits that occurs so often during spirit investigations.

Thus it is will—sacred, human, and demonic—that animates and consolidates Mahikari's universe. Dojo members regain control of their lives, health, and good fortune merely by raising their hands and synergizing human and spiritual wills. This simple technique for changing fate and karma is the source of the church's unyielding optimism. When accidents, misfortune, and destiny are attributed to a hidden will, the world itself assumes a more human face. Life is therefore made more plausible and humane not merely by the ingenuous anthropomorphisms of theology, but by magic itself. Thanks to the extension of the will through magic, the world becomes a more hospitable place.

In the next chapter we shall see how realistic this magic is. In the end, the world of miracles, oracles, and exorcism stands or falls on the truth of the magician's credo: "Hope cannot fail, nor desire deceive." [17]

11 *When Okiyome Fails*

However strong his will, however long his practice, there comes a time when the magician's hope *does* fail. His most potent spells no longer work, prayers go unanswered, elixirs foam up, only to fizzle out, and the frailty of hope and desire alike is exposed. In such straits, where does the magician turn? What does he do or think? To come to the point, what happens when okiyome fails?

All religions are in the business of building and maintaining worlds-of-meaning. We have already seen how Mahikari erects such a world on the foundation of a Salvation Syndrome that describes, or actually generates, a human condition characterized by a generic Problem, an Ideal, and a Way to that Ideal. As a cognitive structure, this world is put together by the logic of bricolage—construction taking place not in the calm of the theologian's study, but in the emotional hothouse of a dojo. There are also various psychological mechanisms that enable people to appropriate the Salvation Syndrome in a personal way, for example, ritual dissociation and the induction of various states of consciousness having potential healing effects. Finally, an unconscious linguistic transformation of indices into signals makes possible some of the sect's theological maneuvers and the magical feats that are the pride of every dojo. These, then, are some of the specific ways in which Mahikari builds its world of religious ideas and magical practice. A Doubting Thomas may regard Mahikari as a vulgar mélange of superstitions, but it is obvious that the faithful, who have experienced miracles for themselves and have seen their own spirit levels go up, find in Mahikari a coherent, real world.

Once religious symbol systems of this sort are institutionalized, they protect themselves by moving into a state of closure. Internal contradictions are resolved, smoothed out, or simply quashed. Information coming into the system from without is accepted only after it has been properly filtered and made congruent with the system's basic presuppositions or axioms. A religion thereby becomes self-perpetuating, its oracles self-fulfilling, its magic self-confirming and virtually invincible.

Some of our best examples of this kind of symbolic closure come from those compact systems of thought we call primitive. I have already pointed out the way in which E. E. Evans-Pritchard emphasized the systemic coherence of Zande witchcraft, oracles, and magic. In its heyday, this network of thought and action was self-sustaining, self-affirming, and closed. Of the Azande, Evans-Pritchard writes: "All their beliefs hang together, and were a Zande to give up faith in witch-doctorhood he would have to surrender equally his belief in witchcraft and oracles." Indeed, so impervious was this system to any fundamental critique that Evans-Pritchard could regard the Azande as victims of their own world of thought. "In this web of belief every strand depends upon every other strand, and a Zande cannot get out of its meshes because this is the only world he knows. The web is not an external structure in which he is enclosed. It is the texture of his thought and he cannot think that his thought is wrong." [1]

The Zande system of witchcraft, oracles, and magic was sufficiently robust to absorb doubt itself. Although doubt was tolerated, it was always sequestered by the concrete situations in which it arose. Thus, unable to rise above its immediate milieu, the Zandes' doubt was never able to survey the ambient system as a whole or become "systematic" in its own right. "Azande are dominated by an overwhelming faith which prevents them from making experiments, from generalizing contradictions between tests, between verdicts of different oracles, and between all the oracles and experience." The vigor of Zande thought was especially apparent in its capacity to transform negative experience into a positive reinforcement of accepted beliefs and customs. "For their mystical notions are eminently coherent, being interrelated by a network of logical ties, and are so ordered that they never too crudely contradict sensory experience but, instead, experience seems to justify them." Thus, "paradox though it be, the errors as well as the valid judgements of the oracle prove to them its infallibility." [2]

Although Mahikari, a small sect in a complex society, cannot match the inner coherence and stability of Zande beliefs in their classical form, the internal "systematicity" of this African culture and its way of handling "negative externalities," if I may use the economist's jargon, provide valuable clues for dealing with similar problems in Japan. In themselves, religious systems are fragile, even friable, creations. The collapse of any part is apt to threaten the entire structure. When we speak of the coherence of these worlds-of-meaning, we are referring only to their capacity to respond creatively to the poking, probing, and testing of outrageous fortune. The coherence of popular religion is therefore situational and probabilistic—in short a systemic propensity. All religions stand in need of a subsystem of maneuvers and rationales that can be called into play to shore up their vulnerable spots. What they need is theodicy.

Whereas conventional wisdom has it that religion is a way of avoiding misfortune, Clifford Geertz aptly points out that "as a religious problem, the problem of suffering is, paradoxically, not how to avoid suffering, but how to suffer." [3] Religion therefore teaches us how to grasp "the damp hand of melancholy" (James Thurber). We have already seen (Chapter 8) that theodicy is related to legitimation as one side of a coin to the other. If legitimation vindicates an excess of good fortune, power, or wealth, theodicy justifies an excess of bad news, failure, or weakness. Thus if we think of religion as a dike holding back the waters of chaos and anomie, theodicy is a finger in the hole that inevitably appears in the walls of that dike. [4]

Religions actually have two very different types of failure to deal with, and therefore two distinct kinds of theodicy to develop. In the first place, they must account for the ultimate frustrations of the human condition. We have seen that they do this not merely by responding to the givenness of human tragedy, but by creatively defining and symbolizing man's plight as a universal Problem within a specific Salvation Syndrome. Thus we are told, for example, that man must suffer and die because of some ritual abuse committed by his ancestors when the world was young, because of his spiritual ignorance or karma, or because the world in which he was born is temporarily under the control of a less-than-perfect demiurge or demonic being. Theodicies of this sort, which are expressed in terms of the Problem of a Salvation Syndrome, can be called *primary theodicies*.

We have already become acquainted with the fundamental elements in Mahikari's primary theodicy: the Problem of mankind is the clouds or dust that accumulate on the soul because of sin, bad karma, and spirit possession. Actually, the primary theodicy is a bit more complicated than this. Karma and the "sins and pollutions" of the past lower a person's spirit level and make him more vulnerable to possession by evil spirits, which in turn cause disease and misfortune. In many cases possession can be traced back to a person's own misconduct in previous lives. In other cases, its causes are in the present life. For example, medicine coagulates in the body and forms tumors. Evil spirits then wrap themselves around these tumors and form malignancies. Surgery, likewise, invites trouble. A church leader in São Paulo, Brazil, writes in *Mahikari* magazine that many cases of meningitis in his country can be traced back to the great number of tonsillectomies performed by Brazilian doctors. In other words, Western medicine is a case of the Problem.

Medicine is only one of the toxins in the modern world. Every day, newspapers remind the Japanese that their country is literally afloat in a sea of carcinogens. Other poisons that Mahikari finds in contemporary society are less tangible but just as deadly. To people who look on all institutions—whether government, industry, religion, academia, or medicine—from a relative position of social, political, and cognitive impotence, the world itself may seem to give off noxious vapors. As members of Mahikari, the Seed People of the dojo believe that the pride, greed, materialism, wars, and filth of modern civilization make an excellent breeding ground for evil spirits of all sorts. Unlike other Japanese, they therefore have a theodicy that accounts for the current condition of their country. Unlike their secular middle- and upper-class compatriots, they also have a Way out of passive resentment and alienation. This enables them to work their way up in a world they both fear and envy, or at least to advance themselves in a religious world of their own making. Ironically, the conditions of modern society reinforce the ethos and worldview of this sect, whose general orientation is both "pre-modern" and magical in nature. Modernity has actually been woven into the fabric of its theodicy.

Occasionally a theodicy will point the finger of blame at some misdeed a person has committed during his present incarnation. For example, in 1968 Tanaka Ichirō, the husband of a woman who is now the head of the Nakayama Purification Center, died of facial cancer. After his death, his widow, overcome with grief, turned to Mahikari. Spirit investigations revealed that when her husband was a boy, he had killed a snake by crushing its head with a stone. Later the snake spirit caused a cancer to appear on his face (homeopathic possession), and after his death, it even tried to kill the Tanakas' daughter with uterine cancer. The daughter fortunately recovered and was married. The day before her wedding, Mrs. Tanaka gave the girl okiyome, and the snake "committed suicide." Later, the spirit of the snake (apparently reincarnated) appeared to Mrs. Tanaka again and promised to "work for the family" from that time on.

In Mahikari, when a person is made to bear the responsibility for his own plight, his mistake generally turns out to be a ritual offense and not a moral sin. Either his butsudan is in the wrong spot or there are "mistakes" in the arrangement of its memorial tablets. Similarly, as we have seen, woodcutters go deaf when they chop down trees in which the god Ryujin performs his austerities; others have disappeared, never to be heard from again, after offending this god by urinating in the woods.

In short, Mahikari gives many reasons for why life so often is— to cite a philosophical inventory—solitary, poor, nasty, brutish, and short. Spirit possession stories that express theodicy generally have the function of exonerating the individual, blaming him (generally for sins committed in past lives) or simply explaining to him why he suffers. In all of these cases, misfortune is said to be Su-god's way of purifying mankind. Through this purification, people are given an opportunity to raise their spirit levels and prepare themselves for the Holy Civilization of the Twenty-First Century. But exactly who or what causes all of a person's woes—Su-god, evil spirits, karma, medicine, the person himself (in present or past incarnations), or his ancestors—seems to vary from one situation to another. Whereas the church's cosmogony seems to place the blame for human suffering on man's own materialism, pride, and greed, the Problem that emerges in individual spirit interrogations is generally rather truncated, tracing grief back only as far as those omnipresent, opportunistic agents of misfortune: evil spirits.

Misfortune, anomie, and the threat of existential chaos are not the only problems a religious system must deal with. Still more serious is *the problem of its own failures*. Each religion has its Job, a blameless and upright man who has accepted its version of mankind's Problem, hoped for its Ideal, and devoted himself wholeheartedly to its Way. All to no avail. His flocks, servants, and family are destroyed, and he himself is afflicted by loathsome sores and religious friends. Thus if the primary theodicy of a religious system is a function of the Problem it imposes on human sorrow, the *secondary theodicy* deals with the ruts, bumps, detours, and dead ends in the Way of religion itself. It is a secondary theodicy that comes into play when okiyome fails.

Not all who join Mahikari get the miracle they were looking for. When a Japanese newspaper published a series of articles on Mahikari in the spring of 1978, its office was flooded with calls and letters from disturbed readers. One man wrote that he was worried about his wife, who had a kidney ailment but refused to take her medicine because she had learned in Mahikari that "medicine is poison." Others told of friends and relatives who had died after they had given up on doctors and turned to Su-god.[5] Nearly every dojo knows about people who have tried okiyome but dropped out when their miracle failed to materialize.

Mahikari obviously is not the only religion that has had this problem. As Bryan R. Wilson points out, it is a built-in weakness of sects that institutionalize a thaumaturgical response to the world: "Thaumaturgy attracts a volatile clientele, and its practice is likely to be local, transient, and haphazard. . . . The difficulty which arises is that of socializing a clientele to the idea that flashes of miraculous power may be associated with, may even depend on, persistent commitment to a regular pattern of worship and a formal system of belief."[6]

After schism, the dropout rate is indeed Mahikari's foremost institutional problem. In Japan, the purchase of an amulet in a temple or shrine seldom, if ever, carries with it any obligation to continue supporting that institution or its priest. On the contrary, religious affiliations of this sort tend to be affairs of the moment, ad hoc and purely functional. The exchange of cash for amulet both recalls the ancient religious formula *do ut des* and effectively puts the purchaser of the amulet in the role of a customer.[7] Understandably, many Japanese who take Mahikari's training course and receive an omitama treat it as they would any other amulet. Some stop wearing it after their initiation and hang it on the wall, expecting it to work by itself. Many see no need to go to the dojo to give and receive okiyome when they can do it more easily, and at far less cost, at home.

Church leaders are by no means unaware of these pitfalls. Yoshida Sensei estimates that at the Nakayama dojo, about 50 percent of those who receive an amulet sooner or later quit the church. Only about 20 percent become active members. This leaves roughly 30 percent who can only be described as lukewarm. Church leaders repeatedly insist that if a person does not continue his shugyo by raising his hand at the dojo, his amulet will become ineffective. Lecturers often point out the sad plight of those who stop coming to the dojo as soon as they have been cured. Because of their "lack of gratitude," these people often suffer a relapse that even okiyome cannot cure. Evil spirits often save their revenge until a person has children, and then attack them. Children should therefore be given okiyome on a regular basis.

Another reason for continuing to receive okiyome, dojo members learn, is to ward off future diseases and accidents. This prophylactic use of okiyome is especially important in the case of cancer, a disease that may spread rapidly once it has set in. Thus the sooner a person begins to give and receive the Treatment, the better. The dojo is the best place for this ritual activity because the healing Light rays of Su-god are said to be especially thick there. Furthermore, because there are so many strangers who drop into the dojo, doing shugyo there gives members a good opportunity to practice "altruism." With arguments like these, the leaders try to create long-term commitments to the dojo. Yet in spite of their earnest importuning, the attrition of the membership continues at a formidable rate.

How does the church deal with the apparent failures of its own ritual Treatment? There seems to be no end to the reasons alleged for the failure of okiyome. Although okiyome is said to be more objective than faith healing, the failure of the Treatment is sometimes traced back to a lack of faith. Sometimes it is said that a person's disease became fatal because he did not join Mahikari soon enough. In other cases the death of a member is attributed to insufficient shugyo: he did not raise his hands enough, or he did not go to the dojo often enough.

For example, a member in Tokyo joined Mahikari after having an operation for throat cancer. After he received okiyome, his condition seemed to improve. According to his daughter, "he began to vomit impurities and have diarrhea all the time," sure signs that Su-god was cleaning him up. But finally the man died. According to his daughter, evil spirits had taken up their abode in a plastic tube that surgeons had implanted in her father's throat, making them utterly impervious to exorcism. In other words, neither cancer nor okiyome, but surgery was to blame for her father's death. Members also die from ritual mistakes. In spite of warnings from Yoshida Sensei, an old grandmother in the Nakayama dojo gave okiyome to the memorial tables in her butsudan. She died six months later. At least one member of the local dojo died when the symbol of Su-god accidentally dropped out of his amulet.

Ancestral spirits often return to tell their families why they died. One man joined the Nakayama dojo after learning that he had stomach cancer. When his condition became critical, he decided to disregard the church's teachings and go to the hospital (taking his amulet with him). After the man died, his son went to the dojo to receive okiyome. There the father's spirit appeared to the son and said, "I'm ashamed that I went to the hospital. I should have stayed home and used my amulet." When the man's widow heard this, she was filled with wonder and took the next training course herself. In a similar case, a man with throat cancer joined the church, but he lost his faith when no miracle occurred and sent his amulet back to the dojo. After his death, he appeared to his son to tell him how sorry he was that he had turned in his amulet and to urge the young man to persevere in the faith.

A common attitude members take toward the ultimate failure of their amulet's power is to say, in effect, what can I lose? When one person told me that with his amulet he would feel secure even in an earthquake, I protested that, amulet or no, even members of Mahikari have to die. "Yes," he replied, "it is only human to die. But if you don't have an amulet, you might get sick and die need-lessly. If you have an amulet and *still* die, it's just one of those things that can't be helped [*shikata ga nai*]."

There are members, however, whose personal encounters with tragedy have nurtured a kind of religious realism that transcends the magician's fond fancies. Although they do not doubt the World of Miracles, these people know that whatever magic Su-god has in store for them, it is not quick, palpable, or automatic. Miss Nakata, the Old Miss who lives beneath the Nakayama dojo, is a case in point. Realizing that it is now too late to marry, she devotes her-self to giving okiyome to others at the dojo, trying to raise both their spirit level and her own. She hopes that thanks to her shugyo, she will not suffer from the same diseases and misfortunes when she is reborn. Her greatest miracles, therefore, lie in the far-distant future and are a matter of faith.

I have already pointed out that compared with shugyo (or prax-is), faith seems to play a minor role in Mahikari. In fact, faith seems to enter a person's life primarily when okiyome fails. The following story illustrates my point.

In May 1976, Wakimoto Takeo, forty-four, the proprietor of a small camera shop in the city, noticed a growth on his abdomen. His wife, Kayako, recalling how much trouble he had been having recently with his stomach, immediately suspected that it might be malignant and insisted that he see a physician. After taking X rays and conducting other tests, the doctor at the local clinic told Mr. Wakimoto that he had a bad case of ulcers. Mrs. Wakimoto, sus-pecting that there was more to it than this, went to talk to the doctor herself. Her worst fears proved to be true: the tests had actu-ally shown that her husband was suffering from terminal cancer of the stomach. Although the doctor did not feel that an operation would help much, he offered to send the medical records to a larger hospital if the couple decided to seek further treatment.

For some time Mrs. Wakimoto said nothing to her husband. But without being told, he too seemed to know the truth. He consulted palmists and began to take various Chinese herbs and miracle drugs. Then one of his friends told him about Mahikari. A month after Mr. Wakimoto's visit to the clinic, the Wakimotos took the training course at the dojo and began to give each other okiyome day in and day out. It was only after they had joined Mahikari that Mrs. Wakimoto finally told her husband what the doctor had said. At first there seemed reason to hope for a miracle. At the dojo they were told that it was because of okiyome that Mr. Wakimoto was beginning to vomit and have chronic diarrhea. By these means Su-god was melting and destroying his tumor.

Shortly after Mrs. Wakimoto took the training course, she became possessed by the ghost of her father-in-law, who had died some twenty years before from cancer. This evil spirit made her have trouble with her stomach too, so that she finally grew extremely emaciated herself. Even though Mr. Wakimoto, as the eldest son in his family, was responsible for the family's butsudan and memorial tablets, he had never paid much attention to them. After the Wakimotos took the training course, they discovered that both the arrangement and the type of tablets in their butsudan were improper. They bought a new altar and tablets from the dojo and sent their old ones to their family temple for safekeeping.

In spite of their diligent shugyo and the changes in their butsudan, Mr. Wakimoto's condition grew worse. The rest of the family urged the Wakimotos to seek medical attention, but they decided to entrust themselves to Su-god, come what may. Furthermore, there was the example of Mr. Wakimoto's sister. Since she had died one year after having a cancer operation, the Wakimotos were convinced that surgery was no solution. Finally, they realized that their family was under a curse. After all, not only Mr. Wakimoto's sister, but his father too had died from cancer. Also, an uncle who had emigrated to Brazil had been operated on twice for cancer of the bladder and was hoping to go to the Tokyo Cancer Center for still another operation.

Although Mr. Wakimoto only half believed in Mahikari, his wife was zealous indeed. After her father-in-law's spirit appeared to her—weeping with joy because they had fed him at their butsudan—her faith became unshakable. Even her husband's rapidly deteriorating condition could not make her doubt the existence and power of Su-god.

Before long, Mr. Wakimoto became too weak to go to the dojo. His wife continued to go, however, to consult with Yoshida Sensei and the ministers about which "vital points" on her husband's body she should focus on. Occasionally the ministers dropped by the house to give her husband okiyome.

Mr. Wakimoto's first spirit movements took place just two days before he died. Even then, since the spirit did not talk, no one could say what kind of spirit it was. The night he died, he ate a large dinner, but he soon developed a violent case of hiccups. When Mrs. Wakimoto was unable to cure the hiccups by using okiyome herself, she called Mr. Murakami, their squadron leader. At 11:00 P.M. he arrived at their home and gave Mr. Wakimoto okiyome. At first Mr. Wakimoto's head moved back and forth, as though some evil spirit were trying to escape from the Light coming from Mr. Murakami's uplifted hand. Then Mr. Murakami began a spirit investigation, asking the evil spirit what part of Mr. Wakimoto's body it had possessed. The hand of the dying man moved to his chest. "Here, here," he moaned. With that he turned his head aside, vomited something black, and died.

After Mr. Wakimoto's death, some of the members of the dojo began to wonder whether Su-god had really helped him or not. Nevertheless, about thirty members came to his wake and gathered around the coffin to give his body okiyome. So that Mr. Wakimoto could go to the astral world and give his ancestors and other spirits okiyome, he was cremated wearing his amulet and holding his prayer book. The members comforted themselves by noting that, after all, it was a miracle that even on the last day Mr. Wakimoto had been able to eat a large meal, and that he had died with a look of peace on his face.

For forty-nine days after Mr. Wakimoto's death, his spirit appeared to his widow every night when she went to the dojo for okiyome. (During this period, according to Mioshie, a spirit can visit its own family with impunity.) Every time he appeared, his wife wept and did automatic writing on the floor. Usually the spirit caused her to write out the names of their two children, Kanako and Hiroshi. Through their mother, the spirit reminded the children always to be kind to one another and to "keep up the good work [*ganbaru*]." "There is no other way to be saved except through Mahikari," he told them. He also predicted the coming of an earthquake. After the forty-nine days were over and her husband's spirit finally disappeared, Mrs. Wakimoto was possessed by four or five of his uncles and aunts, people who had died in the war and in traffic accidents. A number of her own relatives and about a dozen unrelated spirits also appeared to her. All of these spirits (including her husband's) seemed to say about the same thing: they were hungry, but when they learned that she was tending the family butsudan and doing shugyo daily at the dojo, they apologized and shed tears of gratitude.

After her husband's death in July 1976, Mrs. Wakimoto took over the camera shop herself and continued to come to the dojo every day with her children. By November her "fundamental soul" (*honrei*) had been cleaned up and her spirit movements came to an end. Yoshida Sensei then asked her to become a squadron helper (*hanchō hosa*).

Five months after I had had my first interview with Mrs. Wakimoto, I spoke with her at greater length. By this time she had become quite well adjusted to her new life. Her children had taken the loss of their father with such courage that the neighbors were amazed. By the end of the year she had developed a fairly elaborate religious understanding of her husband's disease and death. She now believes that her husband's stomach cancer was caused by toxins he had absorbed over the years: "Every day for twenty years he smoked about forty cigarettes. Three times a day he went to a nearby snack shop for a cup of strong coffee. And then there were all of the food additives. . . . My husband's cancer was caused when evil spirits 'wrapped themselves around' these toxins."

Even though her husband's own spirit experiences had been extremely vague—nearly nonexistent, in fact—Mrs. Wakimoto, with the aid of the ministers, pieced together a spirit story that has helped her accept his death and the other deaths in their family. It seems that Mr. Wakimoto's ancestors were warriors who once executed a number of peasants and townsmen. These victims later became grudge-bearing spirits that returned to this world and possessed the entire family. It was they who ultimately had caused not only her husband's cancer, but the cancers of his father, sister, and uncle. By the time of our second interview, I noticed that Mrs. Wakimoto's language was full of Mahikari doctrines and technical jargon. She even suggested as an alternative reason for her husband's death that his body was not able to keep pace with the "changes in the universe," that is, with the increasing intensity of fire and light caused by the return of the "strict deities." In effect, the church's eschatology was starting to influence the theodicy that Mrs. Wakimoto was constructing. With Yoshida Sensei's help, she also came to see her husband's death as a sacrifice on behalf of the entire family. She believes that her husband—by doing shugyo first in the dojo and then, after being cremated with amulet and prayer book, in the other world—will be able to save his ancestors, clean up his family's "sins and pollutions," and lift the curse of cancer from the family once and for all. Thanks to his sacrificial death, his children have nothing to fear.*

According to other dojo members, Mrs. Wakimoto has become much more open and friendly since she joined the dojo. It was my impression, too, that she radiates a peaceful, outgoing attitude. Since she goes to the dojo every evening, her life now seems to revolve around her religious faith and practice. When she receives okiyome, she says she has feelings of gratitude and enters a state of (Buddhist) non-ego (*muga no kyōchi*) or a rapturous, dreamlike state (*muga muchū*) in which she is absolutely certain of Su-god's existence. When she gives okiyome to others, she feels heat in the palm of her hand. Later, when she goes home at night, she is happy to know that her husband and his ancestors are all content in the astral world. She is gratified to know that Su-god is saving the entire family both in this world and in the Fourth Dimension.

---

* Mrs. Wakimoto's daughter, Kanako (seventeen) is the girl whom Yoshida Sensei used to demonstrate okiyome to me on my first visit to the dojo. Her younger brother, Hiroshi (fourteen) has suffered from headaches and stomach cramps, and believes that he has been possessed by the spirit of a soldier who died in the Pacific War. During the training course, he collapsed when he was given okiyome. Even now he sometimes has fits (*hikitsuke*) when he receives the Treatment.

Because I met the Wakimoto family after Mr. Wakimoto died, I am not sure to what extent he shared his wife's faith. According to some, he remained skeptical until the very end. But Mrs. Wakimoto has become an extremely devout member of the church. As far as I could discern, she has gone through several stages of personal religious growth since she first joined the dojo. At first, she actually believed that her husband could be cured by a miracle. By purchasing a new butsudan, she hoped to be able to reverse her husband's fate and raise the whole family's spirit level. When he began to vomit and have diarrhea, she was persuaded by friends at the dojo that these symptoms were Su-god's way of purging his body of impurities. Thus even her husband's deteriorating condition gave her hope that a miracle was on the way. Her faith in Mahikari became still deeper when she began to have spirit experiences herself. It became unmovable when various spirits appeared to her to beg for food and shed tears of gratitude for all that she and her family had done for them. Before long, however, fond hope gave way to painful truth. Her husband was dying. Still the family refused medical attention. Together they decided that "whether we live or die we will trust Su-god." The faith and resignation of this decision—Peter L. Berger would call it masochism*—clearly reflect a far different attitude from the combination of hope and anxiety with which the couple first entered the dojo.

After her husband's death, Mrs. Wakimoto, with the help of the dojo leaders, began to look for the reason why okiyome apparently had not worked. Had Su-god failed them? Some of the members began to doubt his power, but Mrs. Wakimoto reached new religious insights into her family's suffering. Her husband's death was an atoning, prophylactic sacrifice to protect the entire family from future disease and misfortune. Far from letting them down, Su-god was still at work helping all the Wakimotos get cleaned up. Her faith in these new rationales was deepened by her many spirit experiences, not the least of which was the repeated appearance of

* Mrs. Wakimoto's words are remarkably similar to the statement in the Book of Job that Berger takes as the locus classicus of the masochistic attitude: "Though he slay me, yet will I trust him." See Peter L. Berger, *The Sacred Canopy: Elements of a Sociological Theory of Religion* (Garden City, N.Y., 1967), p. 74. See also pp. 55–57.

her husband himself during the forty-nine days after his death. By continuing to go to the dojo for okiyome, Mrs. Wakimoto gradually got cleaned up herself. The fact that her spirit seizures went away is sufficient proof that okiyome really works. The staff recognized this achievement by offering her a (rather low) position of responsibility.

The miscarriage of magic drives many from the dojo. Because the church promises quick relief, palpable results, and automatic change, its hope is vulnerable to the intractable, shattering realities of suffering and death. Few have the patience or composure to wait for the slower magic of religious consolation. For those who do, the failure of okiyome generally does not destroy faith in miracles but adds new dimensions to it. Thus they conclude that *in this particular situation*, Su-god worked his magic in an unexpected way. The miracle was of a spiritual sort. As in Zandeland, doubt is thus absorbed by a larger network of belief and action. This, at least, seems to be the process at work in Mrs. Wakimoto's case. The theodicy that finally took shape in her mind resulted from the apparent failure of okiyome. Faith and theodicy grew as hope in miracles became faint. Only after her husband's death and reappearance as a spirit did Mrs. Wakimoto's religious understanding of his death become complete.

The Greek philosopher Democritus taught that the universe is the fruit of chance and necessity; this is also the common-sense conviction of most secular people in modern society. But it is a view repugnant to those whose response to the world is basically magical. Such people see in the idea of mere chance the threat of total chaos, and in necessity, the horror of a world blind and insensitive to human weakness and need. Before they can feel at home in the world, they feel they must domesticate necessity and compel it to take their side. If the world is determined, all things must be at least arranged optimistically. If something in the universe is to be loose and undetermined, it must be predictably amicable.

Religions like Sukyo Mahikari criticize the secular or common-sense viewpoint that attributes misfortune to bad luck and natural causation. On the other hand, they are not willing to endure the insufferable simply because it happens. Between chance and necessity they steer a middle course that is, in effect, an extension and manipulation of natural cause and effect. They disclose a new causal sphere in which human intention and superhuman intervention can alter the necessary and control what others call fortune. In Mahikari, this enlarged world of causation is a realm of spirits and purification. It establishes a framework for the practice of a new, spiritual technology that will renew the world and bring about the Civilization of the Kingdom of God. In its own idiom, Mahikari's magical approach to the world is causal, experiential, and rational. When the coherence or credibility of this world is threatened by the apparent failure of okiyome, various theodicies are put into action to "salve the appearances." In this way, the magician's will and hope are actually reaffirmed. In exceptional cases, like that of the Wakimotos, the failure of magic may even open the eyes of the magician to self-sacrifice and a more mature religious faith.

12 *Upward Religious Mobility*

Like people everywhere, members of Mahikari are, to varying degrees, conscious of their station in life. Moreover, they are quite aware of their rank within their own religious community. In my survey the item with the fewest missing values was Question 15: "Describe your responsibility in the dojo." More people failed to answer the questions about their age and sex than this question. Although I have nothing to compare it with, this attention to the issue of responsibility in the dojo seems to indicate a relatively high level of status awareness among members.

Because the term religious status appears repeatedly in this chapter, I should make clear at the outset what I mean by it. There are two fundamental aspects of personal worth or dignity: self-esteem and social status. Although the two do not always coincide, they are inevitably interrelated. To borrow the framework of G. H. Mead, one could say that self-esteem is to social status what "I" is to "Me." A person's sense of integrity and well-being can never be completely divorced from his status in those social groups that matter to him. Although religious status may be considered a kind of social status (insofar as religious communities are societies), it differs from social status in that (1) it is defined, either exclusively or in large measure, by religious notions and rationales (such as concepts of soul, saintliness, ascetic heroism, or a general metaphysical vision); (2) it is recognized and evaluated by fellow saints who share these notions and rationales; and (3) it is legitimated to a large degree by religious or magical means. One would have to admit, however, that a clear-cut distinction between religious and social status can be made only in modern societies where sacred rationales are no longer needed to legitimate the entire social order.

The Organization of Church and Dojo

Like its seven-dimensional universe, Mahikari's official organization is both hierarchical and bureaucratic. Yoshida Sensei likes to compare it to an army. At the top of the organization is the Spiritual Leader, connected to Su-god by "thick spirit rays." The Spiritual Leader is said to occupy herself primarily with religious activities: doing shugyo, presenting Divine Notifications to Su-god, and preparing amulets. She is assisted by a group of older men, personal disciples of her father who now are in charge of running the day-to-day affairs of the church. Some of them also give lectures for the intermediate and advanced training courses.

The country is divided into sixteen regions, the dojos in each being ranked according to size. In 1976 there were six Grand, thirty-nine Intermediary, and eighty-four Small Dojos. Beneath this level there are Preparatory Dojos, Purification Centers, and Evangelistic Outposts, all of which are generally small enough to be located in members' homes. The leadership of the local dojos can be divided into three levels. At the highest level is the staff, which consists of the president of the dojo, vice-presidents, and ministers. The president is often the person who organized and built the local dojo. Sometimes a junior staff consisting of the heads of the local Preparatory Dojos, Purification Centers, and Evangelistic Outposts works in tandem with the staff.

Most of the ministers (*doshi*) are single people in their early twenties who are trained at the national church headquarters and sent to serve dojos throughout the country. Subordinate both to headquarters and to the local lay leaders on the staff, the ministers receive food and lodging from the dojo, but only a pittance as a salary. In some areas ministers have become dojo presidents, indicating a nascent trend toward a clerical professionalization of the leadership. But this does not happen often, and the church continues to be largely a layman's movement. Because of the ministers' low income and demanding work schedules, their dropout rate is quite high. Some quit their church work when they marry.* Others simply lose their faith. I was told by one minister that some of his brethren had "become proud, and even criticize the Savior and Su-god." He assured me, however, that whenever this happens, Su-god punishes the individual and "wipes him out."

One step down from the staff level is a cluster of important offices, including the squadron leaders (hancho) in charge of evangelism and the spiritual guidance of members living in a specific area; stewardship directors (osewanin-kaichō), whose responsibility is fund raising; and leaders of the Mahikari Youth Corps.† The lowest offices include members of the Women's Circle and all of the assistants assigned to work under the direction of higher-ranking officials. These assistants are generally women or recent converts.

All positions are assigned by the staff of the dojo. Names are sent to the Spiritual Leader, who in turn presents them to Su-god. Occasionally, and for no apparent reason, Su is said to turn down even stalwart members. However unfair this may seem, this ritual confirmation of local appointments seems to guarantee the perpetuation of a residual "charisma of office" (Weber: *Amtscharisma*) at all levels of leadership. Every April the staff reviews the positions to be assigned for the coming year. At this time, each person is asked to ponder how well he has performed in his present position. If he wants to continue in the same post, he may nominate himself for it. If not, he can ask to be moved to another spot, or he can simply become inactive for a while. In spite of this rotation system, the more zealous members may occupy the same position year after year.

A person's spiritual powers, or to be more specific, the strength or thickness of the spirit rays coming from his hands, are in direct

---

*Ministers must receive permission from the Spiritual Leader of the church before they can marry. Sometimes she warns them about a bad match or even refuses to allow a marriage to take place.

†The Youth Corps likewise has a hierarchical organization, from its national governor and supervisors down to the children in the local dojo. Each area of the country is divided into specific corps and sub-corps. In addition to being taught Mioshie, children learn how to march and respond to the commands of their leaders. All must pledge their obedience to the Divine Orders issued through the mouth of the Spiritual Leader.

proportion to his position in the dojo. Theologically speaking, rank or office (*miyakume*) is therefore independent of age, family rank, and the length of time a person has been a member. It is said that children who outrank their parents are more effective than their elders in purifying and subduing evil spirits. Also, as we have seen, exorcists often change places with someone of higher rank when their own benedictions fail to dispel a possessing spirit. Because of their superior spiritual power, the dojo staff sets aside one evening a week for what is called the Staff's Purification. In the Nakayama dojo, every Thursday evening the staff gathered to give one another okiyome. After seven o'clock all members were invited to come and receive the Treatment and spirit investigations from the staff.*

Divine Notifications (onenji) also depend on the church's hierarchical organization. A person may become gravely ill and call his squadron leader to come to his home to give him okiyome. If this seems to do no good, the president of the local dojo may be summoned. He, in turn, may have to call the leader of the whole area (*shidōbuchō*). Although the case will probably have been diagnosed by this time (through spirit investigations), the person may still be dangerously ill. If so, the highest-ranking local leader may finally call the Spiritual Leader and ask her to present a Divine Notification to Su-god.†

Before we leave the subject of hierarchy, I should point out two mistaken notions that people often have when they first come in contact with Japan's New Religions. The first is that because these groups are officially organized along hierarchical lines, they are really petty dictatorships in religious guise. The second is that they are intimate brotherhoods, or *Gemeinschaften*, to use Ferdinand Tönnies' word. Some observers compound their errors and declare the New Religions to be authoritarian *Gemeinschaften* pure and simple. This is not the case.

Because the ideology of the New Religions is often redolent of the political and social values of Japan's ultranationalist period (1930–45), it is frequently assumed that they are based on dangerous,

---

* During the Staff's Purification, okiyome is given only to the primary soul.
† Onenji is described in Chapter 10, p. 203n.

undemocratic forms of leadership. Although, to be sure, the highest positions in many of these groups are hereditary, the tone of the authority they exercise is generally more paternalistic and consensual than authoritarian. In all of these organizations, formal, hierarchical relationships are supplemented by informal, horizontal ties. When we study the organization of these religions, it is therefore as important to investigate the kind of unstructured socializing that goes on while members sit in small circles folding newsletters and gossiping as it is to study their official ranking. Study groups, at least successful ones, are seldom dominated by their leaders. Likewise, feasting, whether planned or spontaneous, is just as important for the solidarity of the group as its vertical organization. In short, the hierarchy of these religions is generally authoritative without being authoritarian or dictatorial. Although the highest offices often are hereditary, all other positions are open to members exhibiting talent and dedication.

The New Religions are treated by some as islands of community warmth in a cold and impersonal industrial society. Now, it is true that many people make new friends when they join a New Religion. In Mahikari, working together to promote the Divine Plan produces not only the external growth of the sect but also its inner sense of purpose and camaraderie. Nevertheless, except among the younger members, there is little socializing among members outside of the dojo. Even the younger people usually meet their friends in the context of organized religious activities—while doing shugyo, or putting on a festival or testimonial meeting. Although members frequently travel long distances together to attend festivals, they are not inclined, say, to meet at a tea shop to idle away their time. The tone of social relationships among members is one of close associates "standing hand-in-hand with each other and with God," as the word for member (*kamikumite*) might be translated. Neither a *Gemeinschaft* nor a *Gesellschaft*, the dojo might better be thought of as a *Genossenschaft*, a fellowship of acquaintances.

Of course, not all members are involved in their *Genossenschaft* to the same degree. In my statistical survey, three factors were used to determine the level of their involvement: position (that is, rank in the hierarchy of dojo offices); attendance; and how many of the three training courses they had completed. These three factors constitute our Scale of Involvement.

When we look at the effects of age, sex, marital status, occupation, income, and education on religious involvement, age and sex prove to be the most important factors determining the degree of a person's involvement in general and his chances for attaining high office in particular. In the four dojos surveyed, a substantial correlation between age and position was found ($r = .15$, $p = .001$). The correlation between age and the amount of training a person receives was even higher ($r = .19$, $p = .001$). Since no discernible relationship was found between age and attendance, however, the correlation between age and involvement as a whole (position + attendance + training) was lower ($r = .14$, $p = .001$). If we divide the members into three groups according to monthly attendance (minimum, average, and maximum) and then analyze these groups by age, we find that the cohort of people thirty to fifty-six years old ranks highest in average attendance but lowest in maximum attendance. The attendance pattern of those eighteen to twenty-nine approximates that of members who are fifty-six and older: both score relatively low in average attendance but high in maximum attendance. The degree of attendance seems to be influenced mainly by work schedules and family obligations, which naturally weigh most heavily on those in middle age. The high level of attendance among the younger members no doubt reflects the zealous efforts of the Mahikari Youth Corps. All three attendance levels drop off sharply at the age of retirement, which is about fifty-five in Japan.

When we analyze differences in religious involvement by sex, we find that men predominate in all three aspects of our Scale of Involvement. Although a higher percentage of women attend the dojo infrequently or fairly regularly, men stand out among those who attend most faithfully (men, 40 percent; women, 28 percent). Men are also more likely to take the intermediate and advanced training courses (intermediate: men, 57 percent, women, 48 percent; advanced: men, 27 percent, women, 15 percent). It is therefore no surprise that the highest positions of authority and responsibility in the local dojo are dominated by men, as Table 7 shows.[1] The

Table 7. *Position in Dojo by Sex*

Position in dojo	Female		Male	
	Number	*Percent*	*Number*	*Percent*
None	250	60%	117	46%
Low	150	36	107	42
High	14	3	33	13
TOTAL	414	100	257	100

NOTE: In this table, the first two levels of responsibility have been combined as "low" position; the third is "high."

overall correlation between the male sex and the Scale of Involvement is therefore rather high ($r = .19, p = .001$).

As for marital status, single members are found largely in the Mahikari followership, and married members in the leadership, probably because of the correlation between age and position. Divorced members also tend to be followers rather than leaders: 67 percent ($n = 16$) had no position at all, and 25 percent ($n = 6$) held offices at the lowest level.

Even though there is no one-to-one correspondence between occupation and position in the dojos, the occupational groups with the highest percentage of members having no position at all are farmers (60 percent, $n = 16$) and blue-collar workers (skilled, 57 percent, $n = 20$; unskilled, 50 percent, $n = 31$). Farmers and unskilled blue-collar workers were also the least represented occupational groups in the advanced training course. The occupational groups having the largest percentage of members in low positions were the white-collar workers (low-level, 45 percent, $n = 66$; high-level, 50 percent, $n = 22$). Putting aside the full-time staff ($n = 5$), the skilled blue-collar workers (14 percent, $n = 5$) and high-level white-collar workers (11 percent, $n = 5$) had the highest percentage of members in the highest dojo offices.

Although coefficients of correlation show little relationship between income and the three aspects of religious involvement, we can say that as a member's income increases, his chances of having no position at all decrease. Members whose annual family income is above $6,897 are more likely to hold a position in their dojo than members whose income is below this figure. Thus the probability that a person will hold one of the highest offices is somewhat improved by a high income.[2]

Figure B.2 in Appendix B shows that high-school graduates and members who have had some college education are somewhat more likely to find a position in the dojo than members with only a junior-high-school background. Even so, whereas 26 percent of the high positions are held by individuals with some exposure to college education, 51 percent are held by high-school graduates and 23 percent by people with only a junior-high-school education. The sect therefore can hardly be said to be dominated by an educated elite. On the other hand, education does seem to be one of the qualities the staff looks for when it assigns responsibilities.[3]

To summarize our findings, although high income and education increase the likelihood that a member will hold an important office in the dojo, advancing age and being male are the most important factors in increasing both the member's chances of holding an important office and the degree of his religious involvement in general. Although occupational groups cannot be decisively correlated with the hierarchy of dojo offices, skilled blue-collar workers and high-level white-collar workers do have a greater percentage of members in the highest positions than other occupational groups.

Upward Religious Mobility

We can now try to relate our findings concerning members' religious involvement with their experiences of spirit possession and miracles. There is no real relationship between possession and the performance of miracles as measured by our Scale of Miracles and Scale of Possession. When we examine the coefficients of correlation between the various items that make up the two Scales we find a discernible relationship only between the sheer number of miracles that members experience and the number of spirit seizures they have $(r = .20, p = .001)$.

If the spirit seizures that members have are unrelated to their miraculous experiences, does possession have anything to do with their religious involvement? Does affliction by evil spirits increase or discourage participation in the affairs of the church? Or, to reverse the question, does a person's religious involvement encourage or ward off spirits waiting to possess him? The coefficient of correlation for the Involvement and Possession Scales shows that there is no overall relationship between these two clusters of experience. The kind of involvement in the sect indicated by the office a member holds and the number of training courses he has taken seems virtually unrelated to possession experiences. Of the coefficients of correlation of the items composing the two Scales, only that relating members' attendance to the sheer number of their spirit movements shows any discernible relationship ($r = .23$, $p = .001$). High attendance levels also seem to accompany the belief that a person's whole family has been possessed by the same evil spirit.

Of the potential triangle between possession, miracles, and religious involvement, we have now established that there is virtually no relationship between possession and the working of miracles, on the one hand, and between possession and religious involvement, on the other. Is there any relationship between religious involvement and the performance of miracles? In this case the answer is yes. The strong positive correlation between the Scale of Involvement and the Scale of Miracles ($r = .33$, $p = .001$) indicates that the more involved people are in the church, the more likely they are to experience miracles.[4]

The significance of the relatively high correlation between involvement and miracles can easily be grasped by considering the following points. In Chapter 10 we saw that the Showers Group (those experiencing a relatively high number of miracles) declines with increasing age. But when we compare the Scale of Involvement (itself positively related to age) with the number of miracles members experience, we find that though the Mercy Drops Group (those experiencing a moderate number of miracles) remains larger than the Showers Group, the more involved a person is, the more likely he is to be blessed by Showers of miracles. In other words, miracles abound among the most involved, as Figure 5 shows, despite the moderating effects of age.

A study of the relationship between responses to Question 25 (on thaumaturgical auto repair) and the three measures of religious involvement yields the following interesting results (see Table 8).

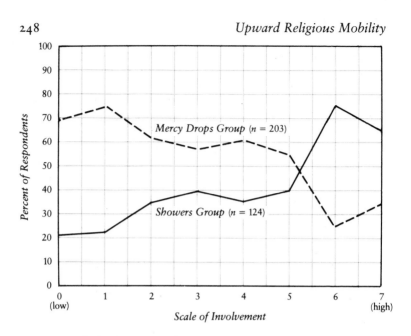

FIG. 5. *Level of Religious Involvement by Miracle Record*

(1) The more doctrinal training a member undergoes, the more likely he is to use okiyome to fix his automobile before trying to fix it in some other way. (2) The higher the member's position in the dojo, the more likely he is to say that he would first use okiyome to fix his automobile. (3) The more the individual attends the dojo, the more likely he is to first use okiyome.

There are several ways to explain this high correlation between religious involvement and belief in miracles. We could say, along with members of the church, that Su-god bestows more miracles on those who faithfully give and receive okiyome at the dojo every week, who take time to attend the advanced training courses, or who accept positions of responsibility in the organization. Or, we could say, from a more cynical point of view, that the more involved a person is in a religion like Mahikari, the more brainwashed he will be. From this perspective, the steadfast believer only *thinks* he is able to move mountains or resurrect goldfish by raising his hand. While both of these explanations are interesting to contemplate, I shall leave them to theologians and private detectives, who are better equipped to adjudicate the matter. A sociological resolution of the problem takes a different tack. What we must explain is not only the positive correlation between religious involvement and belief in miracles, but also the *absence* of any relationship between possession and miracles, on the one hand, and between possession and involvement, on the other. In other words, we must explain both the relationships and the non-relationships in the triangle of possession, involvement, and miracles.

To get at this problem, let us review the way in which people come to Mahikari and get cleaned up. Let us say that Mr. Tanaka comes to the dojo because of angina pectoris. Doctors and pills have done him no good. At the dojo he is given okiyome and suffers a violent spirit seizure. Spirit investigations reveal that he is being possessed by the spirit of a great-uncle who bears a grudge

Table 8. Training Level, Position in Dojo, and Attendance Level as Related to Preference for Thaumaturgical Auto Repair

Category	Would first use okiyome on auto	
	Number	Percent
Training course level:		
I	93	45%
II	68	49
III	48	53
Position in dojo:		
None	100	43%
Low	31	45
High	56	55
Highest	22	61
Attendance level:		
Minimum	53	40%
Average	65	50
Maximum	80	54

against the whole family and has already taken several lives. Week after week he is given the Treatment until his seizures go away. He is told that thanks to okiyome, he and his ancestors are finally getting cleaned up. Both in this world and in the Fourth Dimension, the spirit level of the family is going up, so that Mr. Tanaka and the living members of his family are less vulnerable to attacks by evil spirits. One day he discovers some "gold dust" on the sleeve of his jacket, an omen that Su-god is happy with his shugyo. Finally, his heart trouble goes away—a miracle! Later, he uses the Treatment to heal his wife's stomach cramps, his daughter's acne, and the dog's mange. One day he discovers that he is able to repair the electric fan at the office simply by raising his hand over it. Miracles begin to multiply for the Tanakas. In gratitude to Su-god (and perhaps out of a lingering fear that his heart trouble will recur) Mr. Tanaka repeatedly makes sizable contributions to the church. He comes to the dojo three or four times every week to do shugyo. He takes one of the advanced training courses. Finally, he is asked by the dojo president to become a squadron leader, responsible for three city wards.

Here we have, in a nutshell, the metamorphosis of a Mahikari zealot. Looking at his story, we can see why we found no correlation between the Involvement and Possession Scales. A person who has many spirit seizures is believed to have a low spirit level. If he wants to regain his health, his spirit level must be raised. But to raise his spirit level (religious status), he somehow must get rid of his "low-level symptoms." Therefore, if a person is to improve his religious status, his spirit seizures *must* come to an end.

It is by no means evident that all dojo leaders get cleaned up and overcome their spirit seizures exactly in the way I have described. The coefficient of correlation between the Involvement and Possession Scales, though negative ($r = -.01$, $p = .432$), actually indicates the absence of a relationship, and not a clear-cut negative one. This would seem to indicate that many highly involved members do not undergo any obvious, progressive cleanup, but that, on the contrary, they were relatively "clean" to begin with. Other information from the survey also points in this direction. Staff members are more likely than any other members to admit that they have had only weak spirit movements (67 percent). The fact that 25 percent of them have had no spirit movements at all suggests that not all leaders are susceptible to possession to being with.*

The invulnerability of some people to spirit possession is explained in different ways. It is said that if a person has done sufficient shugyo in his previous incarnations, he will be born in this world with a spirit level high enough to make him comparatively immune to attacks by evil spirits. Likewise, people who are dominated by fire spirits are believed to be less given to the outward displays of possession. Yoshida Sensei explained his own lack of spirit movements by speculating that he had been possessed from birth by a stubborn spirit that simply refused to make its identity known.

Thus far, we have dealt with only the negative side of the elevation of spirit level. That is, we have considered only the ways in which cleaning up sin and pollution, bad karma, and possessing spirits can influence religious status. What we have seen up to this point can therefore be called *the negative demonstration and legitimation of upward religious mobility*. But this is only half the story. Dojo members also need to have positive evidence of their improved condition. This is where magic and miracles enter the picture: to offer *a positive demonstration and legitimation of upward religious mobility*. Whereas the manifest function of miracles is to heal the sick, repair broken wristwatches, and so on, miracles, like religion itself, have latent functions as well. One of these is the legitimation of status within the religious community. In religions like Mahikari, miracles are almost grossly demonstrative. To use Joseph R. Gusfield's word, they are "dramatistic."[5] To some extent this is simply due to their magical nature—magic, as we have seen, tending to be both palpable and quick. Thus if upward religious mobility is negatively legitimated by a spiritual criterion (that is, getting cleaned up), it is positively legitimated, or justified, by a magical criterion. In Thorstein Veblen's words, the elevation of religious status is indicated by a *conspicuous consumption* of okiyome and an equally *conspicuous production* of miracles. Both forms of legitimation are achieved simply by raising one's hand. It

---

* Although the Savior's case is exceptional, it is worth noting that he himself never had any spirit seizures. Nor did he allow others to give him okiyome.

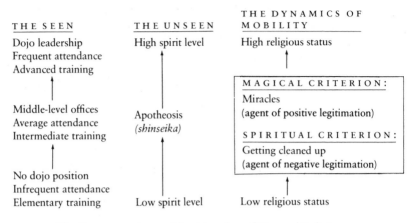

FIG. 6. *The Demonstration and Legitimation of Upward Religious Mobility*

is this magical criterion for upward mobility within the church that accounts for the high statistical correlation between religious status and belief in (and possibly the performance of) miracles.*

The unseen process of apotheosis, the visible creation of a sectarian leader, and the dynamics that legitimate these transformations are represented in Figure 6. The relationship between magic and high office is by no means novel or limited to Mahikari. Half a century ago, Frazer noted that "the public profession of magic has been one of the roads by which the ablest men have passed to supreme power."[6] Three years later, Malinowski corroborated this view, pointing out that "it is an empirical fact that in all savage societies magic and outstanding personality go hand in hand. Thus magic also coincides with personal success, skill, courage and mental power. No wonder that it is considered a source of success."[7] It is also not unusual in other societies practicing exorcism to find

* This high correlation may help explain the "luckier-than-thou" attitude of the Sunshine Children toward non-members. To take just one example from an interview with a member of the Nakayama dojo: "A couple of weeks after I took the training course, I was helping my brother-in-law tear down a house. Suddenly a wall fell on us. Some of the men were badly injured and had to lay off work for three days. Even though the wall fell right on top of me, *I* was able to go back to work the next day. I gave the dojo a special thanksgiving offering."

that people overcome possession by evil spirits as they advance in age, responsibility, and spiritual excellence. According to Oester- reich, it is not surprising to find that "in the case of devout persons having attained a high degree of holiness, possession seems con- fined to the early stages of their career before they have advanced to the higher degrees of ecstasy."[8] Likewise, Walker points out that in Haiti, possession begins with the onset of adult responsibilities and goes away between the ages of forty-five and sixty, "when people become physically and socially dependent upon their chil- dren, who serve them with due respect."[9]

In a similar vein, Samarin found that in some Christian Charis- matic groups (but not all), "a person's rise in status is correlated with a decrease in the use of glossolalia, on the one hand, and, on the other, an increase in the use of other 'gifts,' like interpretation, healing, discernment . . . and prophecy."[10] In more highly struc- tured sects, however, the gift of tongues is a form of legitimation practically monopolized by the leadership.[11] Although it would therefore be rash to generalize in any detail about the use of reli- gious and thaumaturgical criteria as an index of status or power, or their acquisition, it does seem to be a common social and religious phenomenon.

We turn now to a general discussion of the elevation of spirit level (*reisō shōka*),[12] a notion based on three simpler ideas: (1) spir- it level (reiso), (2) the karmic, hierarchical ordering of the universe, and (3) changing karma.

Weber believed that the development of continuous, stereotyped notions about gods and spirits played a decisive role in the evolu- tion of human rationality. He argued, in effect, that before man can be rational or responsible, he must develop a sustained concept of self and deity. The religious discovery of soul and spirit provides a ground for man's self-image and self-esteem, and is therefore the sine qua non for all reform of character and amendment of life.[13] In Mahikari, the gradual elevation of spirit level through okiyome is the measure of the pilgrim's progress. Had he taken Mahikari's elementary training course, Weber would have been fascinated to learn that one of the objects of okiyome is to enable people to live more rational (*gōriteki*) lives. According to Mioshie, every moment that we live we should be bettering ourselves (*takamete iku*). The greatest hindrance to progress is the karma, or the "sins and pollutions," that we and our ancestors have piled up in past lives. This karmic inheritance explains our present troubles—our bad jobs, fickle lovers, and poor health. Thus the Savior taught that just as all the animals, birds, and plants have their own niche in the hierarchy of nature and are bound to their habitats by "unseen chains and cages," so the three worlds of God, spirits, and men are fixed by karma. Paradoxically, the karmic determinism that binds us to our place in the world is also the basis for our progress and evolution. Those who are "children of God" can change their karma, at least to some extent. By accepting fate obediently and at the same time trying to improve and exploit it (*unmei no kaitaku*), they will bring about a change in the Divine Plan for their lives (*shikumi no henkō*). In order to help man break the hold of karma, Su-god has given him okiyome, the upward mobility rite par excellence. He has also shared with man the creative power of kotodama, such as FU.

Although the concept of the "FU-function" is somewhat obscure, it is worth considering as an example of the occult resources for upward mobility. There are two aspects to the FU-function: separating (FU*kiwakeru*) and combining (FU*kiyoseru*), both necessary for the creation and maintenance of the world. Thanks to the operation of the FU-function, Mahikari members "struggle hard" (FU*ntō*) and make "constant efforts" (FU*dan no doryoku*). Sometimes the primary deities use the secondary gods to send temptations, such as money, power, position, and women, to test mankind. Mahikari members must therefore use their FU-function to distinguish (FU*riwakeru*) these temptations from genuine opportunities. Without the FU-function man is like "floating duckweed drifting down a stream." In one of the Savior's oracles, Su-god therefore challenges the church, saying: "The FU-function has been given to you! With hearts inspired rise up!" Thanks to FU and related "functions" (for example SE and MA), members can attain divinity (*shinseika*) and pile up merits (*toku wa toku*).

Mahikari, like most of the other New Religions, emphasizes the active life. It is concerned with changing fate rather than submitting passively to it. Believing that traditional Buddhism promotes an unduly acquiescent attitude toward life, Okada Kotama sought to infuse Mahikari with more positive, activistic ideals. He redefined non-ego (*muga*) as a way for getting rid of the obstacles in a person's life (*muge*). Likewise, he revaluated the notions of throwing self away (*sutemi*) and enlightenment (*satori*) as ways for overcoming resignation (*akirame*). Thus he preached that the Sunshine Children must never allow themselves to grow old. Every year they should double the progress made during the previous year.

Social and Political Values

From a Weberian point of view, although Mahikari's ritual praxis is highly magical, its basic values seem perfectly designed for the promotion of an activistic, this-worldly, and rational "cosmos of obligations." If this is so, one can only wonder whether Mahikari, like so many sectarian movements in the West, is not actually engaged in socializing its lower-class members into the dominant values of the ambient society (for example, the so-called Japanese work ethic). On close examination, do its magical and shamanistic practices and beliefs, which seem so deviant compared with the cultural mainstream, actually support the value system of society at large? This latent function is often served by the Holiness and Pentecostal movements, for example, in the West. Benton Johnson points out that in America, these sects often socialize "marginal, lower class groups in the values commonly called middle class, or more broadly, in the dominant, institutionalized values of the larger society." [14] Furthermore, he argues that the conversion experience itself entails the appropriation of these "higher" values. Is this the case in Mahikari as well?

Although the evidence is sometimes contradictory, sociological surveys have shown that in general, members of religious groups in Western countries tend to be more conservative ideologically and less interested or active in the political process than those who are not members. Members of religious groups have also been found to be more authoritarian and suggestible than others. [15] Do members of Mahikari have similar tendencies? To answer these questions, first we shall look at the Savior's teachings on morals, human relations, and government. Then we shall turn to my survey findings to see how well the attitudes of Mahikari members correspond to Mioshie.

Although the Savior boasted that there were no commandments in Mahikari, he did talk a great deal about "sins and pollution," and about proper attitudes and values. These ethical teachings, which have their foundation in the story of the punishment of the ancient hedonistic Muvians, are closely related to the sect's eschatology. "Ring the jingle bell [*jinguru beru*] of the righteous path of the Sunshine Civilization, the Civilization of the Cross, the daybreak of a new holy century!" The coming civilization will be a perfect blend of material and spiritual culture, with spirit having the upper hand. It will be filled with "non-confrontational love and harmony." The Seed People in training in dojos across the world are therefore enjoined to be obedient, altruistic, and thankful.

The sins that Okada Kotama preached against most vehemently were largely those of people who seldom grace the dojo with their presence: priests, judges, doctors, academics, the rich and the powerful. Priests are supposed to save people, he said, but actually they are interested only in lining their own pockets. Judges will go straight to hell because they sentence people without realizing that their crimes are the work of evil spirits. Doctors, of course, will be damned for giving people medicine (poison) and for performing surgery (cutting through not only the physical body, but the spirit body as well). The sins of these elite members of society all come down to pride and materialism. Secular people like these, Okada warned, preoccupied as they are with "science, theory, plans, meetings, diplomacy, money making, social welfare, and legislation," are no match for evil spirits. Evil spirits, after all, were here thousands of years before science, Western medicine, and the "high-class," self-styled Three Great Religions! As we see by looking at "Modern Man Trying to Catch the Bluebird of Happiness" (Fig. 1, above), Mahikari stands opposed to the hedonism and the intellectual, political, and social ferment that it associates with modern Japan. Social criticism of this sort seems to reflect the kind of counter-cultural mood that often gives birth to genuine social and cultural alternatives.

To draw such a conclusion in this case would be very short-sighted. The resentment that raises its ugly head again and again in Mahikari teachings probably reflects their lower-class origins. As such, it is by no means unusual among the so-called "religions of the oppressed." But resentment of the lifestyle of the social elite does not preclude emulation. Like other New Religions, Mahikari goes to great lengths to attract foreign ambassadors and consuls to its festivals in Tokyo. On these occasions, Japanese politicians, dignitaries, and foreign scholars are regularly invited to give brief, polite greetings bringing recognition to host and guest alike. In 1972 the Savior was happy to have the conservative politician Fukuda Takeo (later Prime Minister) share the podium at the Tokyo Hilton when he received his Saint Denis medal. Because the New Religions are always ready to exploit the prestige of the powerful, whatever class antagonisms they have lie smoldering under the wet leaves of ambition.

Clearly, too, religions like Mahikari, despite their anti-intellectualism, do not completely disown the rationality associated with elite lifestyles. In fact, the internal structure of these large mass religious organizations is often more rational than economic or political associations.[16] We have seen that one of Mahikari's aims is to make life itself more rational. Whereas Okada Kotama taught that "the age of logical comprehension has passed away," his attack on scholarship was really directed against those Japanese scholars who scorned his ideas about Mu, medicine, and parapsychology. He looked forward to a reunion of religion and science that would be climaxed by the development of a "divine science of microscopic and astral grains." His followers today are actively engaged in staging large-scale conferences on these problems, and on that subject so dear to Japan's New Religions: world peace.

Like other leaders of New Religions, when it came to politics Okada seemed opposed to all ideology.[17] In a letter written to President Richard Nixon, he pointed out that "in the universe there are no ideologies"; if the United States and the Soviet Union truly wanted peace, he concluded, they would abandon their artificially concocted "isms." Laissez-faire economics and communism alike had their origins in Christianity and Buddhism, religions that are now passé, he said. Ideology is therefore only a glorified bias that leads to confrontation and strife.

When we examine Okada's political attitudes more closely, it becomes apparent that his own position, far from being neutral, was profoundly conservative, if not reactionary. He believed that the

Liberal Democrats (Japan's main conservative party) were the country's only hope against communism. To warn mankind of the impending destruction of the world, Okada believed, the gods had sent a series of devastating earthquakes around the globe. When the significance of these was not noticed, the gods "turned on a red signal light" and set loose the "spirit of the Red Dragon," namely, the Communist Party and the left-wing Japanese student organization, Zengakuren. Communism is therefore a dire warning from on high.

Democracy, thought the Savior, meant "rule by demonstration." As proof he cited the logopneumatology of the Japanese-English word *demokurashii*, which, he said, derives from another loan word, *demo*, meaning a "demonstration" of social protest. Democracy is therefore only "willful opportunism," and must be associated with the auxiliary water deities and the materialistic (yin) principles of Western culture. Weakened by such foreign ideas, the Japanese have naturally lost their resistance to spirit possession. The introduction of democracy into Japan after the war has caused many people to be possessed by the spirits of their mothers. Offended by the growth of democracy and egalitarianism within the family, these maternal spirits have come back to possess their children. Fathers, on the other hand, are said to be able to put up with these insults, and therefore they are not as likely to take revenge.*

The essence of politics, according to Okada, is "benevolent government" (*tokusei*) and the promotion of human salvation. Mahikari's political mission, therefore, is to replace democracy with a theocracy in which the Savior's teachings will be supreme. To accomplish this, "horizontal" relationships (such as the husband-wife axis in Western families) must be replaced by "vertical" ones (such as the traditional bond between parent and child in Japan). The old pre-war emphasis on loyalty and patriotism (*chūkun aikoku*) and the unity of religion and government (*saisei itchi*) must be restored. In the coming True Light Civilization, god and man will be one.

---

* Actually, according to my statistical survey, maternal and paternal spirits possess their children with equal frequency. Of those who have experienced ancestral possession, about 14 percent have been possessed by a parental spirit. Nevertheless, it is often said in the dojo that the mother's spirit is the more apt to trouble her children.

Rulers will be apotheosized, so that it will not be known whether they are gods or men. Like pre-war ideologists, the Savior believed that the individual (*ko*) is identical with the all (*zen*). That is to say, the individual is to be subordinate to the group.

Like the utopias of other messianic and millenarian movements throughout the world, Mahikari's utopia represents, in effect, a restoration of a golden past. In the new age, Japan will regain the worldwide hegemony she enjoyed in high antiquity. Church publications point out that since ancient times, Japan has been called "heaven," even by other countries. Moreover, it is the only country where the true history of the world has been preserved. The Japanese are mankind's "stem family," the "chosen people" responsible for reviving the spiritual civilization of the world.

In the present degenerate age, however, the Japanese have succumbed to false religions and materialism. For this reason, Su-god made use of Americans in order to bring about a Great Purification of the land—Japan's defeat in World War II. Okada predicted that for a while the "star" (the United States) would continue to reign supreme throughout the world. There would follow a period of harmony during which the "star" and the "sickle" (the Soviet Union) would be brought together. Even during détente, however, the "spirit bodies" of the two countries would continue to be at war. According to one Mahikari lecturer, this spiritual warfare explains why an atomic satellite belonging to the Soviet Union crashed in Canada in 1978.[18] The Savior believed that after their reconciliation, the United States and the Soviet Union would "crush" Japan and then destroy one another. Later, the world will enter a Dark Age, during which the Chinese will come to power. Finally the "sun" (Japan) will rise again, and the world will be filled with a new spiritual Light.

The sun is just one of the symbols of ancient Mu that will be revived at that future time. The swastika is another. This symbol of the ancient Motherland, it is said, calls to mind the nebula or the structure of the atom; therefore it represents the energy of the cosmos itself. The swastika has taken many forms, one being the Christian cross. Even today it is widely used by the Children of Mu in their diaspora around the globe—in India, China, Greece, Rome, England, France, Mexico, Peru, Paraguay, and Scandinavia, not to mention Japan and Germany. The "curved jewels" (*magatama*), which are one of the regalia of the Japanese imperial family, also derive from the swastika of the sunken continent. But the time has now come to reverse the direction of the clockwise-moving swastika (卍) associated with yin forces, Buddhism, and the materialistic culture protected by water and moon deities. The swastika must be made to move in the counter-clockwise direction (卐) of the yang forces, the spiritual deities such as the sun, and the principle of "spirit first, heart second, body third."

That the swastika was also used by the German Nazis cannot possibly be missed by the older members of the church. Even the banners borne in Mahikari processions bear a striking resemblance to those carried by Hitler's troops in their mass rallies. Moreover, it was Okada's custom to review his followers at festivals by having them march before him, goose-stepping in military style. When they reached the spot immediately before the enormous dais where he stood, they snapped their heads smartly in his direction and extended their arms in the Nazi salute. The Savior received their homage by holding up his arm in that rather nonchalant way reminiscent of the Führer himself. Fortunately, these customs no longer seem to be in use.

From this review of Mahikari's social and political ideals, it appears that the organization is counter-cultural only insofar as it is critical of the materialistic liberalism of post-war capitalism and democracy. Many of the values it fosters reflect the ideology of pre-war Japan. Undoubtedly, the Savior's background—born into a family of military men, educated in military schools, spending his young manhood in the imperial guard—influenced his ideals. The Mahikari gospel may represent something of a cultural lag, but in no way is it antithetical to the energetic, practical spirit for which the Japanese are justly renowned.

Like the other New Religions, Mahikari promotes an optimistic achievement orientation that it rewards in its own ranks. Pre-war nationalistic values continue to be felt in Mahikari, but they clearly take second place to the sect's thaumaturgical interests and affirmative pragmatism. Although the church's political ideals may have the latent function of increasing national self-esteem, they are not much different from ideologies nourished in the bosom of other religions. They will lie safely submerged in myth and symbol until pressed into service by new political circumstances or social needs. As we can see in the history of the interaction between the state and religion in modern Japan, the language and values of religion are infinitely plastic. Religions that staunchly supported the nation's military adventures before 1945 became its foremost advocates of peace and international cooperation after that date.

Political Behavior

By looking at the survey findings, we can see how well the official teachings of Mahikari are reflected in the political behavior of its followers. One might expect that people with such a magical orientation to life would not be concerned enough about politics to bother to vote. This is not the case. Of those eligible to vote in the election held on December 5, 1976, 76 percent claimed that they did so. Considering that monthly festivals (lasting three to four hours) were held on the afternoon of the election, this turnout compares very well with the average for the prefecture on that day (77 percent), for Osaka (64 percent), and for the nation as a whole (73 percent). If there is any group in the dojos that could be called apolitical, it is the youth. The younger a person, the less likely he is to vote.

The survey shows that support for the conservative Liberal Democratic Party is stronger among Mahikari members than it is throughout the nation as a whole or in the local areas where the survey was conducted. Although the conservative vote was stronger in sixteen prefectures than it was in the four dojos of the survey, all of these prefectures are largely rural. Members of the dojos, though primarily urbanites, tended to vote as though they lived in the countryside. According to Yoshida Sensei, Mahikari members are forbidden to vote for the Communist Party. Although I have never noticed this political restriction in the sect's lectures or publications, the voting pattern of members seems to bear it out: support for the left-wing parties, the Socialists and the Communists, was generally lower than the national and local averages (see Table 9).

The most interesting influences on the political orientation of members seem to be income and age. Education does not seem to

Table 9. *Voting Patterns of Dojo Members Compared with Those of the General Population*
(percent)

Place	Left wing		Middle		Right wing		
	JCP	JSP	DSP	CGP	NLC	LDP	IND
Nakayama City dojo (*n* = 122)	13%	8%	3%	0%	10%	69%	3%
Nakamoto dojo (*n* = 33) (Nakayama prefecture)	6	15	3	0	6	64	6
Nakayama prefecture averages	19	15	—	13	—	52	—
Osaka City dojo (*n* = 239)	9	16	9	5	14	46	3
Sakai dojo (*n* = 53) (Osaka)	8	15	8	2	15	48	6
Osaka averages	20	18	12	21	3	26	1
National averages	10	21	6	11	4	42	6

NOTE: This table is based on the national election held on December 5, 1976. The order in which parties are listed (from left to right) is the same used to establish the Scale of Political Conservatism in this survey. Party names corresponding to the abbreviations are Japan Communist Party (JCP), Japan Socialist Party (JSP), Democratic Socialist Party (DSP), Clean Government Party (CGP), New Liberal Club (NLC), and the Liberal Democratic Party (LDP); IND signifies independents.

Table 10. *Party Support by Income Level*
(percent)

	Income of voter			
Party supported	Lowest (*n* = 29)	Low (*n* = 150)	High (*n* = 160)	Highest (*n* = 53)
Liberal Democratic Party (*n* = 214)	55%	62%	50%	47%
Japan Socialist Party (*n* = 53)	14	12	14	17
Japan Communist Party (*n* = 41)	17	11	9	9
Other parties (*n* = 84)	14	15	27	26

have any consistent effect, except among Socialists (who decline in number as education increases) and supporters of the New Liberal Club (who increase as education increases). In general, male dojo members are slightly more conservative than females.

As the income of a member increases, he is slightly less likely to vote for the Liberal Democrats and slightly more likely to vote for the Socialists (see Table 10). As income falls, there is a slight increase in the percentage of members who support the Communist Party. But most of the votes that the Liberal Democratic Party loses among members with high income seem to go to the moderates or the New Liberal Club ("Other parties"), and not to left-wing groups.

Support for the Liberal Democrats seems to be strongest among the youngest and the most elderly members. It is primarily among middle-aged members that the Socialists and Communists win their few votes. Because members aged thirty to fifty-six were also those who registered the highest degree of dissatisfaction with society (in response to Question 29 of the questionnaire), we can assume that the disenchanting experiences of hard work and heavy economic responsibility prompt some middle-aged members to turn away from the political establishment. The influence of age on party support is shown in Figure 7.

A liberal reader of this book might expect that the more a member is possessed by evil spirits, or the more miracles a member experiences, the more politically conservative he or she is likely to be. This is not so. Coefficients of correlation show that neither the Scale of Possession nor the Scale of Miracles bears any relationship to the Scale of Political Conservatism. Likewise, there is no correlation between the several items that make up these Scales.

In the case of miracles, however, the overall findings must be modified somewhat by more specific cross-tabulations. Supporters of all the major political parties are nearly equally blessed with healing miracles. But supporters of the conservative Liberal Democrats seem to be the most able, or likely, to perform, physical miracles (39 percent, $n = 82$). They are closely followed, however, by the Communists (32 percent, $n = 11$), and then the Socialists (18 percent, $n = 9$). Supporters of the two most conservative parties

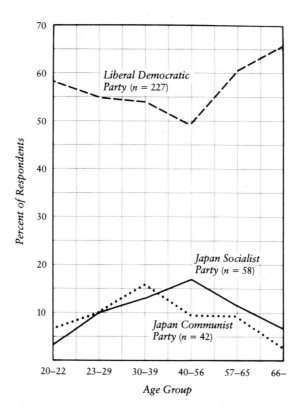

FIG. 7. *Party Support by Age Group*

Table 11. Party Support by Preference for Thaumaturgical Auto Repair

Party supported	Would first use okiyome on auto	
	Number	Percent
Liberal Democratic Party	85	51%
New Liberal Club	19	48
Japan Communist Party	7	42
Japan Socialist Party	9	32
Clean Government Party	2	29

are also the most likely to try using okiyome to repair their auto-mobiles (see Table 11).

When we group members by the number of miracles experienced into the Mercy Drops and Showers Groups, we find that the political conservatives more often fall into the Showers Group, whereas supporters of the left-wing parties more often fall into the more modest Mercy Drops Group (see Table 12).

In short, though coefficients of correlation reveal no general relationship between political conservatism and number of miracles experienced, individual cross-tabulations indicate that in certain situations, conservative members may tend to have a more thaumaturgical response to the world than left-wing members.

Although the relationship between miracles and political conservatism is weak at best, the statistical correlation between religious involvement and conservatism is not. The survey clearly shows that the more involved people are in Mahikari, the more politically conservative they are likely to be. In Table 13 the coefficients of correlation relating the Scale of Political Conservatism to the Scale of Involvement and its components indicate that there is a strong relationship between political conservatism and a member's position in his dojo. There is also a discernible correlation between political conservatism and the amount of training a person receives in the teachings of the sect. Only dojo attendance shows no discernible relation to political conservatism.

Table 12. Party Support by Miracle Record
(percent)

	Number of miracles		
Party supported	None	Mercy Drops	Showers
Right wing:			
Liberal Democratic Party (*n* = 135)	3%	61%	36%
New Liberal Club (*n* = 32)	3	53	44
Left wing:			
Japan Communist Party (*n* = 23)	0	74	26
Japan Socialist Party (*n* = 27)	4	67	30

Table 13. Correlation Between Political Conservatism and Religious Involvement

Scale and types of involvement	Scale of political conservatism (r)	Probability of chance correlation (p)
Position in dojo	.25	.001
Training level	.18	.001
Attendance level	.14	.003
Scale of involvement	.24	.001

Attendance aside, Figure 8 shows the dramatic split that occurs between the political Right and Left when we relate the party support of members to their "commitment" (position + training) to the sect. As the religious commitment of members increases, they are more inclined to support the conservative Liberal Democrats and less inclined to vote for the Communists and Socialists.

The political conservatism of the leadership of the four dojos becomes still more apparent when we look at the political affiliations of the forty-three members who hold the highest positions. In the 1976 national election thirty-six of these people supported the Liberal Democrats. Four voted for the conservative New Liberal Club. Two supported the Democratic Socialist Party, which stands in the middle of the political spectrum. Only one voted Communist. There were no Socialists or supporters of the Clean Government Party (connected with Soka Gakkai, one of Mahikari's religious rivals) in the highest echelon of the four dojos. What little support there was for the two left-wing parties came from members with either a low position in their dojo or none at all, as Table 14 shows.

When we control for age, income, sex, and education, the strong relationship between political conservatism and high position in the dojo is consistently confirmed. In all age cohorts, members in high positions are more likely to support the Liberal Democrats than members with no position. In all occupational ranks except unskilled blue-collar workers ($n = 25$), a positive correlation exists between support for the Liberal Democrats and high religious office. Within the lowest income bracket, only those who have either no position in the dojo or a very low one voted Socialist. At all

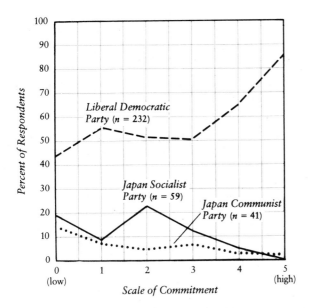

FIG. 8. *Party Support by Religious Commitment*

Table 14. *Party Support by Position in Dojo*
(percent)

	Position in dojo		
Party supported	None (n = 222)	Low (n = 165)	High (n = 43)
Liberal Democratic Party (n = 234)	44%	58%	88%
New Liberal Club (n = 54)	11	15	10
Democratic Socialist Party (n = 24)	8	5	5
Clean Government Party (n = 11)	5	1	0
Japan Socialist Party (n = 60)	18	12	0
Japan Communist Party (n = 42)	14	6	3

NOTE: The first two levels of responsibility have been combined in this table as "low" position. Because of split votes, the third column totals 106 percent.

levels of education, support for the Socialists declines as members rise in the dojo hierarchy.

Although we cannot establish a perfect correlation between political conservatism and attendance, at least between the ages of twenty and fifty-six, support for the Liberal Democrats tends to increase somewhat the more faithfully a person attends his dojo. In all income brackets and at all levels of education, attendance in this age group is positively related to support for the Liberal Democrats.* Among the various occupational groups, attendance is positively related to support for the Liberal Democrats among all but the low-level white-collar workers (where the relationship is unclear) and the farmers (where it is negative). There is, however, no clear-cut relationship between attendance and support for the Socialist Party in any age group. Nor is there any discernible influence of income or education on the relationship between attendance and support of the Socialist Party. Table 15 shows the relationship between attendance and party support.

We can summarize our findings as follows. There is no relationship between political conservatism (measured by party support) and possession experiences. Although conservatives in some circumstances may have a slightly more magical response to the world, there is virtually no overall relationship between political conservatism and number of miracles experienced. Our most significant finding seems to be the strong positive correlation between political conservatism and the degree of a member's religious involvement, especially when measured in terms of his "commitment" (position and training) to the church. How can we account for these findings?

The simplest way to explain this relationship is to examine the way the sect recruits its leaders. We have seen that in Mahikari, leaders are not elected. Rather, they are appointed by the dojo staff. The staff itself is composed of lay leaders and their subordinate ministers. The presidents of the dojos are usually members of Japan's "old middle class" or petite bourgeoisie: small proprietors, owners of small or medium-size enterprises, shopowners, or land-

---

*When we control the relationship between attendance and Liberal Democratic Party support for income, the coefficient of correlation goes up from $r = .14$, $p = .003$, to $r = .15$, $p = .002$, thus establishing a discernible relationship between the two variables.

Table 15. Party Support by Dojo Attendance
(percent)

	Level of attendance		
Party supported	Low (*n = 151*)	Average (*n = 131*)	High (*n = 130*)
Right wing:			
Liberal Democratic Party (*n = 215*)	48%	50%	59%
New Liberal Club (*n = 52*)	11	12	15
Left wing:			
Japan Socialist Party (*n = 58*)	15	17	10
Japan Communist Party (*n = 38*)	15	5	8
Other parties (*n = 49*)	11	17	8

lords.[19] Some of them, like Yoshida Sensei, are actually quite well-to-do. From what I could learn, the lay leaders who build and run the local dojos receive only a modest honorarium from the church, or nothing at all. This means that to be a leader, a person must be financially independent. As in other appointed hierarchies, the leadership of the Mahikari dojos tends to perpetuate its own kind. Appointments also seem to be based on what common sense (that is, social custom) says will make good leaders. In some cases the social criteria for leadership (for example, male dominance) are given explicit theological rationales in the teachings of the sect. Thus the use of these criteria is probably both conscious and unconscious. In any case, leaders tend to be old rather than young, male rather than female, married rather than single. They are generally people who attend the dojo frequently and who have taken one or two of the advanced training courses. Both education and a relatively high income help qualify a person for leadership in the dojos. Finally, in Japan, as elsewhere, there is a natural "elective affinity" between high income and political conservatism. Statistics clearly show that the Liberal Democrats receive much stronger support from Japanese in the higher income brackets than from those with more modest incomes.[20] This helps to explain the tendency in Mahikari for high office (and upward religious mobility) to coincide with the social and political *embourgeoisement* of members.

Occupation also seems to be related, though in a complex way, to the appropriation of the beliefs and praxis of the sect and to the recruitment of leaders. We have seen that a higher percentage of skilled blue-collar and high-level white-collar workers attain the highest dojo offices than any other occupational groups. This trend may be related to the tendency for the leadership to rank higher than the followership in "business mentality" (as measured by Question 30, discussed below). The fact that high-level white-collar workers are the highest occupational group in income may also have something to do with their leadership role. As in other religious groups, the privilege of leadership seems to be, in part, a reward for financial support. That farmers stand next to the bottom of all the occupational groups in their position in the dojos may likewise be attributable to their being the lowest of all occupations in income. No consistent correlations could be established, however, that would enable us to rank occupation *as a whole* among our other criteria of legitimation. Although our information on the occupational groups in the dojos is far from perfect, it does seem that occupations and the styles of life associated with them may have considerable influence on the religious affiliation of members and their ability to appropriate the ideas and practices of a religious group.*

To summarize, the close relationship between religious involvement (especially high position) and political conservatism can be attributed to (1) the built-in prerequisite that leaders be financially independent (because they cannot rely on the church for a stipend), (2) the natural tendency to reward generous financial support with the gift of high office, (3) the staff's tendency to perpetuate its own general class, status, and lifestyle in making appointments to high positions, and (4) the influence of the Savior's own conservatism, a

---

*Farmers, for example, have only a modest miracle record, and they score the lowest of all occupational groups in overall susceptibility to spirit possession. But curiously enough, a higher percentage of farmers than any other occupation belonged to other New Religions before joining Mahikari (46 percent, $n = 11$).

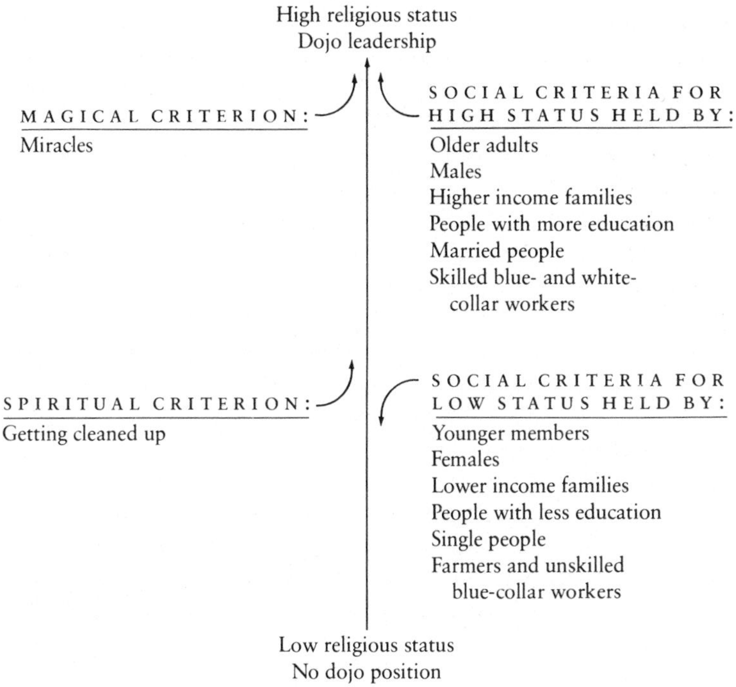

High religious status
Dojo leadership

MAGICAL CRITERION: ⟩
Miracles

SOCIAL CRITERIA FOR
HIGH STATUS HELD BY:
Older adults
Males
Higher income families
People with more education
Married people
Skilled blue- and white-
collar workers

SPIRITUAL CRITERION: ⟩
Getting cleaned up

SOCIAL CRITERIA FOR
LOW STATUS HELD BY:
Younger members
Females
Lower income families
People with less education
Single people
Farmers and unskilled
blue-collar workers

Low religious status
No dojo position

FIG. 9. *The Dynamics of Upward Religious Mobility*

factor that probably increases as people rise to higher positions in the dojo.

We can now round out our analysis of religious status in the dojo by adding social criteria of legitimation to the spiritual and magical criteria we have already discussed. Insofar as position in the dojo goes hand in hand with spirit level—which, in turn, translates into overall religious status—we can now claim at least a rudimentary idea of how (external) social criteria help determine (internal) religious status in the sect. To put it crudely, higher-class members can, in effect, "cash in" their social status for religious status. Figure 9, a modification of Figure 6, summarizes our findings thus far. It pictures the synergic operations of all three sets of criteria on the process of upward religious mobility.

General Social and Political Attitudes

Up to this point, we have considered only the voting patterns of members. In order to see whether members' opinions on general social, political, and ideological issues differ from those of the average Japanese, I included in my questionnaire four items taken from the *Study of Japanese National Character* (hereafter SJNC), a survey conducted every five years (since 1953) by the Institute of Statistical Mathematics of the Japanese government.[21] Although errors were made in transcribing these questions that make comparison difficult in some cases, the results cited in Tables 16–19 seem to indicate that the attitudes of Mahikari members do differ considerably from the national average.

Although the "Other" and "Don't know" options were not included in the Mahikari survey, Question 29 ("How do you feel about society?"; see Table 16) does seem to bring out among sect members a general dissatisfaction with society that is considerably higher than the national average. Whether this difference reflects the growing pessimism about the country's economy since the oil crisis of 1973, or the unrest of the lower classes of Japanese society in general, or perhaps the Savior's own pessimism and lurid eschatological visions, is impossible to determine.*

The question in Table 17 is designed to probe the civil-religious attitudes of the Japanese people. Since the Grand Shrine at Ise is the sanctuary of the clan deities of the imperial family, it is associated both with pre-war State Shinto and with Japanese nationalism in general. After the disestablishment of State Shinto, those who believe that prime ministers should continue the tradition of visiting the shrine can be said to have a traditional or conservative attitude toward the custom. It is not unlikely that they would hold similar attitudes toward other patriotic rituals and customs linking the

---

*By contrast, Gallup polls taken in 1974 and 1977 in the United States (which had economic difficulties of its own during these years) show that the percentage of the population "highly satisfied" with "life in this country" rose from 34 percent to 57 percent. See Surveys by the American Institute of Public Opinion (Gallup), cited in *Public Opinion*, 1, no. 2 (May–June 1978), 22. Although it is impossible to compare directly the results of these two somewhat different questions, the Gallup findings cast some doubt on the idea that economic concerns alone are behind the Seed People's dissatisfaction with Japanese society.

Table 16. Attitudes Toward Society
(percent)

Answers (see NOTE)	Mahikari members	National average (1973)
(1) Satisfied	5%	6%
(2) Rather satisfied	17	20
(3) Rather dissatisfied	31	37
(4) Dissatisfied	46	30
(5) Other	"	1
(6) Don't know	"	6

NOTE: Answers are to SJNC question 2.3d: "How do you feel about society?"
   " Option not given.

Table 17. Civil-Religious Attitudes
(percent)

Answers (see NOTE)	Mahikari members	National average (1973)
(1) Better to go	61%	40%
(2) Better not to go	12	25
(3) Other	27	16
(4) Don't know	"	19

NOTE: Answers are to SJNC question 3.9* (the asterisk is part of the SJNC classification system): "Some Prime Ministers, when they take office, pay a visit to the Imperial Shrine at Ise. Do you think they should, or do you think it would be better if they didn't?"
   " Option not given.

state to religion. Although the "Don't know" option was not provided in the Mahikari questionnaire, members of the sect seem more favorably inclined toward these official pilgrimages than other Japanese. They are also less explicitly opposed to them. These responses seem to reflect a rather conservative or traditional ideological orientation.

The question in Table 18 seems to tap not merely the tension between traditional and modern attitudes, but the difference between what Weber would call *value-rationality* ("Return home immediately") and *goal-rationality* ("Go to the meeting"). If this is so, Mahikari members in general seem to score lower in goal-rationality, or business-mindedness, than the average Japanese, perhaps because relatively few sect members hold positions of managerial responsibility. Thus of all dojos surveyed, members of the dojo in Nakamoto, a provincial town known for its fishing and mandarin oranges, displayed the least business-mindedness. Also, women are somewhat more likely to think that Mr. M should return home immediately than men are. Most interesting, however, is the positive correlation between high office in the dojo and goal-rationality. That is, the higher a person's position in the dojo, the more likely he is to say that Mr. M should go to the meeting.*

Because the words in brackets in the note to Table 19 were inadvertently omitted from the Mahikari questionnaire, our ability to compare members' responses with the results of the national survey is severely limited. The salient aspects of the dojo members' responses seem to be their relatively low level of opposition to the proposal, and their high level of political ambiguity ("Depends on the time and the person") and skepticism ("I can't believe that such an outstanding person exists"). In general, the younger members of the dojos, who have had greater exposure to post-war democratic education, are less happy about entrusting politicians with their country's problems than the older members.†

Although the membership of the four dojos tends to hold relatively traditional social and political opinions, the attitudinal patterns of individual members are impossible to predict. At least, I

---

* When we control for income, we find that at all income levels there is a correlation between high religious office and business-mindedness. Furthermore, high attendance, advanced religious training, and being male—factors that increase a person's chances of becoming a leader—are also positively correlated with the goal-rational or business-minded responses to this moral dilemma. Some respondents tried to get off the horns of the dilemma by writing in the margin of their questionnaire something to the effect that Mr. M should go to his meeting but raise his hand to give Mr. A okiyome from afar, or that he should have the Spiritual Leader present a Divine Notification to Su-god on behalf of his benefactor.

† Many people wrote in the margin of their questionnaires something to the effect that if this "outstanding political leader" were the Savior's daughter, Okada Keiju, they would readily assent to the proposal. Making the church's Spiritual Leader a political leader would, of course, effectively reestablish the "unity of religion and government" (*saisei itchi*) of ancient Mu—the Savior's dream.

Table 18. Traditional vs. Goal-Rational Attitudes
(percent)

Answers (see NOTE)	Mahikari members	National average (1973)
(1) Return home immediately	65%	51%
(2) Go to the meeting	28	40
(3) Other	7	2
(4) Don't know	*a*	7

NOTE: Answers are to SJNC question 5.1: "Imagine this situation: Mr. M was orphaned at an early age and was brought up by Mr. A, a kind neighbor. The A's gave him a good education, sent him to a university, and now Mr. M has become the president of a company. One day he gets a telegram saying that Mr. A, who brought him up, is seriously ill and asking if he would come home at once. This telegram arrives just at the moment when he is going to an important meeting which will decide whether his firm is to go bankrupt or to survive. Which of the following should he do?"

a Option not given.

Table 19. Attitudes Toward Political Leaders
(percent)

Answers (see NOTE)	Mahikari members	National average (1973)
(1) Agree	12%	23%
(2) Depends on the time and the person	37	15
(3) Opposed	22	51
(4) I can't believe that such an outstanding person exists	26	5
(5) Other	3	1
(6) Don't know	*a*	5

NOTE: Answers are to SJNC question 8.1: "Some people say that if we get outstanding political leaders, the best way to improve the country is for the people to leave everything to them [rather than for the people to discuss issues among themselves]. Do you agree with this or disagree?"

a Option not given.

have been unable to establish a statistical correlation among their answers to the questions in Tables 17, 18, and 19 that would establish any unified conservative syndrome of opinion. Likewise, there seems to be no relationship between the general social, political, and ideological outlook of members and our Scales of Possession and Miracles. This means that neither in their political behavior nor in their attitudes are members "made conservative" by spirit possession or miraculous experiences.

When we turn to the relationship between members' involvement in Mahikari and their social and political views, the picture changes completely. Here there are distinct correlations suggesting that involvement in the church promotes (or reflects) not only a conservative turn of mind, but also a more goal-rational attitude. When asked whether the Prime Minister should make the traditional pilgrimage to Ise, those more deeply involved in the life of the church tended to reply in the affirmative, perhaps reflecting their greater exposure to the church's reactionary ideology. Likewise, when asked whether all political questions should be left to outstanding leaders, the more "committed" a person was to the church, the more likely he was to reply affirmatively, or to say that his answer would depend on circumstances. Both of these answers seemed more conservative than those indicating direct opposition to the suggestion or doubt that such an outstanding person exists.* In other words, the replies to the questions in Tables 17 and 19 indicate a clear relationship between church involvement (or "commitment"), on the one hand, and a negative (or ambivalent) attitude toward general democratic procedures and the constitutional separation of church and state, on the other.

Although involvement in the church is therefore related to a member's ideological conservatism, his outlook is not to be associated, *tout court*, with a diehard, head-in-the-sand attitude toward life. As we have seen, responses to the question whether Mr. M

---

* Of the indicators of involvement, only attendance seemed unrelated to a conservative outlook. The more a person attends the dojo, the more likely he is to oppose this paternalistic and potentially totalitarian political solution. But even in this case, opposition to the suggestion was never strong, increasing from 19 percent among those who attend least frequently to 26 percent among those who attend most often.

should return home to his ailing benefactor (Table 18) indicate a remarkably strong correlation between a person's overall involvement in Mahikari and a very rational business-mindedness. The more involved a person is in the church, the more likely he is to say that Mr. M should go to the meeting instead of returning home. Mahikari members in general took a more traditional approach to this moral dilemma than the average Japanese, but those with the highest religious status displayed a comparatively high level of tough goal-rationality.

From these findings, we can conclude either that the leaders of the dojos have been made more goal-rational by virtue of their involvement in Mahikari, or that they have been given their present positions in recognition of their "sensible" outlook. Judging from the way leaders are appointed, the latter is the more reasonable explanation. If so, these findings lend added weight to the importance of social criteria in determining religious status—even in sects with relatively disadvantaged memberships. Having the kind of controlling or teleological rationality associated with a business outlook naturally increases a person's chances to contribute more financially to the dojo and to become one of its leaders. Thus even among the "religions of the oppressed," the spiritual elite is schooled in the wisdom of serpents.

As for the rank-and-file of the church, they are drawn primarily from the conservatives and traditionalists of Japan's labor force. The Seed People are, in effect, the magicians and exorcists of the country's Tory proletariat. For some reason, these people support a conservative political cause that seems to run contrary to their own best interests. Why? Perhaps, since they have a solution to all problems in okiyome, they simply do not need the help of leftwing parties, with their rhetorical preachments on reform and revolution. All they need to do is raise their hands, and their problems go away. Plausible as this explanation may seem, the absence of any correlation between miracle record and political conservatism in our survey makes it dubious. Many members may simply be playing symbolic politics when they cast their ballots, seeking a way to identify themselves with the country's traditional values and imperial institution. Voting is their way of supporting the ideals of continuity and stability in Japan's political culture. Many probably attribute Japan's recent economic success and the improvement in their own circumstances to the long years of rule by the country's conservatives, and simply wish to express their gratitude by supporting the Liberal Democrats at the polls.

Another solution to this problem is to trace the political conservatism of the sect's rank-and-file back to the understandable conservatism of its leaders. Since there is some correlation between income and religious status in the church, there seems to be a natural affinity between high religious status and political conservatism. Well-to-do dojo presidents and staff members are simply voting their class interests when they cast a ballot for the Liberal Democratic Party or the New Liberal Club. This conservatism may very well influence lower-class members, since the predominant ideas of any group tend to be drawn from the conceptual portfolio of its ruling stratum.[22] Still, the influence of the leadership on the voting patterns of members in general probably accounts for only part of the organization's conservatism. The folk tradition itself, by hallowing both the paternal goodness of rulers and the humble obedience of subjects, also plays a part in the mystification of politics. Again and again we have seen how deeply this tradition runs in the family histories of Mahikari members. In short, there seem to be many factors influencing the political outlook and behavior of dojo members.

Deprivation Theory

The origin of sects like Mahikari is often explained as a response to some kind of deprivation, which Charles Y. Glock defines as the various "ways that an individual or group may be, or feel, disadvantaged in comparison either to other individuals or groups or to an internalized set of standards." Glock recognizes five types of deprivation: economic, social, organismic (the deprivation of health), ethical, and psychic.[23] David F. Aberle, who does not deal specifically with illness as a form of deprivation, names four types: the deprivation of possessions, status, behavior, and worth.[24] Whatever categories one chooses to emphasize, deprivation theory itself can be regarded as the sociological reversal of the law of gravity, stating that whatever goes down must also come up. Thus religion becomes a "compensation" for any of several kinds of deprivation. As Liston Pope once put it, describing the Pentecostalist's point of view, "What matters it, then, if a Methodist has more money but has never been baptized with the Holy Ghost?" [25] Deprivation theory seeks to explain why "religions of the oppressed" come into existence in the first place and why they spread, disappear, or change into mainstream churches or denominations. As used by sociologists, its main thrust has been that "sects substitute religious status for social status." [26] We have seen in this chapter that the dojo is, among other things, a status-conferring institution providing a social context for upward religious mobility. Can Mahikari therefore be explained in terms of deprivation theory?

Before going further, I must point out that most versions of deprivation theory entail serious methodological and practical difficulties for the researcher. Theories of absolute deprivation are obviously flawed by their static and mechanical assumptions about human nature. They seem to imply that life is bounded by measurable thresholds of happiness and frustration, and that the emergence of religious behavior can be predicted with thermostatic accuracy. The truth is that such thresholds can be postulated only in the most tentative way and are utterly impossible to measure. Sometimes the alleged influence of deprivation is contradicted by simple fact. For example, the spread of many of Japan's New Religions during decades of economic prosperity would discourage any simplistic identification of social alienation with the growth of these religio-magical responses to the world.*

Today, most sociologists have turned to the more plausible notion of relative deprivation, based on the idea that "people take the standards of significant others as a basis for self-appraisal and evaluation." [27] This statement, of course, does not tell us who these

* Marx mistakenly associated religious opiates with the masses. When we analyze religious affiliations by social class, we often find that it is the religions of the upper middle classes that have a narcotic effect on their adherents. The religions of the disinherited, being far more vital, tend to energize their members for toil and sorrow. Marx was not wrong in seeing religion as a response to man's social and economic alienation. He erred only in failing to see that its roots extend into a far deeper problem: man's creaturely finitude. See R. J. Zwi Werblowsky, *Beyond Tradition and Modernity: Changing Religions in a Changing World* (London, 1975), pp. 106, 113.

significant others are—for example, whether they are social supe-
riors to whose status the person aspires, or others in circumstances
similar to his own. Whether we begin with an absolute or a relative
notion of deprivation, isolating specific deprivations leaves much to
the imagination. Likewise, establishing the connections between
these deprivations and their putative compensations is not as simple
as some might believe. In all cases these connections must be pos-
ited hypothetically by the investigator himself. In spite of their
prima facie similarity, theorizing about deprivations and compensations takes place at a far higher level of abstraction than the
simple description of conscious needs and their fulfillments. Since,
however, the actor is not always aware of his own needs, or even
of the ways he satisfies them, researchers are justified in extending
their search for significant motivations into the realm of the pre-
conscious mind of individuals and groups.

Positing the existence of deprivations and compensations is just
the beginning. One must then go on to assign more specific valences
to each deprivation. For example, does the deprivation of "meaning
in life" play as important a role in the formation of religious groups
as the deprivation of social status or health? Assuming that relative
deprivations can be assigned comparable thresholds, can such
modified thresholds be generalized to apply to all members of a
group, or to all times and places? Reginald W. Bibby and Merlin
B. Brinkerhoff raise four other objections to deprivation theories:
"(1) their *a priori*, tautological-type 'proofs' often preclude the
examination of other possibilities; (2) control group comparisons
are seldom used; (3) deprivation indicators tend to be of an objective rather than subjective type; and (4) little attention is given to
the question of sources of ongoing religious involvement."[28] They
go on to suggest that religious involvement must also be seen as
motivated by "socialization" (being brought into the group as children), "accommodation" (joining to please relatives), and "cognition" (joining to satisfy a quest for the meaning of life).

In addition to its built-in difficulties, deprivation theory has suffered from simple misuse. In religious studies, the greatest misuse
of the theory has occurred when a person's motives for joining a
religion have been confused with the satisfactions he subsequently
gains from membership. Some sociologists have been guilty of

reducing the latter to the former, as when, for example, they assume that a person's motive for joining a group was to upgrade his status—which actually was the *result* of his joining.

If the concepts of deprivation and compensation are to be useful at all, the actor's motives and the consequences of his behavior must be rigorously separated. Let us take the case of the high-level white-collar workers in the dojos as an example. Some 54 percent of this group joined Mahikari for reasons of health, as did 52 percent of all members. They therefore were not any more "relatively deprived" of their health than the average member. (Still, the dominant motive bringing them to the dojo in the first place was sickness.) After they join the church, they tend to respond to the new social and religious possibilities made available to them through membership with considerable gusto. They are among the most easily possessed by evil spirits and among the ablest magicians in the church. They also seem to rise relatively easily to the highest dojo offices. Although their high position can be accounted for in part by their relatively high income, how can we explain their splendid possession and miracle records? Some might suggest that theirs is a case of relative deprivation. Frustrated when they compare themselves with significant others above them in secular society, they turn to the dojo in order to raise their social status. Now, if this is the case, it is not something that we can prove with our limited data. Without further information, we must therefore refuse the temptation to assign more importance to imputed motives (that is, the quest for status) than to the motives alleged by the members themselves (sickness). Their facility for appropriating the church's world-of-meaning can be attributed just as easily to their leadership capacity, imagination, intelligence, or overall ambition as to deprivation.

In criticizing deprivation theory and its abuses, I do not wish to fall into the still more vicious error of treating needs in such a cavalier manner that the obvious relationship between human misery and the rise of religious movements is overlooked. My inclination, therefore, is to be cautious about accepting a full-blown deprivation theory of the origin and spread of the New Religions—especially if it commits us to any mechanical theory of human nature or historical change—and to concentrate on the specific ways

Table 20. Occupational Distribution of Dojo Members

Occupational group	Percent of responses
Low-level white-collar workers (describing themselves as clerks, receptionists, tailors, fortune tellers, beauticians, low-income "salary men," detectives, bank tellers, etc.)	46%
Unskilled blue-collar workers (cooks, gas station attendants, firemen, etc.)	20
High-level white-collar workers (managers or owners of small factories and shops, opticians, calligraphy teachers, real estate agents, public school teachers, etc.)	14
Skilled blue-collar workers (plasterers, carpenters, electricians, etc.)	11
Farmers	8

in which these religions meet specific human needs. Above all, one must avoid the mistake of treating members of these religions as unfortunate wretches in a state of "general deprivation."

Although deprivation theory may be seriously flawed *as a theory*, it does seem reasonable to speak of organizations like Mahikari as groups that respond to and fulfill basic religious, social, and material needs. What are some of the needs, or "relative deprivations," that might possibly account for the growth of Mahikari? One might, at least, propose the six following hypotheses.

People join Mahikari because they are poor. Economic deprivation has long been regarded as one of the more important reasons for the growth of the New Religions. The critical attitude of Mahikari toward the elite professions seems to reflect the resentment that, following Nietzsche and Max Scheler, sociologists have associated with the religions of the lower classes. Most Mahikari members do, in fact, come from the so-called lower classes. The approximate distribution of occupational groups among members is shown in Table 20.

In this survey, as in others relating to Japanese class structure, many of the white-collar workers who "have usually been regarded as middle-class, might more appropriately be regarded as the modern proletariat and labeled as lower-class."[29] About three-quarters of those surveyed could be described as "bourgeois proletarians" (Engels). Others would fall into Japan's "old middle class," or C. Wright Mills's "lumpen bourgeoisie." A few of the high-level white-collar workers (such as the "salary men") would qualify as members of the so-called new middle class. Very few, however, are members of Marx's "lumpen proletariat."

The incomes of these families are not significantly different from those of other Japanese families in similar lines of work. (See Appendix A, Question 5.) For example, in 1976 the average income of a Japanese family of four in which the father, a man of forty with a high school education, worked as a clerk or technician, was about $9,500 a year. A man with the same personal background working in general production earned about $8,365.[30] Were these families to join Mahikari, they would rank in the next-to-highest income bracket, along with about 40 percent of the present membership. Compared with others doing the same kind of work, then, Mahikari members would not have reason to regard themselves as suffering any grievous economic deprivation. In spite of the sect's claim that it improves people's financial situation, only 4 percent admit that they joined for this reason.

Although the Savior promised that Su-god would feed the faithful out of "the storehouse of heaven," it is difficult to say to what extent a member's financial situation does improve after he joins the church.* Studies of social mobility in Japan conducted at about the same time Okada was founding his group show that upward mobility, though far from being fictitious, was largely confined to the middle classes. Those at the lower and higher extremities of the social scale had far less chance of raising their stations in life.[31] If these findings are true today, they imply that the social and economic cards are stacked against most of the families who join the dojo. The financial miracles members talk about are generally small ones that enable them to get through the day, or pay their bus fare to a church festival in Tokyo. But it is not impossible that some members actually do improve their social and economic position by

---

* Okada qualified his promise somewhat by adding that if a person's financial situation did not improve as a result of okiyome, he should regard his poverty as a "temporary purification."

getting cleaned up. Members who are able to give up alcohol and gambling, for example, probably find that they are able to function in the workaday world better than before they joined the dojo.*

One of the young men whom I interviewed, Kitagawa Hisashi, readily discussed his financial ambition. A graduate of Chūō University, Kitagawa now works for a firm selling kitchen sets, water heaters, and bathtubs. Impatient to launch a more profitable career, he regards his present job as merely "preparatory study" for setting up his own business, perhaps a travel agency. Kitagawa could already point to a few financial miracles in his life. When he was a student at Chuo, he was able to find enough money to take a trip abroad. That was his first miracle. Because he missed one of the examinations required for graduation while he was away, Kitagawa was afraid that he would have to spend an extra year at Chuo. (He seems to have been an indifferent college student who spent most of his time mountain climbing.) "Miraculously," after praying to Su-god and talking with his major professor, he was allowed to graduate without taking the exam. In general, he feels that since he received his amulet, his luck has improved (*un ga tsuyoi*). He has not, however, had occasion to perform any physical miracles. He thinks that pollution is caused by factory and automobile emissions, and not by evil spirits. To clean up the air, he concludes, government policy is more important than okiyome. In short, the social and economic attitudes of a member like Kitagawa are a curious mixture of ambition, rationality, and magic.[32]

People join Mahikari because they are uprooted. This explanation has often been used to account for the rapid spread of the New Religions immediately after the war. In fact there is reason to believe that population mobility was an important factor in the growth of these religions at that time. In 1950, 70 percent of the Japanese population lived in the countryside. By 1963, the ratio of rural to urban population had been completely reversed, with 70 percent living in the cities. This enormous disruption created considerable anxiety, especially among families not protected by powerful labor unions or industrial patrons.[33] Although this factor was not covered in the questionnaire, in interviews with members

---

* Mahikari cures alcoholism by exorcising thirsty fox and dragon spirits.

I asked how often they had moved during the past ten years. Judging from their answers, some of the younger members joined Mahikari after leaving their families to go to Nakayama City, but most members have not moved more than three or four times in their lives. The majority have lived in Nakayama City or its environs since birth. My limited information indicates that whereas population mobility may have been a factor in the growth of the New Religions during the 1950's, it is probably less important today.

People join Mahikari because they are uneducated. If by education one means the amount of public education (measured in years) a person has had, this proposition is simply false. When we compare the educational background of members and non-members, we find no reason to speak of deprivation. In 1975, the average Japanese aged twenty-five to sixty-four had 9.2 years of education. Members of the four dojos in the same age group had 10.7 years of education in 1976. Again, in 1975, the average Japanese aged twenty-five to thirty-four had 11.1 years of education, whereas Mahikari members in the same age group who were surveyed the following year had 11.7.[34] This relatively high educational level among my respondents is probably due to their urban background.

Quantity of education obviously is not the same as quality. Since members probably received about the same kind of education as non-members, public school education does not seem to be an important factor in determining who will join the church. Although liberal sociologists like to believe that education causes religion to decline, public education that is constitutionally forbidden to deal seriously with religion is not likely to have much impact on students' personal lives.

People join Mahikari because they are deprived of important social roles. The notion of role deprivation as a motivation for joining a religious group probably has its greatest cogency when applied to domestic status. Applied to public roles (such as occupation or leadership), it seems to be less important. We have seen in great detail how young women deprived of their domestic roles as wives and mothers turn to Mahikari for help. I have talked with several women who believe that they found husbands and became mothers thanks to Su-god's help. Most women are reluctant to admit that they joined the dojo in order to find a husband, but many may, in fact, have joined in search of precisely this kind of "upward domestic mobility."

We have seen that women are more susceptible than men to spirit possession and are somewhat more likely to take a thaumaturgical approach to various problems. Perhaps they are simply fulfilling the sexual role expected of them. It may be that the youth of the dojos and the female members in general find great personal gratification in these possession and thaumaturgical experiences, just as older people and males presumably find gratification in occupying positions of high authority and responsibility. It would therefore be hasty to say that women and young members are more susceptible to possession and more magically oriented *because* they are unable to attain positions of authority in the dojos, or that these activities are a compensation for being deprived of higher status and respect within the church.

People join Mahikari because they are deprived of health. Although I feel that it is odd to speak of the deprivation of status and the deprivation of health in the same tone of voice, many sociologists do regard illness as a kind of deprivation. Since most people go to doctors and not to church when they are "deprived of their health," it is not clear what we gain by talking this way. Whatever the case, it is true that 52 percent of the members of the dojos in the survey originally joined the church either because they were sick or in order to find a cure for a loved one. Healing, therefore, is indisputably the primary motive for the spread of this religion.

In labeling sickness "deprivation," we have still not shown why some people go to a doctor when they fall ill, while others go to the dojo. From my interviews with Mahikari members, the only explanation seems to lie in their family histories. As we have seen, many members can recall that when they were children, their parents consulted mediums, palmists, or faith healers whenever they were faced with a serious crisis. Approximately 29 percent of the members had joined other New Religions before their conversion to Mahikari, and others had undergone "spiritual operations" or exorcism in search of health. Many members grew up in families as steeped in folklore as they were in folk religion. In these families, stories about ghosts, animal spirits, possession, exorcism, and miracles are passed from one generation to the next.

In view of these long family histories of exposure to folk religion, folk medicine, and folklore, why certain people joined Mahikari is not the only question we should ask. Since all healing techniques, traditional and modern alike, are surrounded by implicit networks of cognition and confidence, the sociologist must explain not only why some people turn to religion or magic for a cure, but also why others—even if they happen to be the cognitive majority— turn to doctors. As Bibby and Brinkerhoff point out, the control group is vitally important. To be sure, my answer to this problem only shifts the question from why individuals join healing cults to why their families remained "traditional." A satisfactory answer to this question would take us far beyond my research.

People join Mahikari because they are deprived of meaning in their lives. Since the meaning or purpose of life seems to become more important as highly industrial nations solve their basic bread-and-butter problems, it seems likely that some people turn to Mahikari to help them find their spiritual bearings. Although quite a few people claim that they joined the sect out of "interest" in (or "curiosity" about) miracles, religion, or spirits, many seem to use this response, as we have seen, in order to legitimate a religious affiliation that has actually become a family devoir. Whatever the reason, I am told that more and more people are joining the church not to be healed, but to find meaning in life. These reports may even indicate that the church's age of ingenuousness is coming to an end.

Related to this general deprivation of meaning is the disorienta-tion that many Japanese experienced as a result of their country's defeat in World War II. The growth of the New Religions after the war has often been attributed in part to the collapse of State Shinto and the imperial system. Not a few of these religions have proclaimed themselves the key to world peace, while at the same time promoting, sotto voce, the most offensive kind of ethnocen-trism. Many still espouse the particularistic values of the militarist period, while giving lip-service to universalistic values and even monotheism. Their nationalistic mythologies remind one of the outlook of the idolatrous civil religion of Japan's recent past. It

certainly is not impossible that Mahikari's myth of Mu and its prediction of the global reunion of "government and religion" under
the aegis of the Japanese emperor help compensate for the deprivation the Japanese suffered as a result of their military defeat.
If this is so, one could even argue that such myths are merely the
lower-class version of the faith that the upper classes have until
recently expressed in their country's invincible gross national product. They differ only in their relative lack of polish from some of
the "Japanese Culture Theories" (*Nihonjin bunkaron*), pop-ideolo-
gies that have glutted the Japanese press in recent years.

To summarize our discussion, I find no relative deprivation in the
areas of income and education that would account for the growth
of Mahikari. The only concrete evidence I have of role deprivation
as a motive for joining the dojo is limited to status within the
family. In Chapter 8 we saw that the dojo is an institution for transforming and raising self-esteem. In effect, it empowers people to
overcome passivity and defeat, and assume the active role of shaman or master magician. Thus the Seed People regard themselves
as true shamanistic ascetics (*makoto-gyōja*), religious virtuosi in
supreme control over their own lives and world. In traditional
societies and in religious communities today, such charismatics enjoy the highest respect.[35] The possession-exorcism syndrome in
Mahikari, as elsewhere, can therefore be thought of as an "oblique
aggressive strategy" aiming at "self assertion," to use I. M. Lewis's
words.[36] In Chapter 9 we saw how change in self-esteem is linked
to the upward mobility of a person's domestic status. In this chapter we have seen how the dojo enables people to raise their status
within their own religious community. Raising religious status
seems to be a major function of the New Religions for those classes
in which upward social and economic mobility is difficult. Edward
Norbeck points out that in Soka Gakkai, too, opportunities are
provided "that are probably unparalleled elsewhere in the nation
for rising swiftly in position and—within the sect if not in the
general society—in prestige, on the basis of individual efforts."[37]

There is no evidence, however, that Mahikari members "substitute" their religious status for their standing in society, as Liston
Pope would put it. One could even ask whether such a substitution

is possible. The Ethiopian in the Book of Jeremiah might *think* about changing the color of his skin—or the leopard his spots— but to speak of an actual substitution of one kind of skin, spots, or status for another is clearly an illusion. Nevertheless, it is certainly possible for people to *supplement* their social status and self-esteem with a new religious identity. This kind of supplementary fulfillment of oneself is usually a consequence of joining a sect like Mahikari, and not the primary motive for it. The status that rises as a result of getting cleaned up in the dojo is therefore primarily religious in nature, and in some cases, domestic. It is limited to the member's immediate family and "approval group." One can only speculate whether members' actual social status improves as a result of joining the dojo, but this seems rather unlikely. The financial miracles that most members recount generally have to do with pathetically small economic gains. Members with a relatively high standing in the secular world may actually *lose* status as a result of their involvement in the world of miracles and spirit possession.

Upward religious mobility involves more than the satisfaction of the needs that motivate people to join the religion of the "disinherited" in the first place. Once concrete human needs have been absorbed by thaumaturgical Need—that is, once life's problems have been incorporated into the Problem of life as it is understood in a "church of magic"—an inflationary spiral is apt to develop. As in a consumer economy, demand for miracles is stimulated both by supply and by advertisement (of which there is no lack). After, say, a person's first healing miracle, the Treatment will be applied to more and more needs and problems. As problems are solved, needs and "deprivations" begin to multiply.

In this chapter we have examined a need satisfied by one of the latent or secondary functions of religion and magic alike, the need for legitimacy. We have seen how okiyome and magic act as indices of members' upward religious mobility. Because the mobility they demonstrate is limited only by the Seventh Dimension, apotheosis should be thought of as a scalariform process of legitimation. Consequently, in sects like Mahikari legitimation, and perhaps theodicy too, are *expansible* "plausibility structures."[38]

Although the deprivation theory of the origin of religious sects may stand in need of serious modification, or even demolition, it is helpful insofar as it focuses attention on the importance of concrete needs in the formation of these movements. As problematic as the concept of need (or deprivation) may be, I do not find it as reductionistic as critics are wont to maintain. Individuals who join religions like Mahikari generally see themselves as people in need. As a retreatant in another New Religion once remarked to me, such religions are of no help until one has come to a point of personal deadlock (*ikizumari*).[39] What such people need is not just a "general order of existence," an "ultimate concern," or a "sacred canopy"—the foci of contemporary theories of religion—but a faithful, fertile spouse, obedient children, congenial friends, a job, good health, and a fast and sure way to ward off disaster and death. If, in addition to satisfying these basic needs, a person were to fix his television or run his car without gasoline; improve the taste of his noodles, rice, and wine; heal his cat or bring his dead goldfish back to life—all this, just by raising his hand—who is to say that he could not raise his own religious status in the same miraculous way?

13 *The Cunning of Magic and Reason*

In this book I have described the sociosemantic construction of a magical response to the world. I have suggested that as a religion Mahikari is virtually slow magic, and that as magic it is fast religion. In this concluding chapter, I would like to reflect on the place of magical religions of this sort in the modern world.

Psychologists say that no one completely escapes from the thralldom of magic. All, to varying degrees, are victims of thought's would-be omnipotence and self's private rituals. Retreat into the enchanted forest, or more specifically regression to the magical womb, is as common in politics and science as in religion. Magic can therefore be considered a natural aspect not only of religion, but of consciousness itself. Sartre reminds us that "the act of imagination is a magical one. It is an incantation destined to produce the object of one's thought, the thing one desires, in a manner that one can take possession of it. In that act there is always something of the imperious and the infantile, a refusal to take distance or difficulties into account." [1]

Obviously, not all consciousness is magical. Magic is curbed by Ego's lurking suspicion that not all of Id's fancies correspond to the world-out-there. As a person matures, he becomes increasingly conscious of his own limitations and develops a greater capacity for testing his own grip on reality. Gradually he becomes aware of the distance between will and world, or what philosophers alternatively celebrate and lament as the subject-object dichotomy. Some have even speculated that this primordial differentiation in his world was what gave rise to man's magics and religions. For the first time, man was confronted with the irresistible temptation of devising for himself symbolic avenues for retreating to an archaic state of undifferentiated, infantile bliss. Or so we are told.

Whereas regression, and even dissociative states of consciousness, play significant roles in most of man's religions, religion itself is not exempt from reality-testing. Christian saints, with their dove-like innocence, are enjoined by the Master to be as wise as serpents. Buddhist monks, being their own lamp and refuge, concentrate on samsaric realities until they are freed from them. Confucian sages, setting aside other-worldly speculation and this-worldly superstition, devote themselves to the governing of men. In short, religion, far from being merely the opiate of the masses, has within itself two complementary impulses: one an urge to improve or overcome "reality," the other a courageous drive to probe it and find its limits. Religion is therefore no stranger to the grim truth about the world. We have seen that religion teaches man not how to avoid suffering, but how to suffer *meaningfully*. Magical religions, however, though they also contribute to a more "meaningful" world, search for the short-cut to happiness, for detours around the sloughs of despond through which religion tells us we must go.

In this book we have seen how members of the dojo, by giving full range to the regressive and magical depths of the religious imagination, create a world that is humane, tractable, and seemingly respectful of their place in it. My purpose has been to show how they put this world together. In disciplines that seek to understand worlds that not only surround us but invade our inner space (one thinks, for example, of psychoanalysis) there is always the temptation to place too much emphasis on the ultimate cause of man's ideal creations. Likewise, in religious studies, scholarship has been beset and bedazzled by a succession of monogenetic theories seeking to explain the origin of religion—theories based on animism, totemism, repression, alienation, and group solidarity, to cite only a few. The ultimate origin of man's religions is, of course, shrouded in prehistory and will never be known. Only the ongoing creation of religion and magic is open to investigation.

Perhaps the best way to pursue this study is to follow the lead of, say, medical research, which has learned to look for complex explanations of the origins and distribution of disease, for example, the interaction between heredity, environmental conditions, stress, and so on. I have suggested that the creation of Mahikari's world of magic, exorcism, and omens is made possible by a similar *complex* of symbol-generating mechanisms. Like the *arcs-boutants* of the medieval cathedral, these devices hold together religion's walls, windows, and roofs, thereby creating a sacred space where revelations and miracles can take place. The preceding chapters have discussed the ways in which (1) the schematization of life by Salvation Syndromes, (2) the logic of religious bricolage, (3) homeopathic and catalytic projections, (4) the induction of various states of consciousness, (5) the use of index words as automatic signals, (6) the fulfillment of a subliminal thirst for status and self-esteem, and (7) the generation of a theodicy for life's sorrows all contribute, *mutatis mutandis*, to the unification and perpetuation of Mahikari, both as an institution and as a personal faith.

The sacred space held together by these devices is, of course, the dojo itself. We have seen that contrary to Durkheim's view, such "churches of magic" exist even in the midst of a highly complex, industrial society. This chapter examines the question, Do churches of magic really "belong" in such a society? Before this question can be answered, we must briefly review the history of magic in Japanese culture. Where does magic "belong" in the Japanese tradition itself?

The Tradition of Magic

Unlike the biblical tradition in the West, Japanese religion has seldom tried to stay the force of magic. The tension commonly occurring in other cultures between the rational ethics and metaphysical systems of the elite, on the one hand, and the magic and superstition of the folk, on the other, has been strangely muted in Japan. Buddhism, for example, was introduced into the country as a form of magic. In the middle of the sixth century A.D., the king of the Korean kingdom of Pekche sent a statue of the Buddha, some sutras, and various ritual implements to the Japanese court, together with a letter touting the magical efficacy of Buddhist practices: "Imagine a man in possession of treasures to his heart's content, so that he might satisfy all his wishes in proportion as he used them. Thus it is with the treasure of this wonderful doctrine. Every prayer is fulfilled and naught is wanting." [2] The new faith was alternately blessed for preserving the health of emperors and cursed for sending plagues and droughts. Practical-minded emperors allowed select individuals to worship the new Korean deity as an experiment, that is, to see whether it really would fulfill "every prayer." One of these experiments reveals exactly how magical early Japanese Buddhism was. According to the *Nihongi*:

Mūmako no Sukune, *by way of experiment*, took the relic, and placing it on the middle of a block of iron, beat it with an iron sledge-hammer, which he flourished aloft. The block and the sledge-hammer were shattered to atoms, but the relic could not be crushed. Then the relic was cast into water, where it floated on the water or sank as one desired. In consequence of this, Mūmako no Sukune, Ikenobe no Hida, and Shiba Tattō held faith in Buddhism and practised it unremittingly. Mūmako no Sukune built another Buddhist Temple at his house in Ishikaha. *From this arose the beginning of Buddhism.* [3]

Even after the court turned to the more sophisticated doctrines and rituals of the Shingon and Tendai sects, it continued to look to Buddhism, as it did to Shinto, for this-worldly magical benefits. Heian aristocrats were preoccupied by astrology, geomancy, tantric forms of yin-yang magic, the fear of unlucky directions, and malevolent spirits. Throughout the Middle Ages the warrior class, the new social elite, depending on the land for its own material support, practiced the same agrarian magic used by its peasant underlings. Except for a few thinkers, such as Dōgen Zenji, Shinran Shōnin, and certain Confucianists of the later Tokugawa period, magic was universally practiced as an ancillary to religion, a skillful means (*hōben*) for the enlightenment of the ignorant. More generally, it was practiced simply because of its considerable practical benefits.

Even the eschatology of the New Religions and their predecessors in the Tokugawa period had its roots in the magical utopianism that grew up around the figure of Maitreya (Japanese: Miroku), the Future Buddha. Throughout East Asia, the Future Buddha played an important role in the fantasies of resentment and revenge of exploited peasants. In both China and Southeast Asia, he became the patron deity of social unrest and rebellion. In Japan, the myth of the coming of Maitreya's World (*Miroku no yo*) seems to be a Buddhist superimposition on a far more archaic belief in a paradise beyond the sea (*tokoyo no kuni*). In this mystical land, the gods were believed to be preparing rich harvests for hard-pressed peasants. Many thought that they could hasten the arrival of Maitreya's boat by singing and dancing his praises.*

Like the followers of Okada Kotama in the twentieth century, the medieval believers in Maitreya thought that the advent of the Future Buddha would be preceded by earthquakes and other natural disasters. During the tumultuous events of the nineteenth century, Japanese peasants were attracted to the belief in the magical "renewal of the world" (*yonaoshi*). Because yonaoshi was thought to be a purgation of society and nature alike, it too became a common theme in peasant uprisings. Destroying the property of landlords and the account books of moneylenders was part of a glorious eschatological drama. These movements, however violent, seldom if ever challenged the ultimate legitimacy of the authority and privileges of the ruling classes. Like the magician, the rebel looks for instant relief, not for a new order of things. Although yonaoshi rebellions were generally more violent than the Maitreya movements, when the two came together, as they occasionally did, faith in the Future Buddha added fuel to the already perfervid expectations of the peasants. Landlords sometimes refused loan applications from their tenants, fearing that "Maitreya would come" and cancel the loan.[4] Mahikari has grafted these apocalyptic hopes into its own conservative, nationalistic ideology. But the magic is still there. When the Endtime comes, the triumph of the Seed People will be quick, obvious, and virtually automatic.

Although some voices were raised against the use of magic, the

---

* Originally, the boat was thought to be filled with food for the starving. Later, with the growth of a money economy, Maitreya's bounty was changed into hard cash in the imagination of the oppressed. But the idea was the same: Maitreya would bring immediate, concrete help.

Japanese peasant traditionally mixed his prayers and spells with long hours of hard work.[5] Like Malinowski's Trobrianders, were you to suggest to them that they could raise their rice and vegetables by relying on magic alone, they would "simply smile on your simplicity."[6] During the Meiji period, however, this happy union of magic and industry came under increasing attack by a government determined to build a "rich country and a strong army" (*fukoku kyōhei*) as quickly as possible. It condemned as wasteful many of the "superstitions" and orgiastic "excesses" of traditional folk religion. The practice of mountain asceticism (*shugendō*) was largely forced underground, not to be revived until the American Occupation granted religious freedom to all.

While the government was busy preaching a this-worldly asceticism to the common people, many traditional religious and magical practices were slipping through the back door via Japan's burgeoning new cities. Cities grew up that, in spirit, were villages writ large. As Kamishima Jirō puts it, the Japanese city was really a "second village."[7] The ethos of the Japanese village continues to dominate many of these cities to the present day. Tsurumi Kazuko writes: "On the surface . . . contemporary Japanese society looks like a model mass society. At bottom, however, the primary village community and the fictitious village within the city are still preserved."[8] Little wonder that the New Religions of the post-war period were able to rekindle the spirit of folk religion and magic so easily in the new urban setting. In village and city alike, magic, like religion, continued to exist in both institutionalized and diffused forms (that is, as New Religions and as "superstition").

When we look at the New Religions in the light of this long history of magic and religion, it is they, and not the more prestigious sects such as Zen, that appear to represent the cultural mainstream of the country. Considered from the unbiased vantage point of statistical significance, Japan's Great Tradition virtually *is* her Little Tradition. To this day, taboos, lucky and unlucky years, seasons, and directions (*kataimi*), not to mention countless other "superstitions" of humble origin, continue to influence the activities of the so-called common man. But though magical notions continue to be found in contemporary Japan, it is true that cultural mainstreams change their course. Difficult as statistics on secularization are to interpret, they provide at least prima facie evidence that religious belief and magical practices have declined since the end of the war. Before that, the government's incessant promotion of "civil religion" for its own ends makes it difficult to tease apart what people said they believed (*tatemae*) from what they actually felt (*honne*) about religion.

After the war, State Shinto was disestablished and religious freedom guaranteed by the new "MacArthur Constitution." No longer fanned by the government, the blazing fire of civil religion suddenly subsided, leaving behind only the glowing embers of community cults and family worship. Several statistical surveys indicate a serious erosion of religious faith in Japan during these years. The *Study of Japanese National Character* recorded a progressive decline in the percentage of the population claiming to have "some kind of religious faith or attitude," from 35 percent in 1958 to 25 percent in 1973.[9] In 1963, a poll taken by a television network in Japan found that 23 percent of the population believed in spirits (reikon), though only 18 percent thought there is an afterlife.[10] In 1975, another nationwide survey showed that only 13.6 percent of the Japanese believed in the power of amulets, 12.8 percent in miracles, and a mere 6 percent in fortune telling or divination.[11] If accurate, these figures suggest that religions like Mahikari nowadays represent not the mainstream, but a cognitive minority within a far more secular culture.

The relationship between the secular culture of Japan and the cognitive deviance of the New Religions is no simple matter. For reasons I explain elsewhere, the secularism of modern Japan seems to be about as "situational" as traditional religion and magic.[12] What recent opinion surveys have revealed is therefore not the growth of a committed or philosophically disciplined atheism, but rather the general decline in the need for religion *at present*. The relationship between the secular and the supernatural must therefore be seen within the context of the integrative cognitive style of the Japanese, which the anthropologist Itō Mikiharu likes to call a "logic of relative contrasts."[13] Both the sacred and the secular can be expected to color the lifestyle of most Japanese. Because even the secular Japanese may someday need a little magic himself, he is chary of condemning the occult and the supernatural out of hand. As long as his more religious neighbors seem happy, healthy, and lucky, his attitude is one of "live and let live."

The secular and the supernatural come into conflict only when one or the other does something to upset the subtle equilibrium of Japanese etiquette or the tolerance of its "logic of relative contrasts." In general, what secular Japanese object to in the New Religions is not their magical orientation, but their aggressiveness and exclusive claims. The more aggressive and exclusive a religion is, the more it is disliked by non-members. Soka Gakkai surpasses all in opprobrium. But as we have seen in the spirit history of the Yoshida family, Mahikari members too are apt to arouse the animosity of friends and neighbors by their invasion of privacy. Generally speaking, however, the church's magic gives rise to social or family tensions only when it does not work.

Mahikari poses less of a social problem than more aggressive New Religions simply because it makes fewer demands. Even the most zealous convert will insist that a person can practice okiyome while being a Buddhist, a Shintoist, or a Christian. The social values preached by the sect also make for better relations with neighbors. Many members say that the most important thing for them about Mahikari is its stress on being humble (*sunao na kimochi*). "Instead of looking for others' faults, we should try to get along with people [*nakayoku suru*], and live in harmony with our neighbors [*wa no naka ni ireru*]," one member said. The Seed People therefore strive to be flexible, adaptable, and rational—an ideal strategy for finding one's niche in an industrial society infused with very traditional values. Perhaps their goal is not unlike that of a young man I met when studying a different New Religion: to be "more easily used" (*tsukaiyasui*).[14]

Magic in an Industrial Society

In the minds of many, religions like Mahikari have no place in the modern world. In an age of science and technology, so they say, such archaic survivals can only be detrimental to the health of society. Some, like Sir James Frazer, might even argue that they are a standing menace to the progress of civilization and the modern economy. Some exponents of modernization theory have treated magic and religion alike as impediments to the rationalization of society.

It is instructive to review Max Weber's thoughts on magic, since so much of modernization theory was inspired by his work. For Weber, magic is primarily an ad hoc and emotional way of responding to human need. It promotes a cognitive particularism incapable of generating the universalistic values and religious ethics that he believed provide the backbone for the rationalization of social and economic life. Only from a long-term evolutionary perspective can the contribution of magic to modernization be measured at all. Both the charisma of the archaic magician and the taboos surrounding magic itself contributed to the stereotyping of magical concepts. Magic was therefore the primitive source of most religious phenomena, such as prayer, sacrifice, pastoral care, mysticism, asceticism, and even aesthetics.

Despite its contributions to the rationalization of primitive life, in Weber's view the toleration of magic has become a major impediment to the modernization of society. One of the reasons for the early rationalization of Western civilization was the high level of tension that developed between Protestantism and magic. This tension in turn generated the "disenchantment of the world" on two fronts. The most obvious is the decline of religion and magic due to the progressive "intellectualization" of life. The second, less obvious from the annals of intellectual history, may be even more important: the disenchanting effect of the routines of everyday life in industrial society. Strangely enough, though Weber clearly stated that disenchantment is only a growing *possibility* in modern society, he also regarded it as part of the *fate* of Western civilization. Because *Entgötterung* and *Entzauberung* stripped life and death of their meaning, Weber believed that the very progress of civilization inevitably led to the permanent anesthetizing of the human spirit, until the world would be filled with "specialists without spirit, sensualists without heart." [15]

Whereas Weber wrote at great length about the decline of magic, he rather inconsistently seemed to recognize its undiminished survival in the modern world. Magic seems to have a trans-historical function in the lower reaches of all societies, since "the masses in need are always out for emergency aid through magic and saviors." [16] Although the modern proletariat might be indifferent to the religions patronized by the bourgeoisie, its most oppressed elements (together with members of the lower middle classes in danger of sinking into the proletariat) have an elective affinity for magical forms of religion, or as he put it, the "magical-orgiastic supervention of grace" and the "soteriological orgies" that one finds, say, among the early Methodists or in the Salvation Army. [17]

How would Weber regard a movement like Mahikari? Okada's oracles of doom remind one of the rhetoric of the biblical prophets, but his occultism, thaumaturgical outlook, and class associations would make Weber's "plebeian mystagogue" a more appropriate tag. The mystagogue, who performs "magical actions that contain boons of salvation," differs from the magician only in degree. [18] He is interested less in dogma than in magical salvation. The distribution of his charms and boons provides him with a livelihood that often is passed on to his own children. Thus the mystagogue must be strictly distinguished from the prophet, a type of religious leadership that Weber associates with rationalization and social change.

The persistence of magic and religion poses an interesting problem for Weber, whose notion of disenchantment is based on a complex but unilinear concept of evolutionary development. In fact, he differs from other evolutionists only in his romantic, yet realistic, pessimism. While recognizing the survival of religion and magic, Weber fails to analyze in detail the coexistence of these archaic phenomena with science and capitalism. Because he always linked rationalization to domination (*Herrschaft*) and power (*Macht*), reason in his thought clearly has a winning edge over unreason. One would think that on his own grounds *magic should not exist in the modern world*. This theoretical conundrum seems to be related to his analysis of reason itself. Although Weber distinguished carefully among types of social conduct according to the goals and motivations of the actor, he did not pay enough attention to the relationships between social classes and what could be called the scope of their rationality.

A better exposition of this problem is to be found in Karl Mannheim's clarification of the word rationality. Mannheim distinguishes between two sorts of rationality: substantial and functional.[19] By substantial rationality he means "an act of thought which reveals intelligent insight into the interrelations of events in a given situation"; it is an act that displays "the capacity for independent judgment."[20] Functional rationality, on the other hand, is a series of actions efficiently related to the realization of predetermined ends. In functional rationality, "emphasis is laid on the coordination of action with reference to a definite goal."[21] An example Mannheim uses to elucidate his distinction is that of an army. In an army, the common soldier "carries out an entire series of functionally rational actions accurately without having any idea as to the ultimate end of his actions or the functional role of each individual act within the framework of the whole." The substantial rationality of the army, on the other hand, is the privilege of its commanding officers. The functional rationality of the troops therefore depends "on the plans of certain authorities far removed from the actors," that is, on the substantial rationality of those who alone monitor and command the big picture.[22]

Whereas many modernization theorists simply assume that the masses are automatically drawn into the thought, values, and lifestyle of the elite as society becomes more "rational," Mannheim uses his analysis of the scope of rationality to explain the eruption of irrationalism in the so-called rational societies of Europe in the 1930's. Industrialization, according to Mannheim, cuts down the scope of rationality for the masses.

The more industrialized a society is and the more advanced its division of labor and organization, the greater will be the number of spheres of human activity which will be functionally rational and hence also calculable in advance. Whereas the individual in earlier societies acted only occasionally and in limited spheres in a functionally rational manner, in contemporary society he is compelled to act in this way in more and more spheres of life.

. . .

If, in analyzing the changes of recent years, people had kept in mind the distinction between various types of rationality, they would have seen clearly that industrial rationalization served to increase functional rationality but that it offered far less scope for the development of substantial rationality in the sense of the capacity for independent judgment. . . . Functional rationalization is, in its very nature, bound to deprive the average individual of thought, insight, and responsibility and to transfer these capacities to the individuals who direct the process of rationalization.[23]

According to Mannheim's analysis, though the functionally rationalized masses are capable of self-rationalization (the systematic control of an individual's own impulses), their capacity for reflection and self-observation is diminished. As a result of this process, individuals confronted with the inexplicable breakdown of their society (for example, economic crises and social disorder) are easily thrown into "a state of terrified helplessness," in which they become susceptible to epidemics of totalitarian irrationalism.[24]

To return to Mahikari, Mannheim's discussion of the scope of rationality helps clarify how a religion can seem to be "irrational" (magical, shamanistic, occult) while promoting and rewarding relatively rational lifestyles among its members. Weber treated "Asiatic charms" as cases of irrationality; but okiyome cannot be so lightly dismissed. As long as the dominant mode of the rationality of a class is restricted in scope to the efficient performance of tasks laid down from above, magic is by no means contradictory to reason. By ritualizing optimism, magic enhances the rationalization of life even in an industrial society. The magical response to the world sponsored by the New Religions of Japan indirectly supports the social order by relieving the tensions and anxieties that people in any society have. While some religions narcoticize the masses with their opium, others, including Mahikari, infuse the faithful with energy and self-confidence. Thanks to the democratization of magic, modern believers can face the challenges of life with the courage of the primitive shaman and wizard.

There is room, then, for churches of magic in modern, industrial societies, especially in those where, since earliest times, religion has been geared to the satisfaction of immediate needs and wishes. One of these churches is the Mahikari dojo. There, day after day, members methodically raise their hands to heal the sick, cast out evil spirits, change karma, and prepare themselves for a glorious role in the coming Kingdom of God Civilization. They have discovered in Mahikari what Malinowski found in magic in general, namely, "the sublime folly of hope, which has yet been the best school of man's character."[25] Some have even found in this church of magic a still nobler folly: the courage to say to fate itself, "in spite of all . . . !"

Appendixes

APPENDIX A

Questionnaire and Basic Frequencies

In December 1976 the following questionnaire was distributed to members of four dojos in Osaka, Sakai, "Nakayama City," and "Nakamoto" (a small town of 16,768 in "Nakayama" Prefecture). Some 385 usable responses were received from Osaka, 85 from Sakai, 176 from Nakayama City, and 42 from Nakamoto. The frequencies listed below are based on a total sample of 688 cases. Only when the total number of cases drops below 350 will the number of cases be reported.

When the coefficient of correlation (Pearson's r) drops below .15, no relationship will be said to exist between two variables. The significance (p) of the relationship between variables will also be reported, though it is not strictly applicable to the non-random sampling technique employed here. A relationship will be considered significant only when p is .05 or lower.

Five scales were used in this study. The Scale of Miracles is based on the number of miracles a person has performed and whether he or she has experienced any physical miracles in particular (Questions 26 and 24). The Scale of Possession is made up of three items: (1) the number of spirit movements a person has had (Question 17A), (2) their intensity (Question 17B), and (3) report of multiple possession experiences (Question 20). The Scale of Involvement was constructed on the basis of (1) the number of training courses taken (Question 14), (2) the member's position in the dojo (Question 15), and (3) his or her attendance at the dojo (Question 16). Because in some cases attendance seemed to have a different effect on a member's behavior, it was excluded in the Scale of Commitment, which was constructed merely on the basis of the number of training courses taken and a person's position in the dojo. Finally, a Scale of Political Conservatism was used to assess the political outlook of members in terms of the party they supported in the election held on December 5, 1976. Those who supported more conservative political parties scored higher on this Scale. To create the Scale, political parties were ranked from left-wing to right-wing as follows: the Japan Communist Party, the Japan Socialist Party, the Democratic Socialist Party, the Clean Government Party, the New Liberal Club, and the Liberal Democratic Party.

1. What is your sex?
   Male   38%
   Female   62

2. What is your age?
   Median age   39 years

3. What was the last year of school completed?
   Junior high school   35%
   Senior high school   50
   Some college   16

4. What is your occupation?*
   Firm   26%
   Housewife   21
   Student   16
   Self-employed   13
   Public servant   5
   Farmer   3
   Other   17

5. What is your family's annual income?
   0 to $2,069   9%
   $2,070 to $6,897   38
   $6,898 to $13,793   40
   $13,794 and above   13

6. What is your marital status?
   Single   35%
   Married   58
   Divorced   4
   Remarried   3
   Separated   0.7

7. To be answered by married people who have had spirit movements: Of the ancestral spirits which have appeared to you, which are the more numerous: (a) your own ancestors, (b) your spouse's ancestors?
   Own ancestors   72%
   (Men   86%)
   (Women   65)
   Spouse's ancestors   28%
   (Men   14%)
   (Women   35)

8. Why did you join Mahikari?
   Recommended by a relative   39%
   Newspapers and advertisements   23

*The 322 responses to this question that offered sufficient detail were further analyzed for occupational rank. Occupational rank is therefore based on the respondent's occupation except in the case of housewives and students, where the occupation of the head of the household was used. The results obtained from this analysis are as follows.

Low-level white-collar workers	46%	Skilled blue-collar workers	11
Upper-level white-collar workers	14	Farmers	8
Unskilled blue-collar workers	20		

The percent of farmers in this breakdown is higher than it should be. Farmers were simply easier to identify than others, and therefore they are represented out of due proportion here.

Recommended by a friend 22
Recommended by a supervisor 7
Public testimonial meetings 6
Recommended by a stranger 6
Recommended by person in same place of work 5
Recommended by person in same line of work 2

9. What was your motive for joining?
Sickness 52%
Interest in miracles 22
Interest in spirits 18
Interest in religion 11
Anxiety in the family 9
Anxiety over the impasses of society (politics, pollution, etc.) 6
Financial anxiety 4
Problems with people outside the family 4
Marital problems 2

10. Before joining Mahikari did you belong to any of the other New Religions such as Tenrikyō or Sōka Gakkai?
Yes 29%
No 71

11. Before joining Mahikari did you believe in parapsychology, the Fourth Dimension, UFOs, etc.?
Yes 46%
No 54

12. In the two years before you joined Mahikari did anybody in your family have cancer or some other incurable illness?
Yes 19%
No 81

13. When you were a child, did your parents zealously tend their Buddhist memorial altar (*butsudan*)?
Yes 57%
No 43

14. How far have you gone in the Mahikari training courses?
First level 100%
Second level 51
Third level 19

15. Describe your responsibility (position) in the dojo.*
None 55%
Minor responsibility 16
Important responsibility 22
Highest responsibility (staff) 7

16. How many times a month do you visit a dojo or purification center?
Minimum (under 9 times a month) 37%
Average (10–19 times) 31
Maximum (20 or more times) 33

17. (A) Have you had spirit movements?
No 23%
A few 40
Quite a few 21
A lot 15

* For statistical purposes, leaders of the Mahikari Youth Corps have been ranked with those holding other important responsibilities. In fact, however, there is not simply one continuous vertical line of authority running through the dojo, but parallel ranks running through its different organizations. The four levels of responsibility listed here are an attempt to distill these parallel ranks into a single scale.

(B) Have these movements been weak or strong?

Weak   61%
Strong   39

18. What kind of spirit did these movements indicate?
Ancestral spirit   62%
Unrelated human spirit   53
Animal spirit   26

19. If it was an ancestral spirit, what type was it?
Grandparent   29%
Warrior   27
Father   14
Mother   14
Brother or sister   13
Townsman   6
(Deceased) child   5
Farmer   4
Some other type   33
                    $n = 292$

20. Has the same spirit ever possessed you several times?
Yes   44%
No   56

21. Have you ever been possessed by an evil spirit motivated by sexual karma (e.g., a husband, wife, or lover from a previous life)?
Yes   29%
No   71

22. Do you think men or women have more spirit movements?
Men   15%
Women   54
Same   31

23. To be answered by one person per family: Has the same spirit

ever possessed more than one member of your family?
Yes   30%
No   70

24. Have you ever performed a physical miracle through oki-yome, such as fixing a wrist-watch? Please describe.
(See Question 26B.2, "Physical miracles," for frequency.)

25. If your car broke down, in what order would you do the following:
(a) look for the cause and fix it yourself, (b) give it okiyome, (c) call a garage?
(Those who answered the question chose the following responses as their *first* option.)
Look for the cause and fix it   47%
Give the car okiyome   51
Call a garage   1

26. (A) How many times have you been blessed with a miracle?
Never   3%
Mercy Drops (1−14)   60
Showers (15 or more) 37

(B) Please describe. (Answers were broken down into the following categories.)
Healing miracles   39%
Physical miracles*   36
Coincidental miracles   13
Evangelistic miracles   5
Spiritual miracles   5
Financial miracles   5
Human and/or family relations miracles   2
Academic miracles   2

---

*Because members were asked about the physical miracles they had performed in a separate question, the 36 percent reporting this type of miraculous experience is probably higher than it otherwise would be.

27. (A) Did you vote in the election
    held on December 5, 1976?
    Yes   69%
    No   31

    (B) Which party do you support?
    Liberal Democratic Party 54%

Japan Socialist Party	14
New Liberal Club	12
Japan Communist Party	10
Democratic Socialist Party	7
Clean Government Party	3
Independent	3

Four further questions were taken from the *Study of Japanese National Character*. See Tables 16–19 in the text.

APPENDIX B
Statistical Tables and Figures

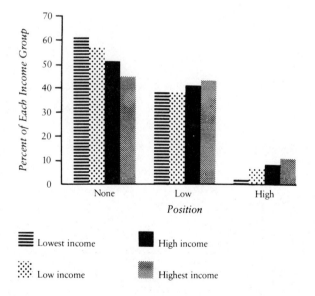

FIG. B.1. *Position in Dojo by Income Level. "Low" position consists of the first two levels in the hierarchy of responsibilities.*

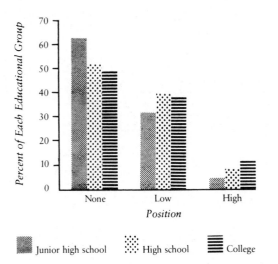

Junior high school   High school   College

FIG. B.2. *Position in Dojo by Educational Level.* "*Low*" *position consists of the first two levels in the hierarchy of responsibilities.*

Table B.1. *Sexual Karma Possession by Sex and Marital Status*
(percent)

| Marital status | Members with sexual karma experience | | |
	Women	Men	Both sexes
Single	48%	39%	44%
Married	28	8	21
Both statuses	34	20	29

Table B.2. *Attitude Toward Thaumaturgical Auto Repair by Income Level*

| Attitude | Income 0–$6,897 | | Income over $6,897 | |
	Number	Percent	Number	Percent
Would try okiyome first	78	55%	82	44%
Would try to determine cause and fix car themselves	65	45	104	56

Table B.3. Miracle Record by Educational Level
(percent)

Education	Number of miracles		
	None	Mercy Drops	Showers
Junior high school (*n* = 119)	3%	70%	28%
Senior high school (*n* = 169)	4	55	41
Some college (*n* = 64)	3	53	44

Table B.4. Correlations Between the Miracle and Involvement Scales and Their Components

Scale or component	Number of miracles		Number of physical miracles		Scale of miracles	
	r	p	r	p	r	p
Position	.1531	.002	.1659	.001	—	—
Training	.3115	.001	.2412	.001	—	—
Attendance	.1494	.003	.2238	.001	—	—
Scale of Involvement	—	—	—	—	.3278	.001

NOTE: A correlation is said to exist when *r* is higher than .15; *p* is said to be significant at .05 or lower.

Notes

Chapter One

1. In spite of its respectable size, Mahikari has received virtually no attention from Japanese scholars. I know of only four short essays on the movement in Japanese and one series of newspaper articles designed for popular consumption published in the *Mainichi shinbun* in the spring of 1978. To my knowledge there are no reliable works on this sect in English.

2. Ino Kenji, Umehara Masaki, and Shimizu Masato, *Minshū shūkyō no jitsuzō: Jūni no kyōsotachi* (The real picture of popular religion: twelve founders; Tokyo, 1972), p. 183.

3. Joseph M. Kitagawa, *Religion in Japanese History* (New York, 1966), p. 333.

4. Erving Goffman, *Frame Analysis: An Essay on the Organization of Experience* (Cambridge, Mass., 1974), p. 13.

5. Kitagawa, p. 335. Italics mine.

6. Max Weber, *The Sociology of Religion*, tr. Ephraim Fischoff (Boston, 1964), p. 117.

Chapter Three

1. See Yoshikawa Yoshio, *Chōnōryoku* (Parapsychology; Tokyo, 1975), pp. 116–44.

2. Okada Kōtama, *Mioshieshū* (Collected sacred teachings; Tokyo, 1967), pp. 130–41 (summarized). The slogan "spirit first, heart second, body third" means that the healing of the body depends on the purification of the inner man by okiyome.

Chapter Six

1. Other sects belonging to this family of religions are Ananaikyō, Seichō no Ie, Sekai Kyūsei Kyō, Ishinkai, Sekishinkai, and Shintō Tenkokyō. See Harry Thomsen, *The New Religions of Japan* (Rutland, Vt., 1963), pp. 127–98.

2. For a sample of his revelations, see Carmen Blacker, *The Catalpa Bow: A Study of Shamanistic Practices in Japan* (London, 1975), pp. 202–7.

3. Thomsen, pp. 128–29.

4. I have heard this fact denied by the Mahikari leaders. But see Ino Kenji, Umehara Masaki, and Shimizu Masato, *Minshū shūkyō no jitsuzō: Jūni no kyōsotachi* (The real picture of popular religion: twelve founders; Tokyo, 1972), pp. 183–84.

5. I can only conclude that the puzzlement Okada is said to have felt when, in 1959, the heavenly voice first told him to "raise his hand" was a pious liberty taken with the truth. Any believer in the Church of World Messianity would have known what it meant to "raise one's hand." It meant jōrei.

6. First called Kannon Kai or Kannonkyō, the sect has also been known as Nippon Kannon Kyōdan and Sekai Meshiya Kyō.

7. Thomsen, pp. 173–82.

8. Okada Mokichi, *Teachings of Meishu-Sama* (Atami, 1968), II, 87.

9. *Ibid.*, I, 63.

10. *Ibid.*, I, 8.

11. I use this rather awkward expression to distinguish these spiritual techniques from massage, *shiatsu*, and other therapies that, however traditional in their conceptual framework, are thought to work directly on the body without the mediation of Spirit.

12. Miyazaki Gorō, *Te: Sono kiseki* (Takehara City, Hiroshima Prefecture, 1964).

13. Winston Davis, "Ittōen: The Myths and Rituals of Liminality," *History of Religions*, pts. 1–3: 14, no. 4 (May 1975), 282–321; pts. 4–6: 15, no. 1 (Aug. 1975), 1–33.

14. Suzuki Gorō, *Te no hira ryōji* (The laying-on-of-hands treatment; Tokyo, 1974).

15. Davis, 14, no. 4, 30–37.

16. James Churchward, *The Lost Continent of Mu* (New York, 1959; paperback), p. vi. Originally published in 1931.

17. *Ibid.*, pp. 248, 250.

18. Cited in Robert Wauchope, *Lost Tribes and Sunken Continents: Myth and Method in the Study of American Indians* (Chicago, 1962), p. 42.

19. Churchward, p. 20.

20. Yamae Kiku, *Nippon ni himerarete aru sekai no seishi* (Tokyo,

1964). Educated in a Japanese mission school, the author describes herself as a "woman's lib" activist who later turned to the world of scholarship.

21. Blacker, *Catalpa Bow*, pp. 35–36.

22. Takie Sugiyama Lebra, *Japanese Patterns of Behavior* (Honolulu, 1976), p. 236.

23. Interrogations in the traditional yorigito rite are called *mondō* or *oshirabe*. They correspond to *reisa* in Mahikari. See Blacker, pp. 53, 308.

24. *Ibid.*, p. 237.

25. Sigmund Freud, *The Future of an Illusion* (Garden City, N.Y., n.d.), p. 56.

Chapter Seven

1. Ikado points out that the organization of these religious institutions is "very similar to, or even more rationalized than economic or political ones." Ikado Fujio, "Trend and Problems in New Religions: Religion in Urban Society," in Morioka Kiyomi and William H. Newell, eds., *The Sociology of Japanese Religion* (Leiden, 1968), p. 110.

2. Peter L. Berger and Thomas Luckmann, "Secularization and Pluralism," *International Yearbook for the Sociology of Religion*, 2, no. 2 (1966), 73–84.

3. See Gotō Yōbun, "S kyōdan Morioka dōjō sobyō: Nyūshin no shūhen o chūshin ni," *Shūkyōgaku nenpō*, no. 20 (1975; Taishō Daigaku Shūkyō Gakkai), pp. 35–43.

4. See Appendix A, Question 11.

5. See Winston Davis, "The Secularization of Japanese Religion: Measuring the Myth and the Reality," in Frank Reynolds and Theodore M. Ludwig, eds., *Transitions and Transformations in the History of Religions* (Leiden, 1980), pp. 259–83.

6. In Soka Gakkai, too, many youths seem to be motivated by spiritual needs, universal goals, and a quest for meaning rather than by physical infirmities. James W. White, *The Sōkagakkai and Mass Society* (Stanford, Calif., 1970), pp. 86–87.

7. This was a familiar custom in Japan before the war, but adopted husbands are now declining in number.

8. Appendix A, Question 12.

9. Some anti-Western sentiment may be involved in this return to kanpoyaku. See Yasuo Otsuka, "Chinese Traditional Medicine in Japan," in Charles Leslie, ed., *Asian Medical Systems: A Comparative Study* (Berkeley, Calif., 1976), pp. 322–40.

Chapter Eight

1. Sigmund Freud, "A Neurosis of Demoniacal Possession in the Seventeenth Century" (1923), in *On Creativity and the Unconscious: Papers on*

the Psychology of Art, Literature, Love, Religion (New York, 1958), p. 265.

2. T. K. Oesterreich, *Possession Demoniacal and Other Among Primitive Races, in Antiquity, the Middle Ages, and Modern Times* (London, 1930), pp. 46–47.

3. Sheila S. Walker, *Ceremonial Spirit Possession in Africa and Afro-America: Forms, Meanings, and Functional Significance for Individuals and Social Groups* (Leiden, 1972), p. 26.

4. Likewise, Walker, in her study of African and Afro-American possession, found that "some people appear quite lucid at times, as if their possession were just an act, yet at other times they appear to be in a deep trance" (p. 30).

5. This seems to be similar, if not identical, to the "sympathetic weeping" (*morainaki*) that Takie Sugiyama Lebra found in the "Salvation Cult." See *Japanese Patterns of Behavior* (Honolulu, 1976), p. 56.

6. Traditional exorcists received the same personal benefit from their art. See Percival Lowell, *Occult Japan or the Way of the Gods* (Boston, 1894), p. 104.

7. Lebra, p. 244.

8. Walker, p. 104.

9. Oesterreich, p. 121. This may be related to the fact that drug-induced abreactive treatment is far more effective for normal subjects who have suffered a temporary mental trauma than for long-term schizophrenics or patients suffering from psychotic melancholia. See William Sargant, *The Mind Possessed: A Physiology of Possession, Mysticism and Faith Healing* (Philadelphia, 1974), pp. 5–6.

10. Merton M. Gill and Margaret Brenman, *Hypnosis and Related States: Psychoanalytic Studies in Regression* (New York, 1959), pp. 78, 198, 215.

11. Sigmund Freud, *The Future of an Illusion* (Garden City, N.Y., n.d.), pp. 77–79.

12. Mircea Eliade, *Myths, Dreams and Mysteries: The Encounter Between Contemporary Faiths and Archaic Realities* (New York, 1960), p. 77. Emphasis in the original.

13. Yoshida Teigo, "Mystical Retribution, Spirit Possession, and Social Structure in a Japanese Village," *Ethnology*, 6, no. 3 (July 1967), 237–62.

14. Ishizuka Takatoshi, *Nihon no tsukimono* (Spirit possession in Japan; Tokyo, 1973).

15. Cited in Oesterreich, *Possession Demoniacal*, pp. 106–7.

16. Likewise, in the African Zar cult, "In most cases the possession manifestation does not represent the original trouble, and does not take place until after the intervention of the priest or healer" (Walker, *Ceremonial Spirit Possession*, p. 110).

17. Oesterreich, pp. 131–375. Similarly, I. M. Lewis draws a distinc-

tion between "unsolicited" or "uncontrolled" possession, on the one hand, and "solicited" or "controlled" possession, on the other. *Ecstatic Religion: An Anthropological Study of Spirit Possession and Shamanism* (Harmondsworth, Eng., 1971), p. 55.

18. For an example of how traditional possession behavior was learned, see Lowell, *Occult Japan*, pp. 185–87.

19. Oesterreich, p. 241.

20. Clifford Geertz, "Ethos, World View, and the Analysis of Sacred Symbols," in *The Interpretation of Cultures: Selected Essays* (New York, 1973), pp. 126–41.

21. Felicitas D. Goodman, *Speaking in Tongues: A Cross-Cultural Study of Glossolalia* (Chicago, 1972), p. 127.

22. John P. Kildahl, *The Psychology of Speaking in Tongues* (New York, 1972) pp. 8, 61.

23. Goodman, p. 136.

24. See James T. Richardson, "Psychological Interpretations of Glossolalia: A Reexamination of Research," *Journal of the Scientific Study of Religion*, 12, no. 2 (June 1973), 206.

25. William J. Samarin, *Tongues of Men and Angels: The Religious Language of Pentecostalism* (New York, 1972), pp. 227–28.

26. *Ibid.*, p. 42.

27. Goodman, pp. 58–86, 153–61; James N. Lapsley and John H. Simpson, "Speaking in Tongues," *Princeton Seminary Bulletin*, 58 (Feb. 1965), 6.

28. Samarin, p. 33. Emphasis in the original. Lewis holds the same opinion regarding possession itself (*Ecstatic Religion*, pp. 45–46).

29. Norman Cameron, *Personality Development and Psychopathology: A Dynamic Approach* (Boston, 1963), p. 341.

30. James C. Coleman, *Abnormal Psychology and Modern Life*, 2d ed. (Chicago, 1956), p. 202.

31. Cameron, pp. 341, 364.

32. See Alfred Schutz, "On Multiple Realities," in *Collected Papers*, Vol. 1: *The Problem of Social Reality* (The Hague, 1967), pp. 207–59.

33. Clifford Geertz, "Religion as a Cultural System," in *The Interpretation of Cultures: Selected Essays* (New York, 1973), p. 90.

34. The same point is made by Oesterreich, who attributes the outbreak of epidemics of possession to the "sight and company of possessed persons" (*Possession Demoniacal*, p. 92).

35. Geertz, p. 90.

36. Arnold M. Ludwig, "Altered States of Consciousness," in Charles T. Tart, ed., *Altered States of Consciousness* (Garden City, N.Y., 1969), p. 19.

37. Sargant, *Mind Possessed*, p. 17.

38. Ernest Hilgard, *Hypnotic Susceptibility* (New York, 1965), p. 25.

39. Kildahl, *Psychology of Speaking in Tongues*, p. 50.

40. Goodman, *Speaking in Tongues*, p. 70.

41. Gill and Brenman, *Hypnosis*, pp. 66–70.

42. Walker, *Ceremonial Spirit Possession*, pp. 86–87.

43. Gill and Brenman, pp. 14, 19.   44. *Ibid.*, pp. 91–98.

45. *Ibid.*, pp. 71–100.   46. Walker, p. 99.

47. Robert White, "A Preface to the Theory of Hypnotism," *Journal of Abnormal and Social Psychology*, 39 (1941), 484–85.

48. Mircea Eliade, "The Prestige of the Cosmogonic Myth," *Diogenes*, 23 (Fall 1958), 3.

49. James George Frazer, *The Golden Bough: A Study in Magic and Religion*, abridged ed., Vol. 1 (New York, 1975), p. 12.

50. See Chapter 3, p. 46.

51. Lebra, *Japanese Patterns of Behavior*, p. 246.

52. Freud, *On Creativity*, p. 265.

53. Goodman, *Speaking in Tongues*, p. 152.

54. On the relationship between the medical notion of energy flows and the religious theme of "pure activity" in Chinese and Japanese culture, see Winston Davis, "Ittōen: The Myths and Rituals of Liminality," *History of Religions*, pts. 4–6: 15, no. 1 (Aug. 1975), 13–24.

55. L. Takeo Doi, "*Amae*: A Key Concept for Understanding Japanese Personality Structure," in Takie Sugiyama Lebra and William P. Lebra, eds., *Japanese Culture and Behavior: Selected Readings* (Honolulu, 1974), pp. 145–54; Takie Sugiyama Lebra, *Japanese Patterns of Behavior*, pp. 50–66; Harumi Befu, "Gift-Giving in a Modernizing Japan," *Monumenta Nipponica*, 23 (1968), 445–56.

56. Walker, *Ceremonial Spirit Possession*, pp. 42–43. See also Gill and Brenman, *Hypnosis*, pp. 83–84.

57. Gill and Brenman, p. 94.

58. Befu, pp. 447–49.

59. Meyer Fortes, *Oedipus and Job in West African Religion* (Cambridge, Eng., 1959), pp. 29–30.

Chapter Nine

1. Carmen Blacker, *The Catalpa Bow: A Study of Shamanistic Practices in Japan* (London, 1975), p. 312.

2. The extraordinary predominance of women in possession cults throughout the world is attested by T. K. Oesterreich in *Possession Demoniacal and Other Among Primitive Races, in Antiquity, the Middle Ages, and Modern Times* (London, 1930), p. 121.

3. Clifford Geertz, *The Interpretation of Cultures: Selected Essays* (New York, 1973), p. 26.

4. Arnold Van Gennep, *The Rites of Passage* (Chicago, 1960).

5. Susan J. Pharr, "The Japanese Woman: Evolving Views of Life and

Role," in Lewis Austin, ed., *Japan: The Paradox of Progress* (New Haven, Conn., 1976), p. 309.

6. Iwao Sumiko, "A Full Life for Modern Japanese Women," in *Text of Seminar on "Changing Values in Modern Japan,"* Stanford University (Nihonjin Kenkyūkai in association with the Asia Foundation, 1977), p. 96.

7. *Japan Times* (Nov. 27, 1976), p. 2.

8. Blacker, p. 312.

9. Unfortunately, my interviews included no clear-cut cases of men who were suffering from sexual karma possession.

10. See Appendix B, Table B.1.

11. *Standard Dictionary of Folklore, Mythology and Legend*, Vol. 1 (New York, 1949), p. 413, "Fox."

12. Toba Sojo was the son of Minamoto-no-Takakuni, the author of *Konjaku Monogatari*, a collection of tales that has major importance in the study of the folklore about foxes.

13. Ilza Veith, "The Supernatural in the Far Eastern Concepts of Mental Diseases," *Bulletin of the History of Medicine*, 37 (1963), 145.

14. Erving Goffman, *Frame Analysis: An Essay on the Organization of Experience* (Cambridge, Mass., 1974), pp. 40–82.

15. George De Vos, *Socialization for Achievement* (Berkeley, Calif., 1973), p. 155.

16. I. M. Lewis, *Ecstatic Religion: An Anthropological Study of Spirit Possession and Shamanism* (Harmondsworth, Eng., 1971), p. 75.

17. Harumi Befu, *Japan: An Anthropological Introduction* (San Francisco, 1971), p. 50.

Chapter Ten

1. See Bryan R. Wilson, *Magic and the Millennium: A Sociological Study of Religious Movements of Protest Among Tribal and Third-World Peoples* (New York, 1973), pp. 24–25.

2. See Appendix B, Table B.2.

3. See Appendix B, Table B.3.

4. See Keith Thomas, *Religion and the Decline of Magic* (New York, 1971), p. 61.

5. William P. Alston, "Religion," in *The Encyclopedia of Philosophy*, Vol. 7 (New York, 1972), pp. 141–42.

6. Dorothy Hammond, "Magic: A Problem in Semantics," *American Anthropologist*, 72, no. 6 (Dec. 1970), 1352.

7. Marcel Mauss, *A General Theory of Magic* (New York, 1972), p. 63.

8. Henri Doré, *Researches into Chinese Superstitions* (Shanghai, 1914–38), Vol. 3, pp. iii–v.

9. See Robin Horton, "A Definition of Religion and Its Uses," *Journal of the Royal Anthropological Institute*, 90, pt. 2 (July–Dec. 1960), 208–9.

10. Mauss, pp. 91, 87.

11. *Ibid.*, pp. 72–73.

12. *Ibid.*, p. 76.

13. Edmund Leach, *Culture and Communication: The Logic by Which Symbols Are Connected* (Cambridge, Eng., 1976), pp. 9–16.

14. *Ibid.*, pp. 29–31.

15. Although one is tempted to make the feeling of sacred awe another criterion for distinguishing between religion and magic, anthropologists have repeatedly shown that neither can be defined on the basis of unique sentiments or emotions. See Horton, pp. 206ff.

16. E. E. Evans-Pritchard, *Witchcraft, Oracles and Magic Among the Azande*, abridged ed. (Oxford, Eng., 1976).

17. Bronislaw Malinowski, *Magic, Science and Religion* (Garden City, N.Y., 1954), p. 87.

Chapter Eleven

1. E. E. Evans-Pritchard, *Witchcraft, Oracles and Magic Among the Azande*, abridged ed. (Oxford, Eng., 1976), p. 109.

2. *Ibid.*, pp. 149, 150, 155.

3. Clifford Geertz, "Religion as a Cultural System," in *The Interpretation of Cultures: Selected Essays* (New York, 1973), p. 104.

4. For a general discussion of theodicy, see Peter L. Berger, *The Sacred Canopy: Elements of a Sociological Theory of Religion* (Garden City, N.Y., 1967), pp. 53–80.

5. "Aru kiseki" (Shiriizu 'shūkyō') (Miracles [series on religion]), *Mainichi shinbun* (March 20, 1978), p. 3.

6. Bryan R. Wilson, *Magic and the Millennium: A Sociological Study of Religious Movements of Protest Among Tribal and Third-World Peoples* (New York, 1973), p. 168.

7. See Winston Davis, *Toward Modernity: A Developmental Typology of Popular Religious Affiliations in Japan*, Cornell University East Asia Papers, no. 12 (1977), pp. 79–83.

Chapter Twelve

1. In Soka Gakkai too, though women are numerically predominant, men hold nearly all high-level positions. See James W. White, *The Sōkagakkai and Mass Society* (Stanford, Calif., 1970), pp. 61–62.

2. See Appendix B, Figure B.1; and also White, p. 73.

3. In Soka Gakkai too, the relatively well-educated occupy "a disproportionately large number of leadership roles" (White, p. 65).

4. Table B.4 in Appendix B gives the coefficients of correlation for the several items composing the two Scales. All of these relationships hold up when we control for age, income, and education.

5. Joseph R. Gusfield, *Symbolic Crusade: Status Politics and the American Temperance Movement* (Urbana, Ill., 1969), p. 166.

6. James George Frazer, *The Golden Bough: A Study in Magic and Religion*, abridged ed., Vol. 1 (New York, 1975), p. 55.

7. Bronislaw Malinowski, *Magic, Science and Religion* (Garden City, N.Y., 1954), p. 83.

8. T. K. Oesterreich, *Possession Demoniacal and Other Among Primitive Races, in Antiquity, the Middle Ages, and Modern Times* (London, 1930), p. 85.

9. Sheila S. Walker, *Ceremonial Spirit Possession in Africa and Afro-America: Forms, Meanings, and Functional Significance for Individuals and Social Groups* (Leiden, 1972), p. 81.

10. William J. Samarin, *Tongues of Men and Angels: The Religious Language of Pentecostalism* (New York, 1972), p. 219.

11. *Ibid.*, p. 217.

12. The notion of upward religious mobility is also expressed in Mahikari by the words *reisō shōge* (raising the spirit level), *tamahi no reisōkai no kōjō* (elevation of the spirit-level-world of the soul), *tamahi no shōka* (elevation of the soul), and *shinseika* (apotheosis).

13. Max Weber, *The Sociology of Religion*, tr. Ephraim Fischoff (Boston, 1964), especially pp. 1–45.

14. Benton Johnson, "Do Holiness Sects Socialize in Dominant Values?," *Social Forces*, 39, no. 4 (May 1961), 309.

15. Michael Argyle, *Religious Behaviour* (London, 1958), pp. 80–92.

16. Ikado Fujio, "Trend and Problems in New Religions: Religion in Urban Society," in Morioka Kiyomi and William H. Newell, eds., *The Sociology of Japanese Religion* (Leiden, 1968), p. 110.

17. See also Winston Davis, "Ittōen: The Myths and Rituals of Liminality," *History of Religions*, pts. 1–3: 14, no. 4 (May 1975), 295–96.

18. "Aru kiseki" (Shiriizu 'shūkyō') (Miracles [series on religion]), *Mainichi shinbun* (March 16, 1978), p. 3.

19. Ino Kenji, Umehara Masaki, and Shimizu Masato, *Minshū shūkyō no jitsuzō: Jūni no kyōsotachi* (The real picture of popular religion: twelve founders; Tokyo, 1972), p. 174.

20. In 1974, for example, only 27.1 percent of Japanese with monthly incomes of 150,000–200,000 yen supported the Liberal Democrats, compared with 49.7 percent of those with monthly incomes above 200,000. See *Kōmei senkyo renmei, sangiin giin tsūjō senkyo no jittai* (Tokyo, 1974), p. 381. My thanks to Professor Bradley Richardson for drawing my attention to these figures.

21. Hayashi Chikio et al., eds., *Nihonjin no kokuminsei* (A study of the Japanese national character; Tokyo [Tōkei Sūri Kenkyūjo Kokuminsei Chōsa Iinkai], 1975), no. 3.

22. See Karl Marx, "The German Ideology," in Robert C. Tucker, ed., *The Marx-Engels Reader*, 2d ed. (New York, 1978), p. 172.

23. Charles Y. Glock, "The Role of Deprivation in the Origin and Evolution of Religious Groups," in Robert Lee and Martin E. Marty, eds., *Religion and Social Conflict* (New York, 1964), pp. 27–29.

24. David F. Aberle, *The Peyote Religion Among the Navaho* (New York, 1966), p. 326.

25. Liston Pope, *Millhands and Preachers: A Study of Gastonia* (New Haven, Conn., 1970), p. 137.

26. *Ibid.*

27. Robert K. Merton, *Social Theory and Social Structure* (New York, 1968), p. 40.

28. Reginald W. Bibby and Merlin B. Brinkerhoff, "Sources of Religious Involvement: Issues for Future Empirical Investigation," *Review of Religious Research*, 15, no. 2 (Winter 1974), 71–79.

29. Edward Norbeck, "Continuities in Japanese Social Stratification," in Leonard Plotnicov and Arthur Tuden, eds., *Essays in Comparative Social Stratification* (Pittsburgh, Penn., 1970), p. 175.

30. *Japan Statistical Yearbook* (Tokyo; Japan Statistical Association, 1977), pp. 398–99.

31. Norbeck, 178–79.

32. For a similar combination of ambition and magic, see James Allen Dator, *Sōka Gakkai, Builders of the Third Civilization: American and Japanese Members* (Seattle, Wash., 1969), p. 87.

33. Ikado, "Trend and Problems in New Religions," pp. 103–6.

34. *Asahi nenkan* (The Asahi yearbook; Tokyo, 1977), p. 591.

35. Max Weber, for example, pointed out that in China, charismatic magicians who were thought to embody the yang were worshiped as living "redeemers." *The Religion of China: Confucianism and Taoism* (New York, 1964), p. 202. In pre-modern Japan, charismatic ascetics and wizards enjoyed the same respect.

36. I. M. Lewis, *Ecstatic Religion: An Anthropological Study of Spirit Possession and Shamanism* (Harmondsworth, Eng., 1971), pp. 32, 203.

37. Norbeck, p. 186.

38. For the concept of plausibility structures, see Peter L. Berger, *The Sacred Canopy: Elements of a Sociological Theory of Religion* (Garden City, N.Y., 1967).

39. See Davis, "Ittōen," pts. 1–3, p. 294.

Chapter Thirteen

1. Jean-Paul Sartre, *The Psychology of Imagination* (Secaucus, N.J., 1972), p. 177.

2. *Nihongi: Chronicles of Japan from the Earliest Times to A.D. 697*, tr. William George Aston. Vol. 2 (Rutland, Vt., 1972), p. 66.

3. *Ibid.*, p. 102; italics mine.

4. Yasumaru Yoshio, *Nihon no kindaika to minshū shisō* (The modernization of Japan and popular thought; Tokyo, 1974), pp. 87–96.

5. For an example of a protest against magic, see Thomas C. Smith, "Ōkura Nagatsune and the Technologists," in Albert M. Craig and Donald H. Shively, eds., *Personality in Japanese History* (Berkeley, Calif., 1970), pp. 140–41.

6. Bronislaw Malinowski, *Magic, Science and Religion* (Garden City, N.Y., 1954), p. 28.

7. Kamishima Jirō, *Kindai Nihon no seishin kōzō* (The cultural structure of modern Japan; Tokyo, 1971), pp. 40–89.

8. Tsurumi Kazuko, *Social Change and the Individual: Japan Before and After Defeat in World War II* (Princeton, N.J., 1970), p. 211.

9. Hayashi Chikio et al., eds., *Nihonjin no Kokuminsei* (A study of the Japanese national character; Tokyo [Tōkei Sūri Kenkyūjo Kokuminsei Chōsa Iinkai], 1975), no. 3, p. 448.

10. Suzuki Norihisa, "'Nihonjin no shūkyō ishiki' kenkyū ni tsuite" (Research concerning the "religious consciousness of the Japanese"), *Shūkyō kenkyū* (Religious research), 38, no. 3 (182) (March 1965), 125–26.

11. *Nihonjin no ishiki: NHK seron chōsa* (The consciousness of the Japanese: The NHK public opinion survey; Tokyo, 1975), p. 285.

12. See Winston Davis, "The Secularization of Japanese Religion: Measuring the Myth and the Reality," in Frank Reynolds and Theodore M. Ludwig, eds., *Transitions and Transformations in the History of Religions* (Leiden, 1980), pp. 259–83.

13. Itō Mikiharu, "Nihon bunka no kōzōteki rikai o mezashite" (Concerning the structural understanding of Japanese culture), *Kikan jinruigaku* 4, no. 2 (1973), 3–30.

14. Winston Davis, "Ittōen: The Myths and Rituals of Liminality," *History of Religions*, pts. 1–3: 14, no. 4 (May 1975), p. 307.

15. Max Weber, *The Protestant Ethic and the Spirit of Capitalism* (New York, 1958), p. 182.

16. Max Weber, *Ancient Judaism* (New York, 1952), p. 223.

17. Max Weber, *The Sociology of Religion* (Boston, 1964), p. 101.

18. *Ibid.*, p. 54.

19. This distinction should not be confused with Weber's own distinction between substantive and formal rationality. See Max Weber, *The Theory of Social and Economic Organization*, ed. A. M. Henderson and Talcott Parsons (New York, 1966), pp. 184–86.

20. Karl Mannheim, *Man and Society in an Age of Reconstruction* (New York, 1940), pp. 53, 58.

21. *Ibid.*, p. 54.   22. *Ibid.*

23. *Ibid.*, pp. 55, 58.   24. *Ibid.*, p. 59.

25. Malinowski, *Magic, Science and Religion*, p. 90.

Index